THIS AIN'T NO HOLIDAY INN

Down and Out at the Chelsea Hotel

1980-1995

An Oral History by

James Lough

schaffner
press

Tucson, Arizona

For permission to reprint, contact:
Permissions: Schaffner Press, Inc. POB 41567, Tucson, Az 85717.

Library of Congress Cataloging-in-Publication Data

Lough, James.
This ain't no Holiday Inn : down and out at the Chelsea Hotel, 1980-
1995 : an oral history / by James Lough.
    pages cm
 Includes bibliographical references and index.
 ISBN 978-1-936182-52-7 (trade pbk. : alk. paper) -- ISBN 978-1-936182-
53-4 (epub) -- ISBN 978-1-936182-54-1 (kindle) -- ISBN 978-1-936182-
55-8 (adobe)
1. Chelsea Hotel. 2. Hotels--New York (State)--New York. 3. New York
(N.Y.)--Social life and customs--20th century. I. Title. II. Title: Down and
out at the Chelsea Hotel, 1980-1995.
 TX941.C44L68 2013
 910.4609747--dc23
                        2013014869

I dedicate this book to my wife, Jennefer Morris-Lough, for cheerfully putting up with my extended periods holed up working in my office.

Author's Note

This book is an independent work of cultural history and commentary. HOLIDAY INN is a registered trademark of Six Continents Hotels, Inc. and is used in the title of this book pursuant to the Fair Use Doctrine. No affiliation with, and no sponsorship or endorsement by, any copyright or trademark owner, any business (including the current owners of the Chelsea Hotel) and/or any individual quoted or described in this book is claimed or implied by the author or the publisher.

Table of Contents

i /INTRODUCTION

Chapter 1 :
1 / CHECKING IN

Chapter 2 :
25 / CHELSEA WILDNESS

Chapter 3 :
57 / THE THREE WISE MEN OF DOPE:
Beat Writers Huncke, Corso, and Matz

Chapter 4 :
107 / THREE CHORDS AND A GRUDGE:
Dee Dee Ramone and the Chelsea Hotel Blues

Chapter 5 :
135 / GETTING BY

Chapter 6 :
147 / STANLEY BARD:
Steel Fist in Velvet Glove

Chapter 7 :
167 / CHELSEA PORTRAITS

Chapter 8 :
223 / CHECKING OUT

Chapter 9 :
235 / 21ST CENTURY AFTERMATH

Epilogue :
243 / FAUXHEMIA:
Does the Death of Bohemia Matter?

250 / WHERE ARE THEY NOW?

252 / ACKNOWLEDGMENTS

253 / ENDNOTES

THIS AIN'T NO
HOLIDAY INN

schaffner
press

An early advertising postcard highlighting the building's safety (above) and a brochure emphasizing the hotel's proximity to the Chelsea Piers (below).

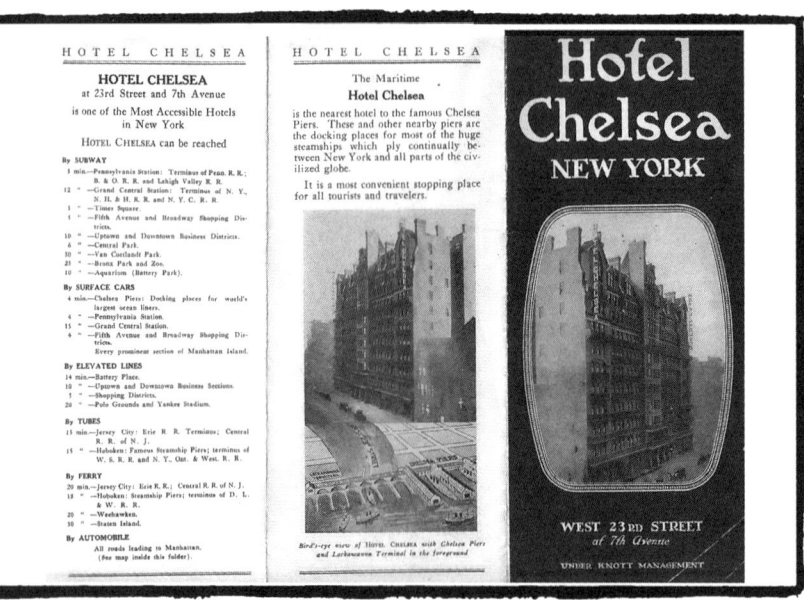

Introduction

At the Chelsea, we used to have this joke. When people were really acting outlandishly and out of bounds, we would shrug our shoulders and say: "Well, this ain't no Holiday Inn!"

—PAUL VOLMER

I finally made it to the Chelsea. For years I had phoned, emailed and snail mailed a small army of free-spirited Bohemians who had lived, loved, partied, created and crashed at the Chelsea Hotel from the 1980s through the 1990s (*Crashed* as in slept on somebody's floor, and crashed as in *crashed and burned*). I tracked down these eccentrics, interviewed them on the phone for hours and hours—my dime. I bought them meals and drinks, urged and cajoled them to be part of this book. I even lent them money. For years, I read every book about the Chelsea Hotel, every magazine article, brochure and blog I could get my hands on. I watched all the movies shot in its venerable rooms and halls.

Now, finally, it was time to get at these eminent Bohemians in person.

I arrived on a dismal New York night in the pouring rain, a hangover from "Tropical Storm Ernesto" that had swept through the city the day before. The air was warm, sodden and dreary, the heavy drizzle would rally into a fierce downpour and withdraw back to a sulking haze. But weather be damned, I was thrilled to be there.

The rain only made Manhattan glimmer all the brighter. The streets shone with red and green streaks, and even if it rained the entire week, wet or dry, it was all New York to me. Let it rain. Who cared? I was at the Chelsea, damnit!

When the cab pulled up to the curb, to my acute disappointment, the entire Hotel Chelsea was shrouded in steel scaffolding. Its brick surface was being tuck-pointed, repaired and improved, like the rest of the neighborhood.

The tuck-pointing would also prove symbolic of something the Bohemians had led me to expect, something they had warned me about time and time again: "The Chelsea has changed. It's not like it was." It had been gentrified, they said, domesticated, tamed like the whole neighborhood, which, since the mid-90s, had turned distinctly upscale. The greasy diners were gone, replaced by uniform Starbucks. The boarded-up storefronts were now upscale spas. The neighborhood dives were now exclusive nightclubs replete with guest lists and doormen who turned the "wrong" people away. Everyone was saying the hotel, the neighborhood, all of Manhattan, had sold out.

I sincerely hoped that the death of the Chelsea, like the death of its former tenant Mark Twain, had been greatly exaggerated. I would dispel this myth and find some vestige of the place's edgy, original energy.

And now I found myself standing amidst my luggage beneath the famous red and white candy-striped awning. I looked inside, waiting before taking the plunge, not out of any sense of wonderment, but to avoid spoiling the photo being shot by a well-heeled young tourist in a mustard-colored sport jacket and spiked hair.

Why all the excitement about arriving at a hotel? Because the Chelsea Hotel is not your ordinary hotel—it's a culture factory on hyper drive. Artists living at the Chelsea have probably produced more great paintings, sculptures, literature, theater, music, photography, and film than any American artistic movement. With an impressive record like this, it's no surprise that myriad myths and half-truths about the Chelsea and its artists have ascended like a flock of blackbirds.

For example, it's not exactly true that Dylan Thomas died at the Chelsea Hotel. He merely slipped into a coma there in Room 215 where he resided. He did the actual dying at St. Vincent's Hospital in Greenwich

Village. But after his bender at the White Horse Tavern, he did utter his alleged last words at the Chelsea: "I've had eighteen straight whiskeys, and I think that's the record."

It's debatable that punk rock icon Sid Vicious killed his girlfriend Nancy Spungen at the Chelsea. True, Spungen was stabbed to death in Room 102, and in the famous photograph, that is her body in the bag the paramedics are hauling out under the hotel's red and white awning.

But, according to insiders at the Chelsea, people who'd lived there forever, it was the small-time punk rocker and heroin dealer Rockets Redglare who murdered Nancy during an argument over money she owed him for drugs. During the fracas, Sid lay innocently sleeping in a heroin stupor.

It is true that Arthur Miller lived at the Chelsea, and Mark Twain. Janis Joplin did in fact "service" Leonard Cohen there on an unmade bed. It's true that the acting legend Sarah Bernhardt, in her penthouse apartment at the Chelsea, slept nights in her custom-made coffin beneath her custom-made pyramid. On the tenth floor, Stanley Kubrick did argue with Arthur C. Clarke over the screenplay for *2001: A Space Odyssey*. The list of Chelsea luminaries goes on and on. Writers Thomas Wolfe, Nelson Algren, Vladimir Nabokov, Gore Vidal, Jean Baudrillard, and others just as famous, wrote books there.

As for musicians, Joni Mitchell, Bob Dylan, Jimi Hendrix and Rufus Wainright composed songs there. Punk rock was practically born at the Chelsea, where Patti Smith penned her lyrics in the room she shared with photographer Robert Mapplethorpe. Not to mention Nico and John Cale of the Velvet Underground who both jammed there, as did Johnny Thunders, Sid Vicious and Dee Dee Ramone.

There were the painters (Pablo Picasso) and film directors (Milos Forman) and actors (Ethan Hawke). We could—and will list the movies that were shot at the Chelsea, the people who were shot at the Chelsea, the hijinks, the tricks turned and the scandals hatched between the Chelsea walls, as well as the ghosts who flitted right through them.

A MAGNET FOR ARTISTS

One thing is certain—these artistic VIPs lived in the Chelsea not because a room there was an elegant status symbol. They lived there because of all the other artists who had lived there before, and because the Chelsea and its managers—the cultivated, visionary Bard family—understood artists and were good to them. Stanley Bard, the hotel's owner and manager, loved the arts and collected the works of his tenants. He even accepted their work in lieu of rent.

Artists loved the Chelsea because they didn't have to put on airs, social masks, neckties, or pantyhose. They could be themselves. And being themselves, often as not, meant being beyond the pale.

Since 1883, New York's Chelsea Hotel provided safe haven for countless cultural creatives. More than safe, the place was positively solicitous to its artists. At the Chelsea, a residence hotel, you could stay as a tourist—or a transient, as they call them—for a few days or a few weeks. Or if you could convince the manager you were an artist worth betting on, he would let you move in as a "permanent resident." In that case you would pay a month-to-month rent, just like renting an apartment. The rooms were dirty but dirt-cheap. The management might even waive your deposit.

But the Chelsea was no typical apartment building. Some have compared its atmosphere to that of an enormous, twelve-story artist's colony—others to an insane asylum. It was also a "fall back" place for artists and Bohemians who were hitting the skids.

"Well," they said, "I can always get a room at the Chelsea."

Of course economy comes with a price. Low rent attracted not only starving artists and Bohemians but also the lowlifes, troublemakers, idlers, petty criminals, rebels, degenerates, drug dealers, pimps and their girls (or boys) and sundry Dick Tracy type characters who populated the hotel's *demimonde*. The Chelsea not only inspired artistic creation—it was an incubator for debauchery, addiction, and crime. Beat poets rubbed shoulders with machine-gun-toting gangsters. Con artists partied with performance artists, and film directors rode the elevators with directors of drug rings. Pimps and their girls fought in the stairwells. To the artists living there, a brush with criminals was part of the hotel's charm, a little danger across the hall.

The guy who got me started on this fool's errand of chasing the Chelsea's counterculture was my ex-brother-in-law Robert Campbell. He later informed me it was a small miracle, convincing so many Chelsea veterans to talk to me in the first place. After all, this was a bunch of streetwise Bohemians who made their own rules and who often as not operated on the other side of the law. Why would they take me seriously? Why wouldn't they assume I was a fake, a poseur, a dilettante? These folks had forever been surrounded by would-be artists and artists manqués smoking in the cafes, talking about getting around to writing a play, bragging about the time they almost started a band. How would I be any different? How many other self-styled writers had shown up at the Chelsea and announced they were writing a book?

Not to mention, I was penetrating a tight inner circle. There's a rule among people who live long-term in residence hotels, in close quarters, and who may harbor a secret or two, a skeleton in their closet: do not blab about your neighbors lest they blab about you. An unspoken oath of silence protects them.

My brother-in-law Robert was a cagey guy. He had waited good and long before voicing his doubts. Because—call me naive—it had never occurred to me that the Chelsea denizens might not want to talk. Not because I'm incapable of self-doubt, but because if these stories were going to get told, *somebody* had to record and compile them. I just advanced forward with the phone calls, letters and emails to the people who had lived in this monstrous red brick ecosystem of creativity.

A COLLAGE OF DECADES

This book covers a decade and a half, starting in 1980 and ending in 1995, when the hotel's new management adopted a "no tolerance" policy and everything about the Chelsea changed for good, if not for the better.

Of course the Chelsea Hotel's cultural scene in the early 80s mirrored the larger cultural scene in New York. Punk rock was still alive and well in New York and in the Chelsea. Dee Dee Ramone, no longer with the Ramones, would move into room 525 and continue writing songs for his former band, plus try to kick his heroin addiction. Johnny Thunders, guitarist in the garage glam band the New York Dolls, partied at the Chelsea with friends and fans.

The Beat writers' most celebrated period at the Chelsea was in the 1950s—*Naked Lunch* author William Burroughs lived there then—but in the 80s, three original Beats still held court at the Chelsea. Gregory Corso, Herbert Huncke, and Marty Matz had made themselves at home, establishing an ad hoc literary salon. It featured some writing, of course, but also a smuggling ring, an illegal gambling parlor, and a continuous lava flow of pot, coke, Valium and heroin, anything they could get their trembling hands on.

The 60's Chelsea scene also survived into the 1980s. Andy Warhol's Factory crowd had made the hotel notorious in the 60s—with films like *Chelsea Girls*. For one, Viva still lived there. The strawberry blonde diva from the Factory days, Viva (Susan Hoffman) was one of Warhol's top-tier superstars and played the lead in several of his films. The poet Rene Ricard still lived there. Ricard had also starred in *Chelsea Girls.* His book *God with Revolver,* a sort of *Basketball Diaries* in verse, had made him notorious. Not to mention Richard Bernstein, living on the first floor, whose colorized photo illustrations for Warhol's *Interview* magazine are still indelibly linked to the magazine's heyday.

Aside from the Warhol crowd, the 60s also returned to the hotel every time Arthur Miller paid a visit to Stanley Bard. And if we stretch even further back in time, a monumental portion of the 40s and 50s had never left the Chelsea. Ensconced on the top floor was Virgil Thomson, Pulitzer-winning opera composer and chief music critic for the *Herald Tribune.* The younger residents got a kick out of holding the elevator for the imperious old queen of the castle.

All of these historical epochs still lived on and even thrived during the 1980-1995 period covered in these pages. High-modernist composers from the 1940s, 1950's Beats, 1960's Warhol superstars, 1970's punk rockers, and 1980's proto-rave trance dancers were juxtaposed in the Chelsea like a living collage of cultural history, all the wisdom and folly of five decades compressed into fifteen years.

With all this cross-generational mixing, the Chelsea was a hopping place to be. But sadly it would only last awhile. The 1990s marked the end of the hotel's 100-year tradition of supporting wild, counterculture creativity. In the early 90s, the Chelsea sang its swan song, its farewell performance, its final creative eruption before the volcano went dormant. The big gears of society were shifting and the Chelsea's little gear couldn't help but spin along. With the dot-com bubble in the 90s, New York—and by extension the Chelsea—came into new money. Neighborhoods were "improved." Gentrification invaded even the shabbiest Manhattan neighborhoods, and artists born without silver spoons needed not apply. If you had to ask, you couldn't afford it.

The 1980s Chelsea Hotel that musician/writer Dimitri Mugianis recalls in later pages as an "aging whore" got herself a 1990's facelift. Along with her wrinkles, out went her patience for laggards. Instead of gently tolerating artist-residents who owed her rent money, she sent them out to the sidewalks and filled their rooms with people who could pay. Many of the new residents were artists, too, but bourgeois artists who had already achieved success or come from families with money. Either way, the new wave of Chelsea tenants lacked the desperation, the urgency, the libidinous wildness that encourages young artists to take risks, to experiment, to launch artistic movements.

Writers Christopher Hitchens and James Wolcott have written at length about New York's big change in the 90s. They almost apologetically lament what was lost when money was gained. In short, New York lost its edge. And so too did the Chelsea.

The fact that the scene had to die is what makes the Chelsea's 80s to 90s grand finale so poignant, so painful, so hilariously raw and alive. I have had the great luck to interview dozens of residents who were there, at the heart of the scene before it frittered away. They were card-carrying Bohemians when it was still possible to be so, when rent was low and expectations high.

NEW YORK'S 1980s COUNTERCULTURE

In 1980, where this book begins, New York was limping along to escape the previous disastrous decade, marked by the city's near bankruptcy and appallingly high crime rates, the 1977 Blackout and its attendant looting, not to mention the atmosphere of high anxiety triggered by the Son of Sam murders. The clichéd images of New York featured heaps of garbage on the sidewalks, graffiti-covered subway cars and decrepit buildings whose entryways smelled of piss. It would still be twelve years before Mayor Giuliani entered the picture and used draconian means to clean up the city.

In the early 80s, the youth counterculture was no longer a unified movement. Remnants of 60's idealism survived, but hippies were showing their age. Few 80's Bohemians had illusions about world peace and the Age of Aquarius. Sex, drugs, and rock and roll were still popular, but not *corporate* rock and roll. Not Robert Palmer, not Boston and certainly not Styx. Punk rock's angry revolt, while alive and well in New York, never reached the mainstream. Although the Bohemian counterculture was alive and well, a conservative parallel universe was simultaneously taking shape with a fresh generation of kids, kids not interested in rebelling against anything except the 60s. Short-haired kids wearing Polo shirts with pastel sweaters draped over their shoulders. Kids in Sperry Topsiders sailing shoes. Instead of fighting the power, they wanted the power. Instead of studying Religious Studies and Environmental Design in college, they majored in business. Instead of peace, love, and utopia, they *wanted* money and success—everything their parents' generation distrusted. These kids *liked* Ronald Reagan.

And Ronald Reagan, just elected for his first term, with his wife Nancy as poster girl, declared the infamous War on Drugs that has raged longer than the wars in Vietnam, Iraq, and Afghanistan combined.

But back to the 80's counterculture, the Bohemians. What did it mean to be a Bohemian New Yorker in the 1980s?

First, like Bohemians of all eras, those of the 80s were deeply skeptical of received values. The pieties of state, school, church, family and the American Dream were to be scrutinized with a cold eye. "Question Authority" was a slogan you saw on buttons and bumper stickers, as well as the omnipresent "Circle A" of anarchy. Much of this skepticism came out of punk rock's disaffected, working-class resentment. In the words of punk rockers Sid Vicious and Johnny Rotten: "No Future".

In this nihilistic atmosphere, the mantra was: "Don't make promises you know you won't keep."

Naturally, most Bohemians mocked the Reagan Revolution's slogan, "It's Morning Again in America," and the "Greed is Good" creed. Most viewed pop culture as the tool of big business and Madison Avenue. Instead, they had turned their attention to "alternative" movies, books, and bands, before big business and advertising co-opted this concept for their own ends. Before you could buy Doc Martens in any color of the rainbow.

Eighties Bohemians may have been skeptical, but they weren't paralyzed by cynicism. They still *did* things. They started bands, they published 'zines, they made paintings and videos and performance art, even if some of them didn't have much talent. Punks distrusted virtuosity as a surrogate for authentic feeling, which was usually anger. These Bohemians didn't rely on the internet, movies, and TV for their diversions. They didn't live on screens. "If you don't like what's on the news," Paul Krassner once said, "make some of your own." The acronym *DIY* (Do It Yourself) was as popular as *Question Authority*. Be self-sufficient, self-reliant, self-actualizing.

No one becomes a Bohemian for the money. Many consciously chose poverty to avoid being swept away by the routine pandering and trifling anxieties of the marketplace. Granted, some were just lazy. But the result was the same, boiling daily life down to what really mattered—your next meal, your next minute. Poverty has a way of focusing you on the present. It draws you out of dreamtime into the reality of an empty fridge.

If a little money did happen to come in, you enjoyed a night out at a cheap mom-and-pop restaurant or diner down the block. Otherwise, you made due with Ramen noodles boiled on a hotplate, or if you were lucky enough to have one in your room, an old gas stove. Given a choice between dinner and a joint, you'd have to think about it.

Nowadays, the primacy of money has changed everything in the U.S., in New York, and at the Chelsea. Nowadays, the same one-bedroom costs literally ten times as much as it did in the 80s. In fact a room at the Chelsea now costs *more* than the average Manhattan apartment. Money drives the Mercedes called Manhattan. Individuality and eccentricity take the bus. Gentrification, boutique hotels, prefab Olive Gardens and Home Depots are the coils tightening around the Chelsea. No more getting on bended knee to beg Stanley Bard to give you a room. In fact, the new owner, busy with intensive renovations, isn't admitting anyone into the hotel. No doubt, if he does, it'll be the moneyed elite, standing surrounded by their Louis Vuitton bags, checking in while dialing their iPhones. But that's another story. For now, let's go back to the energetic 80s, when rooms were cheap and anything was possible.

The Chelsea's famous art-bedecked lobby featuring Joe Andoe's horse painting and Renata Goebel's papier-mache woman on a swing.

CHAPTER 1

Checking In

*It is strange how people seem to belong to places
—especially to places where they were not born.*

—CHRISTOPHER ISHERWOOD, *The Berlin Stories*

THE LOBBY: A ROGUE'S GALLERY

When the spiky-haired tourist had taken his photograph and proceeded out the big glass front door, I hurriedly grabbed my bags and stepped out from under the candy-striped awning and inside the Chelsea's famous lobby.

The place was stone quiet and more cramped than I'd envisioned. Artwork was ubiquitous, paintings crammed up and down the yellow walls. There was the ornate Victorian fireplace, its mantelpiece sporting Rene Shapshack's[1] bust of Harry Truman.

Of all people to honor on the mantel of the anti-establishment Chelsea Hotel! The little bullet of a president from Missouri who dropped the atom bomb on Japan. The symbol of true blue America fair-and-square, showcased prominently here at Bohemian Central. No doubt the hotel's manager and part-owner Stanley Bard had long-since transcended the irony. No doubt he could wax on about how, back in the day, he had bartered X amount of Shapshack's rent for the statue and how much its value had multiplied over the years.

The quality of the Chelsea's lobby art is up for dispute. Its placement on the walls didn't seem to follow any organizing principle. Larry Rivers'[2] pop-art masterpiece "The Dutch Masters" hangs prominently in all its glory, but what's with the huge, goofy, amateurish painting of a black flowerpot? To the right of the fireplace, there's a nice Phillip Taaffe[3] pinwheel abstraction, but over there, above the display case full of travel brochures, there's a tinsel metallic curly-cue contrivance that hurts the eyes.

My brother-in-law Robert Campbell states it more plainly.

ROBERT CAMPBELL

In the lobby, you've got some of the crappiest artwork you ever saw in your life. Some of it looks like artwork you'd see in the waiting room of a doctor's office. But there's some stuff that's good.[4]

The real reason for the art's spotty quality may be simpler.

MARY ANNE ROSE

Stanley took the best paintings home.

Stanley Bard, the hotel's manager and part owner for over fifty years, has denied accepting artworks in lieu of rent payments (the hotel's co-owners would have probably disapproved). But the residents know better. Not only was the lobby chock full, but every hallway on every floor was lined with paintings, prints, and drawings. Every stairway was plastered with artwork strung up in diagonal rows. Mobiles hung from the ceilings—sculptures rose from the floors. Did the artists just donate their work out of adoration for Bard and the hotel?

The Chelsea's abundant art may not be worth all that much. In a recent legal dispute between the hotel's owners, the artwork—so much that if they pulled it all off the walls you'd think the building would collapse—was appraised at a total of only around $900,000. More evidence that Bard took the best stuff home.

As I carried my bags through the lobby, I recognized, to my left, the cubby-like room I'd seen in movies, the iconic little space with the payphones and the marble floors. In the 1980s, cell phones were almost nonexistent. And despite the fact that two-thirds of the residents were not transients, but "permanent," living there indefinitely, the Chelsea was still, after all, a hotel. As with any hotel, outgoing phone calls made from your room were outrageously expensive. So residents plodded down to the lobby's payphones.

JULIE EAKIN

In the middle of the night or whenever, we'd always be going down there in pajamas. Calls cost a dime. You'd pull the doors shut—it was one of those glass jobs, so you could see all the business going on in the lobby as you were sitting in there talking.

What made the little phone room iconic wasn't the marble floors or the phone booths themselves, but what happened there over the phone, from the ordinary to the sublime: lovers arranging rendezvous, having knock-down drag outs, ordering pizzas or pot. Actor Ethan Hawke, understanding the payphones' symbolic resonance as the counterculture's Communications Central, featured them in his movie *Chelsea Walls.*

Architecture is Frozen Music

You can't talk about Chelsea culture or people without talking about the building itself. A building's character, after all, shapes the characters inside.

DIMITRI MUGIANIS

The Chelsea is almost like a beautiful fortress. Architecturally, it was gorgeous! There were balconies I liked to sit outside on. In addition, inside, the staircase is beautiful, and there were working fireplaces in the rooms. I know they've fixed the hotel up now, but the state of disrepair it was in when we lived there, was so charming, like a beautiful old whore whose beauty was fading.

JULIE EAKIN

The building was a little macabre—it was much disheveled when

I lived there with Dimitri. It was not kept well, nothing like it is now. It was much dingier—it wasn't cleaned as often. Almost anybody could easily sneak up the back stairway into the hallways.

It cost five hundred dollars a month for a big, square room with a beautiful fireplace that didn't work. There were the two bays with the front doors and the balcony, and it had beautiful parquet floors and tall ceilings that must have been twelve feet high. The bathroom was outside in the hall and was shared by two other apartments, one on either side.

The Hotel Chelsea has an ugly-duckling sort of stateliness. Built during the transition between Victorian and Edwardian periods, it shows the influence of both. Call it Awkwardian. If you were to show an innocent bystander a picture of the building, they might guess it was an old insane asylum, back when straitjackets were in vogue. With its high gables, skinny chimneys, its homely-ornate brick façade, and florid wrought-iron balconies, the Hotel Chelsea is gothic, at least in the literary sense of the word.

The hotel's fortress-like construction had its advantages, especially when it housed a bunch of hard-living libertines. Its builders made the interior walls extra-thick for two reasons, the first being so residents wouldn't be bothered by their neighbors' noise; the second was to prevent fires from spreading from room to room. In fact, the builders poured sand, a dependable fire retardant, between the building's steel girders to prevent this from occurring and risk engulfing the whole hotel. When Chelsea rooms have caught fire, they may have burned themselves bare, smoke and flames surging outside through the windows, but the adjoining rooms were not affected.[5]

The unburnable Chelsea Hotel was built in 1883 during the great surge of the Industrial Revolution, a time of opulence, ostentation and robber barons. In fact, Mark Twain (maybe during his own nights at the Chelsea?) coined the period "The Gilded Age."

The Chelsea still bears traces of these lavish times. At the time it was built, it was New York's tallest building, towering over the city at an awe-inspiring twelve floors. It was not designed to be a hotel, but a "co-op," similar to today's condominium complexes, where people could purchase their units and own them. But what units! The apartments, especially those on the top floors, were enormous, their square footage running in the several thousands. The penthouse apartments were comprised of two stories, and when viewed from the outside, it almost looks as though a giant crane had lifted a few two-story houses and placed them side-by-side on top, creating an exclusive little neighborhood on the roof.

If New York was doing well during the Gilded Age, the Chelsea District positively thrived. The Chelsea Hotel sat at the epicenter of New York's Theater District. Playhouses, opera houses, and vaudeville houses were strewn throughout the neighborhood. The world-renowned actor Sarah Bernhardt made her home in one of the Chelsea's penthouses. The pyramid she had built for her roof survives to this day. As a wealthy celebrity, Ms. Bernhardt could afford such extravagances. Where there's a whim, there's a way. But most actors were dirt poor, exploited by the big theater syndicates and struggling to form labor unions. Still, the scores of less well-heeled actors kept the Chelsea District lively.

Unfortunately for the Chelsea district, around 1905, theater owners found bigger, cheaper spaces to build music houses and cabarets on a street called Broadway. The entire theater district packed up and moved north. You know the rest of the story. With its lively theater scene gone, the Chelsea neighborhood began to decline. The wealthy Chelsea dwellers moved on as well. The building was turned into a hotel, albeit a "residence hotel" that had rooms for tourists (whom Chelsea insiders called "transients") and actual apartments for permanent residents. The Chelsea remained so until very recently: one part hotel, two parts apartment building. While it is best known for its artists, it is also renowned for its unique design features. For instance, you can't mention the hotel's architecture without referring to its staircase.

JULIE EAKIN

The central stairwell, in particular, is a really resonant, romantic space. It goes up for ten flights and has the wrought iron banister all the way up—it's very identifiable.

PETER JOHANSSON

You can see the famous stairway in a lot of movies, like *The Pro-*

fessional, which was shot at the Chelsea. Look at that movie, and you'll see how the Chelsea used to look. There's a scene where a very young Natalie Portman is sitting and smoking a cigarette, dangling her feet. They show you an eagle's eye view of the stairs with their black and white tiles. That movie really gives you a feel of what the inside of the Chelsea was all about.

I approached the cluttered front desk area. Up to the right, there hung a painting by Abstract-Expressionist Herbert Gentry,[6] a nice painting of spontaneous, swirling brushstrokes forming themselves into human figures, but it was grimy, in sore need of a cleaning. No different, I guess, than the rest of the Chelsea.

I had assumed the hotel's staff would be bored with starry-eyed tourists brimming with questions about the hotel's history. But the desk clerk was an affable, talkative man, perfectly willing to play up its reputation. He escorted me up the ancient elevator—*Creak! Clang!*—and down the quiet hallway. Same as bellmen anywhere, he insisted on helping me carry my two small, lightweight bags into my room, and waited politely for his tip.

A Man's Cave is His Castle

When I saw Room 626, my heart sank. It was dim and shaped like a narrow wedge. No doubt, the owners had split it off a larger room to double the money collected from the same square footage. The furniture was period Salvation Army. The view out the enormous window was not of 23rd Street, but of the little concrete courtyard in back, glistening wet, where a single aluminum chaise longue reclined next to a fruit crate on which to set your drink. My room, I realized, was in back.

Almost every long-term resident I had spoken to referred to their room at the Chelsea not as a *room* but as a *house*. They would say, quite unselfconsciously, "Once there was a party at Marty Matz's house for Herbert Huncke," or "One of his junkie friends used to go over to her house and do drugs and get all freaky." Of course there were no actual houses. They were *rooms*, usually tiny, cramped rooms, barely big enough for a twin-sized bed. Was this misnomer just a Chelsea tradition, a piece of local jargon that residents absorbed by osmosis? Was it wish fulfillment? Call it a house long enough and it will become one? Or was there something so comfortable about the Chelsea's atmosphere that turned a little room into a pleasant, inviting home?

Because my room was in back and off the street, it was surprisingly quiet. No street noise floated up through the window, no shouts from the sidewalk or taxi horns. Sadly, the back rooms had no balconies. (At the Chelsea, balconies are prized real estate). But if I left my room and walked down to the end of the hallway, I could step out a big, unscreened window and get some fresh air on the fire escape's tiny landing.

Left alone in my cramped abode, I found myself rummaging for history. I examined every piece of furniture for artifacts left behind, a matchbook or a little plastic cocktail sword. Maybe a novelist or rock star had scribbled a message in the closet's dark corner. I checked behind the big framed mirror hanging on the wall—nothing. But sure enough, when I pulled out an empty drawer of my flimsy old dresser, there was a poem written in bold black marker on the bottom:

> *Two dollars*
> *and*
> *another steel car ride*
> *from fresh*
> *sights*
> *and*
> *new sounds*
> *all containing*
> *the same*
> *stale urine*
> *smell*
> *embedded in the*
> *New York City*
> *sidewalk*

Beneath it, in red marker, a critic had penned a response:

> *Go back to Peoria, sucka!*

At the Chelsea, such missives-left-behind are not uncommon. Julie Eakin, who moved into her room during the mid-80s, found a giant fresco scribbled onto her wall.

JULIE EAKIN

We got our room from a couple who had to break their lease. I think they were from New Zealand. They had left us a jar of marmalade on the mantel, and two black coats in the closet—one woman's coat and one man's coat. They were our sizes perfectly, and they were very hip!

Also, painted in black on the wall, was this huge argument in dialogue. It was huge! The part that I remember said, "You started it!"

It was Room 319, which is on the front of the hotel, just to the right of the lower part of the famous Hotel Chelsea sign. There are two French doors that lead out onto the balcony there. We actually had a hot plate and a toaster oven in our room, because that was the only way we could cook. It was probably illegal, due to fire codes, but I'm sure they knew that we were doing it, because all we had was a bathroom sink in the corner. So we would make Thanksgiving dinner in the toaster oven!

When my mom visited, I think I did begin to see it through her eyes. There were extraordinarily huge water bugs and roaches. She was absolutely appalled. I don't blame her! I remember watching her clean my phone at some point, and thinking, "Oh, it never occurred to me to clean a phone!"

DAVID LAWTON

It was such a dump! Those couple of floors, the second and third floors, we still regard as "the dump floors." The rooms were a mess, the hallway smelled of pot and cat piss![7]

But this didn't deter our young artists, for whom cleanliness was beside the point.

DIMITRI MUGIANIS

Moving in was great! There were all these other young people who were doing things, creating things, and the older people who were doing things, those people I had always looked up to. At one point, in the course of a single month, Tom Waits was living there, Don Cherry[8], Ornette Coleman's[9] trumpet player, was there, and Gil Scott Heron[10] lived there too. You could talk to these people in the hallway!

The very first day I lived there, I opened the door and was going to go out to the store, and Julian Beck,[11] from the Living Theater, was opening the door next to me. I looked at his face—which is a helluva face—and I just closed the door! I was terrified! But I said to myself, "Wow, this is a great place!"

DAVID LAWTON

It was such a wacky universe, with little celebrities passing through! Anthony Kiedis from the Chili Peppers for instance, and you'd see minor celebrities passing through for short periods of time.

ROBERT CAMPBELL

Everybody who moves into the Chelsea wants to know what famous person once lived in his or her room. Big Paul [Romero] had Bob Dylan's room, 319, where Dylan wrote "Sad Eyed Lady of the Lowlands." John Wayne had also lived there. Sarah Bernhardt. Arthur C. Clarke[12] wrote *2001: A Space Odyssey* at the Chelsea. And Julian Schnabel,[13] the painter who made it huge in the 80s, lived up there, the guy with the busted plates. And my friend Scott Covert had Dylan Thomas' room, either that or maybe it was O. Henry's.[14]

PAUL VOLMER

There was this vibe of history going through there. There are the plaques outside, with the names of Brendan Behan[15] and all these luminaries. And you're in your late teens or early twenties—even into your thirties—before you get your teeth kicked in. You've still got the idealism. You want to write, and you want to perform, and you think your shit doesn't stink. It was a great place to do that with a bunch of other people doing it at the same time.

In the hotel's long history, people moving into the Chelsea saw themselves as following a light, or at least a rose-tinted glow: the Chelsea Hotel's glimmering, shabby romantic allure. But before any of them were accepted inside, they had an appointment to keep. They had to sit down face-to-face with the Keeper of the Gate: Stanley Bard.

The Bard of 23rd Street

Who was Stanley Bard? Let's let him speak for himself. Once, when Bard was talking to long-term resident Mary Anne Rose-Gentry, he asserted matter-of-factly, "I am this hotel."

This is no exaggeration. On a day-to-day level, Bard—a slender, well-dressed man, articulate in speech and with gentle, doe-like brown eyes—was Chelsea Hotel Central, its manager and part owner. You could see in his eyes, sensitive but always darting left and right, glancing at something over your shoulder, that Stanley Bard was the Watchman. He loved watching what went on at his hotel. He loved his job, arriving punctually at five a.m. and departing twelve hours later. He handled the gritty day-to-day operations, and in a building as big as the Chelsea, where hundreds upon hundreds of people went about their lives, handling all those details was no small matter. It was Bard who admitted new tenants into the building, managed the hotel's budget and its staff of desk clerks, bellmen, night guards, maintenance people, and room maids.

Bard also dealt in real estate, calibrating the balance between the hotel's short-term transients and long-term residents, tracking room reservations, signing and updating leases, and—famously—collecting payment. He dealt with anything from room repairs and renovations to heart attacks, ambulances and visits by the police. Some say Bard would phone and warn a resident as police caught the elevator up to a room for a surprise drug bust. When the cops arrived, all they found was a toilet still hissing. It was Stanley who handled the hotel's pr, making sure its reputation as a haven for the arts stayed strong. And pristine, which wasn't always easy considering the treachery, lechery, and debauchery that sometimes went on behind its walls.

Stanley Bard knew every one of his residents. He knew their quirks, their eccentricities, their dogs. More important, he knew who owed him money and exactly how much.

For any hotel manager in any hotel, all this would have been a demanding job. But at an artists' hotel like the Chelsea, Bard's job required a different set of skills: the inspirational talents of a coach, the patience of a babysitter, and the tact of a diplomat. And when these didn't do the trick, he could transform himself seamlessly into the hectoring debt collector, a role he performed with aplomb.

Stanley Bard—befitting his oracular last name—was as much an artist as his tenants. His masterpiece was the Chelsea Hotel.

JUDITH CHILDS

He made it possible for creative people to create. He's a kind of genius himself. He got along very well with the artists because they're also mad geniuses.

Sweet Dreams are Made of These

The Chelsea promised different things to different people. Maybe they wanted artistic fame, or at least some new artist friends, famous or not. Maybe they were attracted to the hedonistic pleasures promised in a "rule-free" zone. Most of them aspired to become characters in the Chelsea's history, heroes in the place's epic, eccentric story.

In our own lives, most of us remember our "firsts"—our first day of school, first time driving a car, our first sexual experience. We recall our enthusiasm and dread as things got started, as we girded up our loins and stepped through the door.

When the painter John Zinsser arrived at the hotel, he had also "arrived" in more than one way. His paintings were beginning to sell, he was building a name for himself, and he had just gotten married.

JOHN ZINSSER

My wife and I were looking for a place to live. She was from small-town Michigan, near Toledo, so the Chelsea Hotel had always been a romantic notion for her. We were looking at rental buildings, and we went around the Chelsea and talked to Stanley.

Stanley's office was beautiful. That's where I first met him, when I interviewed with him to be accepted into the hotel. He had all these accordion files stacked up to the ceiling. He ushered you in and sat down across from you. I told him a story about visiting Virgil Thomson at the Chelsea when I was a kid. I told him I was a painter, and at that time having a lot of success.

"Great!" he said. "You're perfect!" There was no check into my finances or anything.

The price there was competitive with other rentals we had looked at.

Then he showed me these horrible rooms. He would show you the worst, crappiest room possible, and his description of it was like he was showing you the Palace at Versailles. The largesse he brought to showing these rooms! Then he would quote these outlandishly high prices with a straight face!

It was such a perverse performance, but so true to Stanley's double-sided character.

Our first place was room 725, the top floor where they have the cast-iron balconies. It had French doors. It had the classic small hotel room feel. But the view, when you looked out the French doors at the brocade of the ironwork on the balcony, was classic and beautiful. High up over the street below. But the room didn't have much detail, so I painted everything white and tried to make it look 1960's Chelsea Girl style.

High and Dry: Paul Volmer

Paul Volmer's move into the Chelsea "was more like being thrown up on the beach." He had just finished his degree at NYU and was lacking direction and money. A thoughtful, introspective and idealistic native of Rhode Island with wavy ginger hair, fair, freckly skin and sensitive blue eyes, Volmer came from working class roots. His mother wanted him back in Rhode Island doing something practical. She suggested assistant manager at the CVS. "You just have to work," she informed him. "You don't have to enjoy it."

Paul knew he couldn't settle for that. He had long admired Andy Warhol and Preston Sturges, the director of screwball comedies, and he wanted to be a writer.

With a small loan from a New York businessman friend of his father's, Volmer gathered enough money to pay the damage deposit for a tiny room. But he hadn't solved the problem of making a living. Wanting to be a writer, he found himself a waiter. Over time, though, he ingratiated himself to Stanley Bard, who finally agreed to hire Volmer as a bellman and night watchman.

With his new position at the hotel, Volmer became privy to two worlds. As an employee, he could observe the hotel's management and operations. But being night watchman was beyond ordinary at the Chelsea. At night, he was witness to—and part of—the hotel's lush, subversive night life.

The scene was perfect for an aspiring writer looking for material. But instead of pulling back and acting the detached observer, Volmer couldn't resist immersing himself in the scene and becoming part of its creative milieu.

PAUL VOLMER

I had read this book called *Edie*,[16] about Edie Sedgwick. She lived at the Chelsea Hotel full time, and she was one of Andy Warhol's Chelsea Girls. Each of these incredible, spirited people also has their fatal flaw that the Chelsea seems to reveal to them. Whatever drugs or mayhem they're susceptible to, it's there at the Chelsea for them.

So Edie helped inspire me to hitchhike to New York. Every two hours I had to walk the floors of the building because there were fire regulations that required it for safety's sake. Late at night was when the ladies of the evening would come in. It was also when the drug addicts would be up and out, and that's when the lost souls would be wandering around. There's a whole other world between night people and day people. I didn't really realize that until I worked the graveyard shift there.

Stanley Bard chose most of the residents because they were creative, they were artists of one kind or another. So people who lived at the Chelsea, or who visited there, used to ask me, "What is your art?"

I'd tell them, "You're looking at it. My art is my lifestyle."

Oh No, Marlowe's Back!

Next was Marlowe West, mellow Marlowe, the dark-haired, handsome, laid-back hippie whose trademark word was "beautiful."

When West moved in as Volmer's roommate, he was already a seasoned veteran of the counter-culture. During the late 60s and early 70s, the chameleonic West had shocked his parents when he left Long Island, tossing aside his acceptance letter to Parson's School of Design. Instead, he followed his dream to Hollywood. There, he spent his flower child period hanging with the rock legend Frank Zappa and his groupie entourage, the GTOs.[17] After Hollywood, he moved to New York, where he often dropped by the Chelsea to visit his close friend Jobriath,[18] for whom he was singing backup.

A decade later, West took the final step and actually *moved into* the Chelsea during his own glam-metal rocker period as the lead singer of a band called Skin Tight.

West kept his day job, which, in this Bohemian milieu, was quite unorthodox. Every morning he drove back to Long Island to work his steady nine-to-five job at a big defense plant, General Dynamics Armaments and Technical Products. When his shift was over, he would drive back "over to the Chelsea Hotel and be this mad superstar!"

Skin Tight's drummer and guitar player had already found a room there, where they met up with a Chelsea dweller, Nicholas (Nicko) Gentry, son of the Abstract Expressionist painter Herbert Gentry, a longtime resident. Nicko was an accomplished musician and became Skin Tight's bassist.

Through Nicko, the band discovered that the bellman/night watchman Paul Volmer needed a roommate. Marlowe went to meet Paul and their friendship was born.

West's reputation at the Chelsea preceded him.

MARLOWE WEST

What was funny was that people at the hotel's front desk remembered me from almost ten years ago, when I used to hang out at the Chelsea with Jobriath. "Oh no," the front desk people said when they saw me, "Marlowe's back!"

PAUL VOLMER

Marlowe is very flamboyant. He would make all of his own costumes for his band, wild things like sequined vests and leather pants with open gaps on the sides and criss-crossed drawstrings up the gaps—all his own creations in the heavy metal fashion.

There was only one problem—an issue that would haunt West for his entire stay at the Chelsea. He moved in without checking first with Stanley Bard. This was taboo. Meeting Bard in person was standard protocol: you sat down for your interview with him, and he gave you a thumbs up or down depending if you were "right" for the Chelsea. "Right" meant you were either a successful artist or you had potential to become one.

Bard sometimes also factored in your ability to pay rent, the precise calculus of which is still unknown. But West ignored the protocol, strutting through the hotel's front doors, flitting right past this little procedural detail, and landing smack in bellman Paul Volmer's Room 218.

The room was a strip of empty space between two beat-up mattresses pushed against the walls. It had a sink and a window with a view of an alley. To West's dismay, the room was a pigsty. Volmer was not famous for his housekeeping.

MARLOWE WEST

When I first stepped into Paul's room, I thought "I'm coming in with two buckets of paint!" I got yards and yards of tulle, and hung it down from the ceiling so it would screen off the half of the room where my bed was. After my designing efforts, the room was pretty neat, though.

Volmer confirms that Marlowe added a little Goodwill glamour to the room.

PAUL VOLMER

There was only one overhead light fixture in the middle of the room. We experimented with different colored light bulbs, but most of the time we had either green or blue. And we painted the room a really light purple, so the room had this purply-green otherworldly atmosphere. Marlowe put satin sheets on his bed, beautiful purples and reds. And over his bed, he had a purple mesh canopy he devised. He also built a little light table with white glass over it and lights underneath. He was very whimsical. We would put little toy dinosaurs, knick-knacks and plastic palm trees on the light table. Something to illuminate the room at night.

MARLOWE WEST

And then things got fun.

Prior to West's appearance on the scene, Volmer's messy room had already evolved into something of a salon where budding young artists, musicians and writers could connect, a place where parties happened, parties that Volmer generously kept supplied with the usual social lubricants.

PAUL VOLMER

The scene at the Chelsea was the remnant of the Warhol scene there. It was very interactive. You were in this many-roomed hotel with many different artists and types of people. Just hanging out with your friends in the rooms and talking about art and writing. I loved to talk about literature. People would bring tapes of their music over to play for you, someone might bring their painting for you to look at, and they were excited that they accomplished it. Or if they couldn't get anything going, they were depressed about it, and at least they had someone to talk to.

And now with Marlowe's interior décor upgrades, the salon had Bohemian-style glamor.

MARLOWE WEST

Just before I left California, there had been a sale at Paramount Studios, and a friend of mine bought these great big cardboard barrels filled with glitter, one gold and one silver. So I took a bagful of each back to New York with me, and on Friday nights we would sit on the balcony and throw glitter down on all sorts of people coming in and going out of the hotel's front entranceway. On the sidewalk in front of the hotel, there was always glitter.

Carolina Boy in Manhattan:
Robert Campbell

When Robert Campbell moved into the Chelsea, he was as different as possible from Paul and Marlowe. Campbell was a North Carolina boy, a chatty, friendly, outgoing rock guitarist from a town called Hickory. He wore blue jeans with Brooks Brothers shirts, dark hair nearly reaching his waist pulled back in a ponytail, and granny-style wire-framed glasses.

ROBERT CAMPBELL

I was twenty-three or twenty-four, and for some reason I had decided I wanted to meet lots of people and get as wild as I could. I planned to straighten out when I was thirty. Of course, it didn't work out that way.

Soon after moving to New York, he got a day job at Atlantic Records proofreading album covers. But living in New York and having a job weren't enough—he wanted to live at the Chelsea.

ROBERT CAMPBELL

I went up and told Stanley Bard, "Hey look, I work at Atlantic Records. I want to live here."

Bard showed Campbell a room for which the word small would be too grand.

ROBERT CAMPBELL

I think it had previously been used as a paint closet. I think it used to be Peter Brook's[19] room. I instantly liked it.

Small room be damned, Campbell used his gregarious personality and knack for bringing the right people together to rapidly become a "Chelsea socialite," known for the parties, jam sessions and social happenings that blossomed in the overcrowded space he shared with his girlfriend, the painter Carol Schmidt.

NANCY ROGERS

At the impromptu gatherings in Robert's room, there were a lot of people who had guitars, so there were a lot of cover songs being played. But there was always a mix of what was played—from the Ramones to the Beatles to Johnny Cash. It was definitely very open as far as musical styles, not this narrow view that if you weren't punk-influenced, you weren't respected. If you came in and you played the accordion, and played polka songs, somebody would grab an electric guitar and they'd say, "Hey, let's figure out how we can jam together." And everyone would respect that, and even enjoy the diversity of it.

JOHN ZINSSER

Robert and his girlfriend Carol were our immediate neighbors whom we shared a hallway with. But the wall we shared with Robert was very thin. He would stay up all night, every night with friends, playing records. So as far as a place to live, it was hellacious because of his night-time habits. But in a way, I didn't mind—it was a package deal—it came with the Chelsea.

DIMITRI MUGIANIS

Robert would say the wrong things—always—to the point where it was wonderful! Once, he took our friend Patrick to see a friend who was a blues singer. Robert introduced Patrick to his friend this way in Harlem: "Patrick, this is the black guy I was telling you about." Another time, Robert looked at me and said, "Dimitri, you've got *Jew* hair!" Now Robert was never racist. I knew that for a fact—but he just didn't know what to say! He came from Hickory, North Carolina and dropped himself down in the middle of this scene at the Chelsea. He would just do the wrong thing. He was a big kid!

DAVID LAWTON

Robert was the master of malapropisms.[20] Famously, when Robert decided to give Dimitri some advice about his band Leisure Class, he said, "You've gotta do something like Debbie Gibson!"[21] He was trying to make the point that you need to make a pop record to break through. "You've gotta be like Debbie Gibson, man!" Paul and I looked at each other like, "Hmm, what can we do with that advice? Maybe we need to play more malls!"

Debbie Gibson or not, Campbell made his own guitar-playing skills known through his Room 227 jam sessions.

ROBERT CAMPBELL

I wanted to be a rock star. I thought that would be cool.

It wasn't long before he received a call on his hotel phone from a real rock star. Dee Dee Ramone had heard about Robert and invited him over to his room to jam. This led to that, and pretty soon Campbell was a full-fledged member of the Dee Dee Ramone Group. Dee Dee wanted to start out by playing blues covers, the same way the Rolling Stones had done. And southerner Campbell happened to know all about the blues. This is how Campbell took his swipe at rock stardom.

Beat the Devil: Dimitri Mugianis

Hailing from Detroit, Dimitri Mugianis hit the ground running at the Chelsea. He was a charismatic twenty-year-old, armed to the teeth with intellectual firepower and an enchanting smile. From one angle he looked like Marlon Brando, from another like Errol Flynn, but his most striking characteristic was his voice. Its scratchy-energetic timbre belonged to a man who had traveled to the dark side and survived. He arrived in Manhattan with his beautiful girlfriend Julie Eakin and his eleven-piece band, Mr. Unique and the Leisure Class. Complete with a horn section and a back-up choir, the whole ensemble migrated to New York around the same time. If they couldn't make it there, to paraphrase Frank Sinatra, they couldn't make it anywhere.

DIMITRI MUGIANIS

Detroit is a great place. But when I came to New York, it was like "Ahhh! I'm *home!*'" And then you move into someplace like the Chelsea, it was "Yeah! This is what I want to do, man!"

Shortly after moving in, Mugianis and his fellow band member David Lawton were riding the elevator down to the lobby, and who should step in but Tom Waits.[22] Daunted by Waits' status, they didn't dare speak to him. But sensing opportunity for his band, Mugianis kept one of The Leisure Class's demo tapes with him at all times.

DAVID LAWTON

The next time Dimitri saw Tom Waits, he actually got a demo tape into Waits's hands.

Some time later, we ran into Waits again and asked if he'd listened to our tape. In that gravelly voice of his, he said, "My lawyer says I can't listen to your tape."

Mugianis's more lasting brush with fame came from a chance encounter at a used bookstore, where he ran into one of his all-time counterculture heroes. He had always been inspired by the Beat writers Jack Kerouac and Allen Ginsberg. One day, while thumbing through some old books, he encountered the quintessential Beat writer, Herbert Huncke, the very man who had given young Kerouac and Ginsberg the term "Beat." Mugianis and Huncke became fast friends.

Huncke introduced Mugianis to other Beat icons like Gregory Corso and Marty Matz. Here was this kid from Detroit actually hanging out with the Beats he had idolized!

But there was a dark side, a little matter that kept these old Chelsea Beats so beat: they were—every one of them—junkies. They used every day, all day, and they pulled Mugianis into their desperate habit. He too became a junkie. Down the road, because of heroin, he lost a girlfriend and later a wife, not to mention his eleven-piece band. He damned near lost his life.

The Chelsea Appeal

Why has the Chelsea Hotel proven so attractive to fledgling artists, not to mention such already successful luminaries as Dylan, Joplin, Warhol, Waits and a thousand others? It's not exactly a luxury hotel. It is worn out, run down and used up. So what is it about the place?

For one, it's more about human relations than bricks and mortar. Artists, especially Bohemians, know when they are genuinely welcome instead of merely tolerated as "talent." Stanley Bard and his family sincerely liked artists, and the artists could feel it. There was nothing patronizing in the hoteliers' attitude toward cultural creatives. Artists aren't known for swimming comfortably in the mainstream. They have foibles, they have eccentricities, and they want a place to live that will either be supportive of them or leave them alone. At the Chelsea, both options were available. As with any cultural subgroup, likes attract. Like blood cells swimming through a network of vessels, all leading to a single heart, people seek places where they can hang with people who share their values, priorities, and interests.

For our four Chelsea newcomers, this single heart was the Chelsea Hotel, floors one and two.

PAUL VOLMER

The bottom two floors were where Stanley would usually put people who first came to the hotel. These were generally young, or the outcasts of society like prostitutes or criminals or runaways. These were the least desirable rooms with the least desirable people. As you went up the floors, there were strata, just like a mirror of society's economic strata. The poorer people were on the lowest floors, and as you went up in floors there would be nicer rooms, until eventually when you reached the top, where there were penthouse apartments with actual gardens on the roof. The wealthy people lived up there.

You were not allowed to go up on the roof. Only the people who lived on the top floor had roof access. From what I understood, the rooms up there were much nicer—the places with the stained glass and all. Those were people who kept, for example, exotic pets and such. Tom Waits was there, and so was Philip Glass.[23]

DIMITRI MUGIANIS

It used to be that New York City would pay hotels to house families on welfare. So on the bottom floors, there were welfare families living at the Chelsea, four people living in a tiny room and being paid a lot of money. There's a guy we shared the bathroom with in the hall, a little man and his wife and their daughter, who seemed sort of developmentally challenged, living in this very small room, probably without any fresh air or circulation.

It would be nice to come up with a metaphor to describe the scene with the poor on the bottom floors, rich on top. Something alchemical, the chaos swirling on the bottom floors providing fuel that fed the hotel's creative fire, inspiring the artists who lived on the more expensive top levels.

It would also be nonsense. The fact is, the upstairs and downstairs people lived very separate lives. They rarely socialized together. Though united to some degree by the Chelsea walls, or more accurately Chelsea ceilings, the wealthy dwellers of the upper floors knew next to nothing about the feral inhabitants of the floors below. They didn't want to know. When the wealthy upper-floor people heard rumors of the Chelsea's raucous, outlaw reputation, they often couldn't believe people were talking about the same hotel! They insisted their building—with its nine-inch, sand-filled walls—was peaceful and quiet, far removed from the madding crowd.

Nevertheless, no matter their social status, open-mindedness was the rule. The upstairs and downstairs people, remote and different in so many ways, were united by their gratitude to the Chelsea and their love for—and fear of—Stanley Bard. Wealthy or poor, they were all odd birds in the same big cage.

MARLOWE WEST

I just thought the Chelsea was where all the freaks were magnetized to. It's where everybody felt comfortable.

If you walked around wearing animal skins and Viking horns, as did a guy named Don Normal, or if you wore a three-piece suit and carried a briefcase, either was okay with both management and residents.

Truth be told, some of the residents took rather drastic advantage of the *laissez faire* atmosphere. Where eccentricity is encouraged, excess follows. Permission to dress differently, think differently and behave differently tends to deliquesce into decadence. You begin to flirt a little too casually with danger, to mix with criminals or mix your drugs—both of which can send you to the hospital. Or worse.

ROBERT CAMPBELL

The Chelsea was so wild it was like an insane asylum. And the Chelsea was also a microcosm of society. There were low-lifes there, there were ordinary people, and there were insane people, and rich and famous people, and you could feel the sense of history, and the outrageous stories of all creative types—not only unbelievably outrageous, but true.

*Bellman/night watchman Paul Volmer (at right) with cat
and Nicko Gentry hanging out in a typically
cramped room at the Chelsea.*

CHAPTER 2

Chelsea Wildness

Furry people, too. Werewolves of Chelsea. Limited always to the 2nd Floor, where the cleaning staff entered with caution, eyes down for glass, peering through the door into the bath, the discipline of homicide detectives.[24]—JOHN CALE

I n the early 1960s, the Pulitzer Prize winning playwright Arthur Miller, still licking his wounds after his failed marriage to Marilyn Monroe, moved into the Chelsea Hotel because at the luxurious Plaza Hotel where he used to live, he hated feeling he had to wear a tie just to go down and pick up his mail.

Some forty years later, long after he had left the Chelsea, Miller wrote an essay for *Granta* called "The Chelsea Effect." His treatment of the Chelsea was droll, portraying manager Stanley Bard as an obdurate optimist, the kind of Pollyanna who, to keep up his positive front, must sink deep into denial about what actually went on between the walls. According to Miller, Bard was "simply not interested in bad news of any kind."

Miller appreciated that the hotel "was a house of infinite toleration," but with some reservations. He had issues with the hotel's insular quality, its pervading atmosphere of unreality. Filmmaker James Rasin described the ambiance in a similar way.

JAMES RASIN

You just walked into the Chelsea and the world disappeared. It's like you were walking into a whole different world, like a warp zone.

After a few years, Miller moved out, fearing that at any given moment he was in very real danger of physical harm. The Chelsea offered both miracles and murder.

Where did Stanley Bard stand amidst the hotel's dreamy treachery? Was his airtight optimism just shrewd public relations? Was Bard a genuine idealist, or just a master of spin?

Real Chelsea dwellers have attested that the wild events you're about to read are factual, actual, and accurate, even if they're not the sort of events Stanley Bard—salesman to the core—liked to peddle.

JULIE EAKIN

I think anything was permitted, honestly. I don't remember any hotel people ever coming into our room.

JUDITH CHILDS

One thing there really aren't, at the Chelsea, are lots and lots of amenities. But there's lots and lots of *laissez faire*, which is much more important than amenities, isn't it!

The Attack of Dainty Adore

One such individual who may have pushed the "all is permitted" ethic past Bohemian boundaries was a drag queen named Dainty Adore. The corpulent Dainty dressed up like Little Bo Peep in a gingham pinafore and a curly blonde wig, and minced around carrying a parasol and singing opera in falsetto.

And now Dainty had become obsessed with Paul Volmer, who planned to become the Warhol of his age. Volmer admired Warhol's ability to dispassionately observe the scene he created, quietly watching whatever insane sex and drug exploits careened around him. As night watchman, Volmer would run into all sorts of people. Sometimes he'd invite them to his room, talk to them, interview them about their lives.

PAUL VOLMER

I had a very inquiring mind. But I swear, I wish I hadn't been so open to Dainty Adore. When I did my nightly rounds, Dainty Adore was always in a bathrobe, sort of waiting for me. Even though he was kind of weird, he was friendly to me and I would talk to him.

Then later on, I started hearing from people in the hotel that Dainty Adore had a crush on me. He was spreading all of these rumors about us as lovers, and everyone was beginning to think the worst of me.

MARLOWE WEST

I thought Paul and Dainty might be having a thing together, and I was thinking, *Paul is going out with a drag queen?*

I asked him, "Paul, you're hanging out with *her*?"

Plus, because Paul was hanging out with Dainty, Dainty would start talking to me in the lobby, as if I were a friend of his. If people were watching, I'd be saying, "I don't know him!"

Dainty was like one of those pink elephants with ballet slippers. I can't fall for that. I don't even like *real* girls who act like that.

PAUL VOLMER

At that time, my actual girlfriend Neicy and I would break up periodically. During one of these periods, I was somewhat depressed, and I guess I told Dainty that Neicy had left again.

The next day, Dainty knocked on my door, but I was so depressed I didn't want to talk to anybody. "Go away," I told him. "I'm not in the mood to talk right now."

After I closed the door, I heard a sound like something pushing against my door, like someone had squished something against it. I opened the door and Dainty was gone, but there was a mashed cake stuck to the door. Apparently, to be sympathetic, he had made me a cake.

I shut the door, thinking, *Oh no. Why do I need this?*

Inside my room, the table I was sitting at was right next to the door. The Chelsea has doorframes with little windows above the frames. It's a solidly built building, the Chelsea. So I'm sitting at my table, and all of a sudden I hear a rumbling in the hallway outside, sort of like the sound of a charging elephant.

Now Dainty was normally a gentle person, but he weighed 300 pounds. He ran full throttle, hit my door, and with a tremendous crash right next to me, he bashed this huge door frame down, making bricks and dust fly. And there he was just standing in shock, as if he were thinking *What have I done?* Then he ran away.

Meanwhile, the manager Stanley and the bellman had heard the tremendous crash. The doorframe and the door itself probably weighed hundreds of pounds. They ran upstairs, and found me sitting at my table covered in plaster and dust. They just looked at me.

"What happened?"

"Well," I said, "I want you to know it's not true that Dainty and I are in love."

I started telling them this whole story about Dainty's love for me. Everyone was quite appalled. They couldn't really believe that I hadn't provoked this.

Ironically, over my many years there, I later became friendly with Dainty. Bygones became bygones.

But it did bring up a question. In a place like the Chelsea, where weirdness was encouraged, where did you draw the line? Exactly what was *too* weird?

Indeed Volmer brings up one of the key philosophical issues that pervaded the Chelsea and all Bohemian enclaves. In a community that prides itself on tolerating, even encouraging weirdness, when was weird too weird for *weirdos*?

But is it Real?

A dependable source of wildness was a young woman named Fuchsia Gold, whom bellman Paul Volmer befriended while making his night watchman's rounds. Fuchsia came from a wealthy family but said goodbye to all that in order to pursue a career as exotic dancer and dominatrix.

PAUL VOLMER

Once, I was having a Halloween party in my room with my room-mate Marlowe. I had invited Fuchsia. Now I also had an ex-girl-friend who had already come to this party. She was waiting in my room with her new husband. They were suits, very straight. He was a pharmacist and she was an executive secretary. So they came to my little funky Bohemian room at the Chelsea and they were sitting on the bed waiting for this party to start, just a little get-together with my friends. I went down to the lobby to wait for Fuchsia to come in, so I could tell her about my party and send her up. But while I was waiting for her to show up, one of her slaves sat down next to me.

I had met him before—I'll call him Nelson [not his real name]. He was sort of overweight and dumpy with a whiney little voice. He worked as a truancy officer, which I thought was funny. He would let Fuchsia tie him up and spank him.

So this slave Nelson and I started having this discussion in the lobby about whether S&M was real love. I contended it wasn't. He had all these arguments why it was. So while we were having this discussion, Fuchsia showed up in the lobby. She was dressed in full regalia with the patent-leather hip boots and her whip. When she saw Nelson, just to mess with him, to frighten him, she said "Nelson, what are *you* doing here!"

Nelson jumped up with a start and ran up the stairs. He knew the party was in my room, so he bolted up there. And Fuchsia literally cracked her bullwhip behind him, the full length across the lobby. I wish I had a picture of it. So Nelson ran into my room and cowered against the wall. And Fuchsia chased after him into my room, cracking the whip and laughing. But she was just mess-ing with him, and we continued on with our party. Meanwhile, of course, my straight ex-girlfriend, the executive secretary, and her boyfriend the pharmacist, were watching this spectacle. They were absolutely dumbfounded.

The Master of Malapropisms

If Volmer was collecting friends from the demimonde, North Carolinian Robert Campbell was acquainting himself with the Chelsea in his own way. In his paint closet of a room, Campbell was applying his gregarious manner and his Southern-style talents for conversation and storytelling to start a noisy little scene of his own.

PAUL VOLMER

Robert was working at Atlantic Records and met a lot of people there. His room was a very amusing place. It was a very small, very skinny room that basically only had a bed pushed over on one side. Robert would invite people over to jam, people from inside or from Atlantic or wherever. Musicians would be jamming in his tiny room and it was really lively.

STEVE HOUSE

You'd go to Robert's room, and it'd be packed with people. He'd be out on the balcony, standing over his little Hibachi grill, and say, "Come on *in*, man! I'm making freaking quesadillas!"

NANCY ROGERS

Within an hour or so there'd be half a dozen people there. Or more. That would create its own party. And of course you can't talk about the Chelsea without acknowledging the ever-present drug scene. I remember a person coming to my party once and saying they'd been offered five different drugs in the half block between the subway and my apartment. But that was nothing compared to the Chelsea Hotel! People smoked weed like cigarettes. People were drinking. But there were also cocaine, heroin, and acid.

Maybe it was because I was in my twenties and early thirties, but I don't remember it as a negative thing. I remember it being a lot of fun!

ROBERT CAMPBELL

I had two rules for anyone who came into my room. The first rule was you could never say the "N-word." I just didn't go for that stuff. My second rule for people in my room was you couldn't smoke cigarettes. You could smoke other things, but no tobacco. I never physically kicked anyone out of my room for breaking either one of those rules. I would just turn off the music and say, "Hey, you know what? We gotta go somewhere. I've got this errand I forgot all about." But I made my rules known, so if anybody brought a friend to my room, I'm sure they were warned before they came in—"Don't say the 'N-word' and don't smoke tobacco."

Looking back on it, the tobacco rule led to one of my grossest ego wipeouts. It happened when I had the writer Kinky Friedman[25] up to visit in Room 723 after I moved up there. Now, I was friends with Herbert Huncke, the old Beat writer. Huncke wanted me to meet Kinky Friedman. I was a Southern guy and I was always drunk and always talking shit, and evidently I had impressed Huncke and his friends with my Southernality. So these guys thought I might want to meet Kinky Friedman.

I knew who Kinky Friedman was. I knew about his band, Kinky Friedman and the Texas Jew Boys. I knew that he also wrote detective novels. I had even read some of them, but books are like toilet paper to me—use 'em and consume 'em—and to be honest, I thought he was a hack as a writer. I was just a pompous little ass. So finally Kinky Friedman came up to my room.

In all of his books, Friedman mentions that he doesn't like people who won't let him smoke cigars in their houses. And here I am, the guy who will only let people smoke weed in his room at the Chelsea. If people smoked tobacco—I didn't care if there was a blizzard outside—they had to go out on the balcony. So when Kinky was in my room, I wouldn't let him smoke his cigar, but then I went ahead and rolled this big fat joint and lit it up. It killed him.

We got into a disagreement about the history of my room. Kinky took issue with my saying that 723 had been Janis Joplin's room. But Stanley Bard himself told me that Janis had lived in my room. Stanley also told me that one night someone painted, "Janis, you are the best fuck I ever had," on 723's door. This someone had been pissed at her.

And then, later on, in one of his books, Kinky Friedman made a point of saying that Janis Joplin's room at the Chelsea was some *other* room, not my room, 723. Which is definitely not true.

In this way, Kinky got his revenge on me. After I read that, I always felt like writing him a letter.

The ironic thing is that now I smoke cigarettes. About a pack a day.

The Marvelous Missteps of Marlowe West

Mellow Marlowe West—by day the lead singer in the glam metal band Skin Tight, by night a factory boy at General Dynamics—was making his presence known at the Chelsea in his own way. He brought humor to the Chelsea, usually at his own expense. After a series of ridiculous misfortunes, he assumed the mantle of the sacred trickster, the Holy Fool. Holy Fools may have been a dime a dozen at the Chelsea, but Marlowe played the role in singular style.

ROBERT CAMPBELL

Marlowe was the nicest guy you would ever see, but he was always doing something screwed up. He had these cowboy boots with metal caps on the toes to make them look cool. Well Marlowe was helping this lady who had a whole bunch of groceries to get into the front door of the Chelsea. So he held the door open with the toe of his boot, and it shattered the window. From then on, Stanley Bard hated Marlowe.

MARLOWE WEST

I went to buy some groceries and was wearing boots that had these big metal shin plates that I strapped around my legs. I came to the door of the Chelsea, and all of the management were sitting there in the lobby having a meeting. In order to open the automatic front door, they had to push a button inside. I had my arms full of groceries, and I kept pushing the buzzer and pushing the buzzer, and nobody was getting up to push the button to open the door for me. I had both arms full of groceries, so I started knocking on the door by kicking it—kick, kick, kick—as if to say "Hello! Here I am." And the door broke. It just shattered into a million pieces.

I had to pay five hundred dollars to replace the door. After that, Stanley and the rest of them just hated me. I told them, "Well, you got a new door out of the deal!"

Another event was a little more serious. I loved Paul Volmer's roommates Neicy and Therese. Neicy defined the word voluptuous. Brunette, pouty lips, lots of body going on, and this childish little giggly voice. She was very cool. I don't know if she and Paul were actually a couple. Later on, they lived together. I think she played along with being his girlfriend, but I don't think there was a physical thing.

So one time I managed to get a date out of Neicy. She had convinced me she wasn't really Paul's girlfriend, so I didn't feel like I was cheating him out. I had a lot of money at the time, and I bought her a bouquet and some champagne. But when I got there, she was lying up in her loft in a *bitchy* mood! So there was no date. She did, however, take the flowers and the champagne. That's how I ended up with this chick Marilyn.

Neicy had closed me out, so I was sitting down in the lobby thinking, "What am I going to do now?" And this woman Marilyn comes along, all flirty. It was like the last catch of the day or something!

Marilyn was ugly as sin, but she did herself up to look like Marilyn Monroe, and she had this cute little Marilyn act about her. No one else was around, so suddenly I was hooked up with Marilyn. She wanted to party, so I said, "Oh, I just got back from Florida and I found this new drink called Sex on the Beach." Some kind of peach brandy mixed with a liqueur. We found all the ingredients and went up to her apartment and started getting drunk. She had a fire escape right outside her window, which she treated as if it were her balcony. So Marilyn and I went out on the fire escape, having a picnic and getting casual out there with our drinks.

All of a sudden, she was really loaded. She started acting as though I was trying to come onto her sexually, and she wasn't going for it. But I wasn't coming on to her at all! Even so, she went inside from the fire escape and shut the window and locked it. All of a sudden I was stuck outside on the fire escape! On the 8th floor! She wouldn't let me in and it was dark outside.

I started creeping down the fire escape, but I tripped over somebody's flower pots. And then I just fell, I fell off the fire escape! I landed on the roof of the church next door. It's incredible because I was wearing a necklace made of silver baubles—they looked like big ball bearings but they were hollow. These baubles dropped off and fell all the way down to the alley. The top of the church was at the level of the Chelsea's sixth floor. I fell from the 8th floor to the 6th floor, and landed on my back, bent over the top of a chain link fence that ran alongside the church roof's edge. The fence kind of sprung me flat on my face and I passed out. Later, I woke up on the roof. The fence pole was totally bent.

It was a miracle—I was so close to the edge. Then I looked down and saw my necklace lying shattered all the way down in the alley six floors below.[26]

My back was really screwed up so I tried to sue the Chelsea Hotel. My lawyer confronted Stanley about it, and Stanley told him that I had no business being out on the fire escape in the first place. And I thought I was going to get rich or something.

Instead, they said, "We're going to countersue."

Chelsea Girl Killed Jimi Hendrix?

Devon Wilson was a beautiful, troubled fashion model best known for being one of Jimi Hendrix's closer girlfriends—a member of his inner circle whom Marlowe had met in Los Angeles during his flower child period in the late 60s.

Not long after they met, Devon Wilson plunged to her death out of a ninth floor window at the Chelsea. It'd be easy to write her death off as just another casualty of the early '70s. But her suicide, or murder, creates ripples that spread wider than her own life. It also adds a new and telling piece of information to the puzzle surrounding the death of rock icon Jimi Hendrix.

MARLOWE WEST

In 1971, somebody pushed Devon Wilson to her death from a window at the Chelsea Hotel. I don't know anything about who did it, but it was one of those mysterious things. Some people apparently didn't like some of the things she was talking about, and they wanted to squash all of that.

In my closet, I still have a purple-fringed leather jacket that belonged to Jimi Hendrix. A lot of people who saw it were really impressed by it—others thought I was full of shit. It should be in a museum—it's worth a million dollars, but it's sitting in my closet now as if it were a piece of crap!

I have tried to get in touch with people about it, but there's no label on it saying it belonged to Jimi Hendrix. Every time I've tried to bring it to light, people have disputed my story.

This is how I got the coat. One time my cousin Marquise of the GTOs and I came to our home in L.A. Miss Mercy introduced me to two new girls at the house. One was Angela Burdon, the wife of Eric Burdon[27] of The Animals. The other girl was Devon Wilson. And Devon had been a girlfriend of Jimi Hendrix. She was also supposedly the niece of Quincy Jones.[28]

These girls stayed with me, Marquise, and Miss Mercy for a few days because they had just come in from England. I was this boy from Long Island thinking, "Wow, this girl is a model, she's going with Jimi Hendrix, *and* she's Quincy Jones's niece!" I was young and overwhelmed by all of this fame.

But Devon Wilson was distraught. She told Marquise and me that just before she came to Los Angeles from England, she had seen Jimi at this party. She made him a cup of coffee and put a tablespoon of heroin in it. She said the only time they were sexually intimate was when they were on heroin, which made Hendrix feel all lovey-dovey. Otherwise, Jimi was always being absconded from her. Guys would get him to jam with them, or the chicks would be all over him. Devon used this ploy: "I'm going to get him stoned on heroin and be intimate with him." But what she didn't know was that Hendrix had been partying on heroin all day. The tablespoon of heroin she put in his coffee was the straw that broke the camel's back. And he overdosed and died!

And now Devon had a terrible guilt complex about giving Jimi Hendrix his final dose of heroin, and she would tell people about it, maybe as a sort of confession to relieve her feelings of guilt.

The questions surrounding Jimi Hendrix's mysterious death in London—and Devon Wilson's plunge out a Chelsea Hotel window—may never be resolved.

Devon Wilson, about whom Hendrix wrote the unflattering song "Dolly Dagger," was hardly a bedrock of emotional stability. According to John McDermott and Eddie Kramer, Wilson was extremely insecure but hid her fears under a tough, streetwise persona. Although she was a bewitchingly charismatic, talented model and actress, her taste for seducing superstars like Mick Jagger and Brian Jones distracted her from her own career. Not to mention her heroin addiction. She was also known for carrying around massive amounts of drugs.[29]

Her relationship with Hendrix was a continual power struggle, a brutal dynamic they both seemed to enjoy, or at least felt compelled to act out. On the one hand, she assumed the role of his guardian and protector, but then she would sleep with other men to make him jealous. Once, at party where Mick Jagger cut his finger, Wilson elbowed her way in to suck the blood off as Hendrix watched.

The night before his death, Jimi was at a party hosted by Kit Lambert, manager of The Who. Afterward, he went back to London's Samarkand Hotel, where he'd been staying with a German artist and skating instructor named Monika Danneman. She spent the night with Hendrix and later testified that, the next morning, after waking up next to him, she had gone out on a quick errand to buy cigarettes. When she came back to their room, Jimi Hendrix was dead in bed, suggesting that Hendrix had been fine when she left, but died before she returned.

However, according to Carmen Geddes,[30] Monika Danneman's story is full of holes and contradictions. Danneman said she found Hendrix dead around 8:00 a.m., but records show she didn't dial 999 (Britain's 911) until around 11:00. She did, however, phone the bad news to rocker Eric Burdon and to Gerrie Stickells, one of Hendrix's roadies, between 8:00 and 9:00. So why did she wait three hours to call the authorities?

Also, Danneman testified that on the pillow next to Hendrix's head, there was a spot of vomit. The ambulance drivers said it was not a spot but a flood. She said she rode in the ambulance with Jimi—the ambulance driver said she never set foot inside. She told Eric Burdon that Jimi was still alive in the ambulance, and said the hospital staff told her they might be able to save him. But hospital admissions records stated that Hendrix was dead on arrival. She said she viewed the body at the hospital morgue, but hospital employees said the only person who showed up to identify the body was Gerry Stickells, the roadie.

Danneman's overall reputation didn't make her the most credible source. Later, in 1995, another of Hendrix's lovers, Kathy Etchingham, sued her for alleging that Etchingham lied about her sex life with Hendrix in her book *The Inner World of Jimi Hendrix*. Etchingham won the suit. Nevertheless, Danneman persisted in calling Etchingham a liar. For this, she was convicted of contempt of court. Two days later, Monika Danneman was found dead of asphyxiation in her Mercedes, most likely a suicide.

Nonetheless, parts of Danneman's story about Hendrix that fateful night at the Samarkand Hotel are probably true. Nothing in her testimony contradicts Devon Wilson's claim that she accidentally overdosed Jimi Hendrix by slipping heroin into his coffee.

Hendrix's death shattered Wilson. According to Sharon Lawrence, "Devon felt unshakeable guilt about the various ways she'd let him down."[31] She lamented nonstop about how she'd taken advantage of him. And authors McDermott and Kramer both affirm the sad fact that at Hendrix's funeral, Devon, "in a fit of hysteria, tried to throw herself into the open grave."

Exactly what happened at Kit Lambert's early evening party? Devon Wilson may very well have spiked his coffee, as she claimed, so Hendrix would make love with her. Despite her cheating heart, she loved him with a wild passion. Two nights before his death, when Wilson found Hendrix and Danneman sitting together at Ronnie Scott's club in Soho, Wilson literally kicked Danneman out of her chair.

Some questions: at Lambert's rock and roll party, would Hendrix have really been drinking *coffee*? Was he trying to sober up? If Devon Wilson had made up the story, wouldn't slipping it into an alcoholic drink be a more plausible lie? Sometimes the truth, or at least its appearance, lies in quirky particulars. As Mark Twain said, a good lie depends on the details.

And finally, if, two years later, someone pushed Devon Wilson off her balcony at the Chelsea Hotel, who was it and why?

Monika Danneman went out of her way to insist she had no idea Jimi was dead early that morning. Did it really take *three hours* to realize it? A good guess is that after she phoned Burdon and Stickells around 8:00 a.m., she commenced to freak out, flush drugs down the toilet and clean the apartment of incriminating evidence before the cops arrived—quite a clean-up job, requiring three hours. She then went so far as to create a Jesus-returns-to-Mary tableau. To "prove" she didn't just let Hendrix lie there dead for three hours before calling the cops, she "brought Hendrix back to life" at the hospital. Talk about resurrecting a god to save your soul. Or your ass.

The troubling fact remains that Devon Wilson claimed she deliberately dosed Jimi Hendrix with heroin, causing his overdose, and she was from that point overwhelmed by guilt. But if she had dosed him at Lambert's party, wouldn't he have overdosed right away, while still at the party, instead of later that night? If she had injected the heroin into his arm, he would have OD'd right away. But a buzz on *ingested* heroin can last up to eight hours. Hendrix would have had ample time to arrive at the hotel, hang out with Monika for a while, go to sleep while the dose was taking effect, and then, while sleeping, die of the overdose.[32]

The drama surrounding Hendrix's death eventually played out in Los Angeles.

MARLOWE WEST

So one night we all went out to the Whiskey A Go Go[33]—Devon and Marquise and Angie and Mercy. And Devon had some of Jimi's clothes, including this purple-fringed coat. Hanging out with these groupies and this coat, I was suddenly like the most famous boy in Hollywood! Everybody knew the groupies. And Devon had a crush on Marquise, even though Marquise was straight. Devon kept on spooning coke into everybody's noses. We weren't really wild like that, with the drugs. But Devon had an arsenal of coke and heroin with her. She was really a wild girl! But finally, when they left our house, Devon gave Marquise the purple coat as a gift and said "Thanks for letting us stay!"

Then one night, Marquise got raped. Two men dragged her into an alley and raped her. She was wearing that Jimi Hendrix coat at the time. After that, she couldn't stand the coat—it reminded her of the rape. So I gave her twenty-five dollars for it. And I still have it in my closet. Someday, somehow, maybe it'll come to light that this was really Hendrix's jacket.

Devon left our place a few days after she had arrived. She and Angie Burdon went to live at Arthur Lee's place, the guy from the band Love.[34] That was the last time I ever saw Devon Wilson.

Years later, when I lived at the Chelsea again, it turned out that a guy named David Kramer[35] was doing a documentary about Jimi Hendrix. Robert Campbell turned me on to Kramer.

"You should get hold of Marlowe," Robert told Kramer, "because Marlowe has Jimi's coat."

Then David Kramer called me up and said "What's with the coat?" He had a really intimidating voice.

I told him the story of the jacket.

"Well," he said, "there are some people who don't want this information known."

So I was thinking, "Whoa, did I step on the Mafia's feet or something?" It startled me very badly. "Oh my God," I thought. "I'm in trouble!" I knew Devon had been pushed out of the Chelsea window and there had been some bad connections involved. Then, when I was trying to get through to Jimi Hendrix's estate, there were people in their twenties answering the phone and telling me that I was wrong about the jacket. I would say to them, "You weren't even *born* at the time! How can you tell *me* I'm not telling the truth?" It's like they were saying to me, "Go away and shut up. Just be glad someone doesn't push *you* out a window!"

Check In to Check Out

We can't ignore the topic of Chelsea suicides. Hotels have long served as attractive spots for those who want to kill themselves. Anonymity is a factor—sometimes you wanna go where nobody knows your name. It's a big enough problem that experts are writing articles about hotel staff members being so traumatized after discovering suicides that they need treatment for PTSD.[36]

The Chelsea has its own hundred-year history of suicide stories. But Stanley Bard rarely talked about these dark punctuation marks in the story.

The existentialist writer Albert Camus wrote, "There is but one truly serious philosophical problem and that is suicide." Meaning, with the opportunity to kill yourself available at all times, one had to think hard to decide. This sort of pessimistic, deliberative suicide is one way to go.

Although many Chelsea residents were philosophical in nature—choosing a Bohemian life can be seen as a philosophical act—Chelsea suicides were rarely statements planned in advance. Most killed themselves in moments of acute panic, despair, or some kind of booze or drug frenzy. And at the Chelsea, where a cornucopia of methods was always available—a handful of pills, a small arsenal of weapons, and two very picturesque drops (one via an outside window, the other via the hotel's spectacular central staircase) the Chelsea made suicide convenient.

Long-time Chelsea resident and surf guitarist Tim Sullivan was around for a few.

TIM SULLIVAN
There was one experience when a woman jumped out of her

window on the ninth floor. It was May twenty-six, which is significant. I was in my room playing music on my keyboard. The weather outside was nice so I had my window open. From there, you can get a good view of what's going on outside, and I saw something coming down—swoosh—like a bird. Then I heard a bang, or more like a clang. There used to be a manhole right in front of the hotel's awning. She landed right on the manhole cover, and that's what made the clanging! She had already slit her wrists, and then ran and jumped out her 9th floor window past the Hotel Chelsea sign, and she landed right in front of the awning.

Then, *exactly* one month later, on June twenty-sixth, a guy on the ninth floor—the same floor the woman had jumped from—jumped down the gap inside the spiral staircase. The very same day, *exactly* one month later. And from the *same* 9th floor.

ROBERT CAMPBELL

The spiral stairwell used to come all the way down to the lobby, but people kept jumping down the stairwell and killing themselves. So they closed up the stairs on the second floor and put a cover over the front desk so people wouldn't jump down there and kill the clerks and management working at the front desk.

This little piece of renovation is one of the hotel's oddest architectural features. The stairwell simply stops and the hole is sealed in with a hardwood floor surrounded by a little brass railing, kind of like a pen for children or small animals. Who would guess it was built to protect the front desk clerks from falling bodies?

JULIE EAKIN

When Dimitri was living there later, in 1989, he and I went out to see Spike Lee's *Do the Right Thing* at a theater just down the street. When we came out of the theater, there were ambulances in front of the Chelsea. We walked down the street and into the hotel's lobby. Somebody had dived from one of the upper stories down to the slate bottom at the base of the stairwell. And the stairwell is narrow, probably three feet by twenty feet. He had dented this slate floor at the base of the stairwell with his head! His head dented the slate floor! But he was actually still alive, because he was drunk!

While most Chelsea suicides ended their spontaneous lives with spontaneous deaths, there was the occasional planner.

ROBERT CAMPBELL

Sometimes at the Chelsea people would check in to check out. My friend Scott Covert who lived there knew this guy there who had AIDS. This guy was just so sick, and so tired of it all, he decided to kill himself. So Scott got him this mondo cut of heroin, which was like ten bags, a bindle, or whatever they call it. And then the guy with AIDS, because he was going to kill himself, put up all of his belongings for sale. I bought his turntable.

But at the last minute, instead of checking out, the guy *chickened* out. On top of that, he wanted all his belongings back. I wouldn't give him back his turntable. I did have a feeling he was going to chicken out—otherwise I probably would have bought more of his stuff. He took the heroin himself all right, but not all at once to kill himself. He took it in smaller amounts just to get high.

Our last suicide harkens the stereotypical image of yellow police tape stretched across a hall. The painter John Zinsser was around when the police showed up.

JOHN ZINSSER

Once, on the sixth floor, somebody apparently checked into the room to commit suicide. Afterward, there was a policeman posted outside of the room, which was down at the end of the hall. All day, he was sitting on a chair down there in the hall, and my wife, who was in the fashion business, had these big piles of fashion magazines. So she took the policeman this big stack of magazines.

"Here, you want something to look at while you're sitting here?"

"Oh thank you, thank you," the policeman said, "You're so kind."

Then he looked at her and said. "You wanna see the body?"
She declined.

PAUL VOLMER

When all the craziness went on at the hotel, I had learned that you had to keep your wits about you.

So I had this saying: "If you're not composed, you're decomposed."

A Cure for Pain

One's personality dictates one's preferred drug. For the cynics among the artists, like the Beat poets, drugs like speed made life endurable. You could gaze at the world's squalor, hypocrisy, delusion and power games, and still feel tolerably good. For optimists like the 1960s hippies, pot and LSD were the stick from which the psychedelic carrot hung: *Get your utopian future right now and avoid the rush.* For an overly sensitive type, heroin dulled the pain. Coke and speed made the meek in spirit feel invincible.

The Chelsea had a drug for every type.

PAUL VOLMER

Therese, who was Neicy's and my other roommate, sort of looked like Betty Boop. This was during the Reagan era, when Nancy Reagan used to say "Just say no to drugs."

"Don't say *no*," Therese would say, shaking her finger. "Say no, *thank* you!'"

At the Chelsea you could buy whatever quantity of pot, small or large. The hotel's pot scene was very capitalistic and competitive. Several different dealers had it for sale, so you could pick the best. I myself stuck to smaller quantities. The types of pot varied. It wasn't the hydroponic stuff that they have now. It was mostly stuff that came in bricks, smuggled into the country, but it was good stuff because in New York City we had all the main connections.

ROBERT CAMPBELL

One time I met somebody at a bar.

"Hey," he asked. "Where do you live?"

I told him I lived at the Chelsea.

"Oh. I heard there was a pot store there," he said.

"What are you talking about?"

"I heard you could go in there and get ten or twenty different kinds of pot, and you just pick what you want."

"*Damn*," I thought. "I've lived here two years and I didn't know *that*!"

Then, I found out that there really was a pot store at the Chelsea. The guy who ran it worked another job as a roofer.

He had people waiting in line to visit him. But first you had to phone him at a certain time. Then once he told you to come by, you would visit his place.

He had a really nice apartment with nice artwork. It didn't look like a stoner's apartment or anything. Then he'd call you into this back room that had no windows. He had these little file boxes in a cabinet, like in an old-style library card catalogue. He'd pull the box out, and it had six or eight different bags in it. Each bag had a colored sticker on it, a color code indicating what type it was and how much it cost.

He'd say, "Okay, this is Colombian. This here is Humboldt, and these over here are Thai sticks," and he'd tell you how much each of them cost. You could say, "Well, I'll take three ounces of that right there, and two ounces of this over here."

Here I was, up from North Carolina, and it just blew my mind!

It was nice to know you could go there and you didn't have to get just one thing. It was like a candy store!

JULIE EAKIN

The bathroom we shared in the hallway, you could never tell who was coming in or out of it. You just wouldn't know who was using your bathroom. Its door had this really telltale, noisy, creaky swing. The doors were solid, probably oak, and really strong, and they had this real finality whenever they shut. In the middle of the night, the door was constantly slamming shut with people going in and out. Then in the morning, you'd go in and there would be blood on the walls from people shooting heroin in there! So that became part of the lyrics to Dimitri's song, "Blood Hotel":

> There's blood on the walls
> Of poets and patriots

Do Not Exceed Recommended Dosage

Where drugs are plentiful, overdoses follow. Some ODs killed—others got you on Letterman.

PAUL VOLMER

Because the ethic was so free, and because there were drugs everywhere at the Chelsea, people could easily find their Achilles' heel, that one drug that would cause them to go over the edge and travel into reaches they never would have gone. They would burn out spectacularly.

There was a guy named Adrian, an artist who flipped himself out on forty hits of LSD and became the samurai who frightened David Letterman. Adrian was a painter who also wrote epic poetry, and he was a little bit pompous. He was in his twenties and always wore three-piece suits. He had a very rigid bearing, and would talk in a sort of educated, slightly snobbish manner. But he was an okay guy, and a very good painter, and he somehow made a living painting, which was difficult to do.

Adrian burned out quite spectacularly. A friend of mine at the hotel didn't deal drugs, but somehow he had gotten hold of something like forty hits of acid. And he thought, "Well, I'll sell a few to friends here and there." The painter Adrian bought every one of them. His downfall was this single batch of LSD. He bought all of those forty hits from my friend, and when he was taking them home in his pants pocket that night, it started to rain. Adrian got soaked, and the skin on his leg absorbed all forty hits at once. He lost his mind.

Around this time, a couple of gay guys lived in the hotel, leather guys who had all sorts of elaborate S&M gear, hats and vests, gauntlets, shin plates and spiked shoulder pads. And by the way, these leather guys, Nick Bienes and Rhea Gallaher, were successful authors of trashy novels, writing under the name of Judith Gould.[37] Their most well-known novel was called *Sins*, which Joan Collins made a TV movie out of, so these two guys were kind of established. It was funny, everyone thought, that these gay leather guys were making good money writing trashy novels for women.

So Adrian's leg absorbed these forty hits of acid. And while he was tripping his brains out he went to these gay leather men and borrowed these leather boots and shin plates, and a leather skirt and shoulder pads and spiked gloves, gauntlets, the works. He had goggles and a sword. He looked like a heavy metal Samurai!

I was walking into the lobby and saw him. "Adrian," I said, "What's up?"

"Paul," he said, grabbing his sword, "I'm taking on the world." He was basically wandering around the lobby freaking people out. Not to mention he was behind on his rent.

So when I was on my rounds later that evening, I walked by my room. Some of my friends were in there watching TV.

"Adrian's just been on television!" they said.

"What?"

"Yeah, he was just on Letterman." Letterman used to go out onto the streets with a camera crew and just goof on this person or that. So Letterman had pulled up in his limousine, and he saw Adrian bent over looking into a shop window. Letterman said, "Oh, look at that weirdo over there!"

At that, samurai Adrian turned around in all his freaked-out heavy metal glory, and started walking towards David Letterman. Letterman saw him coming and screamed at the limo driver, "Get me out of here!" They peeled rubber. Adrian got his fifteen seconds of fame.

So Adrian lost his ability to pay his rent and had to go back home. I think it was Atlanta.

The filmmaker James Rasin achieved a small miracle by accidentally causing Beat writer Herbert Huncke, one of the heaviest, most experienced heroin users alive, to overdose.

JAMES RASIN

When I once went to Thailand, I was thinking, "Well, what gift am I going to bring back for Herbert at the Chelsea?" In Thailand, you can buy prescription drugs over the counter. So I bought him a bottle of five hundred ten milligram Valiums. They were in the real bottle from Roche Labs in Switzerland, all sealed. Five-hundred of them for sixty dollars. So I brought them back in and went over to see Herbert in his room. "Herbert, I brought you something." I pulled out this bottle of five hundred Blues, and his eyes just popped out of his head. His lover Louie grabbed them, and I went back home.

The next day, Dimitri's calling me up. "You *jerk*! Herbert's totally goofed out! He's been crapping his bed all day long, and I'm stuck here cleaning the sheets! You just drop these five hundred pills on these guys and you take off?"

I didn't know!

He said, "You should have just given them to me, and I would have sold them, and we could have given the *money* to Herbert!" The pills could have sold in the U.S. for six dollars each, which would have been three thousand dollars for us. But that wouldn't have been as dramatic, would it! I wanted to pull out the bottle of five hundred Valiums and watch Herbert's face. The pills were gone in a couple of days. They finally gave the leftovers away.

Karma later walloped Rasin when he himself overdosed at the hands of Huncke.

There are drugs and then there are drugs, and the mood changed at the Chelsea when crack cocaine entered the picture, along with its cousin, ice.

ROBERT CAMPBELL

One night, this guy Eddie had been hanging out with Paul at the front desk when Paul worked there. They were both getting all messed up on something. Now, because Paul worked the front desk, he knew exactly which rooms were resident rooms and which were transient rooms, so Paul knew who he could play pranks on—the tourists. He would phone tourists and say, "Hey man, what'd you come to the Chelsea for? You want to party down? I've got some ice!"[38]

I never saw ice except one time. It's like smoking crystal methamphetamine. I guess it's become a big problem in Hawaii and Japan. It's ten times worse than crack, which is ten times worse than hell. That night Paul was hanging out with Eddie. For fun, Paul would call these people and say, "Hey man, I've got some ice!" So in response to his call, this real witch and warlock who were visiting the hotel came down to the front desk. They were going to make a porn movie there the next day. By this time, Paul's friend Eddie was totally wasted, so the witch and warlock never got their ice.

The next day, Paul comes down and asks me, "Hey Robert, you mind if I borrow your vacuum cleaner?"

"No problem. Here it is."

Now Eddie, after partying all night with Paul, had puked all over Paul's room. And Paul vacuumed up all the puke with my vacuum cleaner! He brought the vacuum cleaner back to me without even cleaning it off! It had all the puke still in it and it stank!

I screamed at him. "You ruined my vacuum cleaner!" I couldn't believe that he had done that. I guess that time I was the one who got pranked.

PAUL VOLMER

Crack really changed the whole atmosphere. It was a bad little plague there in the late eighties. Once, a guy who was on crack threw me against the wall in the hotel lobby. Crack and regular cocaine were very easy to get, especially because of the prostitutes there. It was commonplace for them to be taking crack. My friend Nicholas (Nicko) Gentry, a rock musician from Sweden, had lived there various times between Europe and America. Then he got involved in crack and he had to go back to Sweden. He couldn't live in the U.S. anymore. Crack was so tempting and easy to get. It is incredibly addictive, and whatever money you had, you would spend it on the drug until the money was all gone. I remember Nicko being so emaciated before he left; he looked like a skeleton with skin.

Bohemian Physical Fitness

You might be under the impression that Chelsea residents did nothing but sit around drinking, taking drugs, and creating art when they could cram it into their busy schedules. But many residents took physical fitness seriously. Not everyone could win gold at the Chelsea Olympics, so intense training was key.

Paul Volmer received some self-defense training from two guys named Terry and Eddie.

ROBERT CAMPBELL

For about two weeks, this guy Terry went into the lobby every night and did some damage. I don't know what his story was, but for some reason Terry hated the night desk clerk, and he would go up to the front windows of the hotel and smash them. Every single night for two weeks he would smash the windows. And then the next morning he would go down there and give them a check to pay for the windows.

PAUL VOLMER

Terry lived on the first floor, actually in Sid Vicious' old suite, which probably had the worst vibe in the whole hotel. Terry was a complete, raging alcoholic. Someone would call the police because he was such a screaming lunatic, and one time when the police went in his room, I saw them tie him up in a straitjacket. The guy was so defiant that he spit into the police sergeant's face as they were tying him down to bring him to jail. He would also break the front desk window every couple of months. And as long as he paid for it, Stanley just looked the other way.

When I came on there as the security guard, I didn't want Terry's window breaking to continue, so I stared him down and told him it wasn't going to happen anymore. One night I was sitting at the desk as night watchman. The desk clerk was talking to a potential guest who wanted a room, and that person then went away. A minute later—*crash*—the window breaks again! Of course I thought that it was Terry who broke the window. I was totally annoyed. I jumped out from behind the desk into the lobby, thinking I was about to confront Terry. But it turned out that the desk clerk had said something that pissed off this potential guest, and *he* had smashed the window. This guy was an even stranger maniac than Terry! He clocked me as soon as I stepped out. I found myself fighting this *new* guy in the lobby!

Now there was a little old lady named Marilyn who always sat in the lobby of the hotel with her walker next to her. She always had a wig on, but it was a cute wig, a jet black pageboy with short bangs. Interestingly, before she retired, she had been a nurse at a mental hospital. And she witnessed this fight. This guy and I fought in the vestibule until the guy finally left. The day after the fight, she filled me in about what had happened. She said for a good five minutes I had been fighting this guy punch-for-punch like in a boxing match until eventually he ran out the front door. She also said that when we were fighting, I had seemed completely out of it. I didn't even remember a bit of it because I was knocked out, unconscious, *during* the fight! And this old lady, having worked in a mental institution, knew a thing or two about violence.

Here's another example of things getting a little too real for some visitors. There was a time I was feeling somewhat down because my girlfriend had gone away for a while. So I said to myself, "I'll have a little party in my room." I invited a few of my friends. I was a bike messenger at the time, and I decided I would invite some punks to the Chelsea. Because Sid Vicious supposedly killed Nancy at the Chelsea, the hotel had become sort of a shrine for punks who came to pay their homage.

So I went into the East Village, found people with the spiki-est hairdos and the most punked-out costumes and asked about a half dozen if they wanted to come to the Chelsea to my little party. I bought a case or two of beer and a barrel of ice. About thirty punks showed up, and a bunch of them were sitting out on the balcony. Being punks, they started spitting on passers-by. Some of them were yelling, and one of the people on the street threw a bottle back up at them, smashing it against the hotel's stone wall. The punks started throwing bottles back at him, and there was this little exchange. Inebriated, I was leaning against the wall, just watching.

And then I saw this kid go by outside, Eddie, whose vomit I had vaccumed up some time before. Eddie was a gangly kid, may-be six-foot-five, who had a very strange expression and manner about him. Almost no one ever talked to him. But at the time I had a very outgoing girlfriend, Neicy, and she had talked to him once in a while. He was a strange character, but I decided I would play a joke on Eddie.

I shouted out, "Eddie, you wanna see something funny?" I winged my can of beer by him. The beer put out a plume of spray as it went. I didn't hit him but kind of splashed him a little bit with beer and foam. Then I went back into the room and joined the party.

Not too long after I'd thrown the can at Eddie, I heard a huge crash on my room's door. If you don't watch it, the psychos will come to your door, especially if you have anything to do with them. Eddie had picked up a large metal fire extinguisher and thrown it against my door. When I heard the bang, I opened it and looked outside into the hall. There was this fire extinguisher lying there on the floor. I sort of pushed it to the side and went back in the room.

Then, bang! I heard something else. A few minutes later, I went out and saw that he had hit my door with one of these stand-up ashtrays from the lobby. I knew it was Eddie because through my keyhole I had caught a glimpse of him running away. And he was yelling stuff too. I had freaked him out by splashing beer on him.

I said to myself, "It's better not to even deal with this guy."

Then, just a few minutes later, I heard a *third* bang. I looked out, and this time it was a steel electric typewriter that he'd thrown against the door. The typewriter put a dent in the door.

And after his third try, I said to myself, "Well, I should go out there, and talk to the guy, get rid of him, whatever." I went out there and now he had a metal rod that he had picked up from a construction site—a rebar, a quarter inch in diameter and maybe a couple of feet long. He started swinging it back and forth at me like a sword.

I decided, "Well I'm going to disarm him." So I went to grab the bar, and instead of my catching it like I thought I would, he hit my elbow with it. It gouged right into my elbow, sending this rivulet of blood down my arm. It didn't hit any major blood vessels, but it definitely bled a lot. My whole arm was covered with blood. I walked back into my room to get something to sop it up. Eddie just ran away; he was really just a punk kid, you know, probably about nineteen.

When I got back into the room, all of these punks saw that I was covered with blood. Now as far as these punks' heroes Sid and Nancy went, Sid was known for cutting himself with beer bottles onstage and for self-mutilation and blood and stuff like that. If you're a punk, you're supposed to be able to handle blood. But as soon as they saw my arm dripping with blood, they swarmed out of my room, tripping over each other to get out. Those punks got their dose of the real Chelsea!

Chelsea Tryouts

We'll wind up the Chelsea wildness with a tale of one young man who showed up to audition for the Chelsea. His case was heartfelt, emotionally bare. The following event also explores the philosophical question:

When is weird too weird?

PAUL VOLMER

At one point, I was interviewing for roommates. At the time, I had an audiotape of U2 with their song "When Love Comes to Town" that they did with B.B. King. So when I was interviewing for a roommate, this short guy comes over. He was very neat in appearance, wearing a dress shirt, a sports jacket and slacks. He had close-cropped hair. He came into the room and we were chatting about the various questions that a roommate might want to know. I wandered out to the balcony.

"Well, here's the balcony." I was talking over my shoulder while he was still back in the room. And as I was talking, he interrupted.

"Can I get more comfortable?"

"Sure, fine," I said. I thought he was going to take off his jacket or something.

When I turned around, however, he was completely naked except for a pair of white socks. Meanwhile, I had this U2 album going, and it came to the song "When Love Comes to Town." Now I was a person who prided myself on my Warholian, dispassionate, "I'm almost not here" attitude. Just a detached observer.

This naked guy said, "Oh I hope this is okay."

"Oh, it's fine!" I said, thinking I didn't want to rile this nut up.

When it came to B.B. King's guitar solo in the song, he started playing air guitar with his dick! He was a really good air guitarist. I was dumbfounded, still trying to be Warholian, but also asking myself, "How am I going to get him out of the room?" The song ended, and he said, "Oh, let's listen to that one more time!" and he started going for the rewind.

I jumped in front of him and said, "No, no, I think maybe you should leave now."

The spell was broken. He looked shocked and hurt. He put on his clothes and left. I don't think he was trying to come on to me at all. He never looked at me in a lecherous way. I think that's just how he felt comfortable, and he probably felt, at the Chelsea, this is where you could do these sorts of things.

Beat writers Marty Matz (left) and Herbert Huncke
Gregory Corso (bottom)

CHAPTER 3

The Three Wise
Men of Dope:

Herbert Huncke,
Gregory Corso, and Marty Matz

"... they were slinking criminals, like Elmer Hassel,
with that hip sneer ..."

—JACK KEROUAC, *On the Road*

It was the winter of 2002, in the tiny Delta town of Sumner,
Mississippi when Robert Campbell, my brother-in-law and ex-
Chelsea dweller, turned to me:

"Hey, y'ever heard of Herbert Huncke? I used to live next to
that guy."

I had never heard of Herbert Huncke, and I was a writer with a
Ph.D. in literature.

Robert maintained that Huncke (rhymes with *funky*) was the
first Beat poet. I countered that I had read *On the Road* several times
and never heard of Huncke. I had also read the works of the less li-
onized Beats: Orlovsky, Ferlinghetti, Corso, and Cassady. I had been
to my fair share of Allen Ginsberg's poetry readings and a lecture

he shared with William Burroughs. I had lived in San Francisco, Denver, and Boulder—all Beat cities—where I drank beer at bars where the Beats drank beer. I talked with Diane DiPrima about her dabblings in the occult. I once ran into Peter Orlovsky in a crosswalk.

Yet, I had never heard of Herbert Huncke.

The very next Sunday morning—no joke—I was reading the newspaper and my eyes landed on a book review of—what else—*The Herbert Huncke Reader,* hot off the presses. It characterized Herbert Huncke as part lowlife conman, part brilliant storyteller and part guiding light to the Beats. Not only *a* Beat writer, but the *first* Beat writer, exactly as Robert had claimed. In fact Huncke was the man who gave the word *beat* to the Beat Generation.

I did more research and found that, indeed, the aging, withered Herbert Huncke whom Robert had befriended was a dark luminary, a Baudelaire of 42nd Street. Huncke was the Beats' urban psychopomp, who guided the young Jack Kerouac, Allen Ginsberg, and William Burroughs through New York's mean streets, its seamy side, the underworld of petty conmen, drug addicts, winos and prostitutes that was 42nd Street in the 1940s. When they met Huncke, this swarthy little guy who was a brilliant conversationalist, Kerouac and Ginsberg were just two antsy, middle class Columbia students, and Burroughs just out of Harvard. They found more reality in Huncke's gritty, close-to-the-bone New York milieu than in the rarified oxygen of Professor Lionel Trilling's office.

Huncke not only walked the mean streets—he wrote about them. At his best, he was a very good writer—his best work equal to Kerouac's. But Huncke is also remembered for introducing them to the word Beat:

Beat meant beaten up, broken down, bottomed out. It also meant cool. A beat person saw through the dominant social codes of the time, the rules dictating that the good life meant wearing a gray suit to work and religiously mowing your lawn. Beats bridled under the suffocating postwar peer pressure with a sneering indifference they had earned precisely by hitting bottom.

Like Huncke. Beat.

The term stuck. Only later did San Francisco columnist Herb Caen denigrate Beat into *Beatnik,* which he christened after the Soviet satellite Sputnik hit space in 1959. Apparently Caen thought the beatnik poets were "way out there." But beatniks were not Beats. Beatniks were mainstream trendies, poseurs, imitators who, almost a decade later, flooded into the cafes in their turtlenecks, berets, and trim goatees.

During Huncke's old age, he lived at the Chelsea Hotel, where he hung out with fellow Beat Chelsea dwellers Gregory Corso and Marty Matz, plus an ensemble of gangsters, activists, hustlers, not to mention legions of tourists (mostly European) who wanted to meet the Beat phenomenon. Despite Huncke's cult hero status, he was broke, and the rumor was that Jerry Garcia of the Grateful Dead was paying his rent for him. Even though Huncke was in his mid-seventies, he was still active, still writing, still hustling for a few dollars to feed his longtime heroin addiction, and still managing to get himself—and his Chelsea colleagues—into lots of trouble. Most said it was worth it.

ROBERT CAMPBELL

The very first time I saw Herbert Huncke, he was standing in the lobby of the Chelsea Hotel. He was a wrinkled old guy wearing a trench coat, and I wasn't too impressed. As far as I was concerned, he looked like a lowlife.

Huncke always tried to put a hard front on at first. But the truth was, when you got to know him, Huncke was always really friendly and gracious.

William Burroughs, in his book *Junky*, remarked on Huncke's hard front. When the thirty-two-year-old Burroughs met Huncke for the first time, Burroughs had gotten hold of a real Thompson machine gun (Tommy Gun) and a bunch of morphine in Syrette™ form—tiny toothpaste tubes with needles. Burroughs wanted to make some money by selling the gun and the drugs. Through a mutual friend, Huncke expressed special interest in the morphine Syrettes. But when the two met to make the deal, Huncke gave Burroughs a withering stare that felt like Huncke wished him dead. "Waves of hostility and suspicion flowed out from his large brown eyes like some sort of television broadcast," wrote Burroughs. "The effect was almost like a physical impact."

Burroughs didn't mention *why* Huncke had given him the evil eye. Burroughs, befitting his wealthy background, always dressed up. That day he was wearing a nice topcoat and snap-brim hat. No one Huncke associated with dressed like that. He thought Burroughs was a cop.

Later the two became close friends, including a stint when Huncke farmed marijuana plants on Burroughs' Texas ranch. Over the long term, the pendulum of their friendship swung often between closeness and distrust. Occasionally Burroughs would visit the Chelsea, where Huncke spent his last years.

So would many others.

STEVE HOUSE

I went to the Chelsea, and so help me, God, sitting in a chair on a high floor, in a large apartment, there was Herbert Huncke: the real Herbert Huncke. This little, tiny shriveled guy in a chair talking enthusiastically. He wrote his name and number on a napkin for me. I still have the napkin.

But it was Dimitri Mugianis who penetrated Huncke's inner circle. At the time, Mugianis had been working hard to promote his band Mr. Unique and the Leisure Class. They had played CBGBs, the Knitting Factory, and Cooper Union, and developed a cult following. But Mugianis had also developed a nasty heroin habit and was selling drugs to support it. It would be fair to say Mugianis and Huncke became acquainted through a mutual friend: heroin. Even so, the friendship was deep and real.

DIMITRI MUGIANIS

A friend of mine, Roger Richards, ran the Rare Book Room on Greenwich.[39]

One day I was in there, and it turned out that Herbert Huncke was there too. I had always admired his writing and his life. So I extended an overture to him. I said, "Oh, you're Herbert Huncke!"

He looked at me and said emphatically, drawing the words out, "No. Big. Deal."

JEROME POYNTON

When you sat there watching people go in and out of Huncke's room at the Chelsea, it certainly seemed like his place was the place to be. He was a very welcoming person, and had such a great ability to tell stories. And of course if you were interested in drugs, all the better! I myself never used at all. So, as far as I was concerned, it wasn't *just* a drug scene. Far from it.

TIM SULLIVAN

There was nothing like smoking a joint with an eighty-year-old guy. Huncke would roll a really big joint, and I'd get a sense of what these old guys were all about.

DAVID LAWTON

I can be kind of laconic and dry, and I used to push Huncke's buttons. Sometimes you'd be at some of these parties, and somebody would take out a joint and light it up. Immediately, two or three other people would say to themselves, "Well, I have to share *mine* too!" So you'd have two or three big fat joints circulating.

This particular time, as a joint was being passed to me, I said, "Hey, I'm good. I need to catch my breath."

"*Oh!*" Huncke would say, with deep sarcasm. "So *you* can evaluate how much partying you can do?" Huncke was personally offended that I didn't want another hit. To him, you had to stand there and do it all!

JULIE EAKIN

Herbert loved Dimitri, and I'm sure any friend of Dimitri's was okay by him.

Herbert read to me his short story, "The Evening Sun turned Crimson." It's extraordinarily beautiful. Herbert loved women. He was kind of a dandy, and he was small physically. I guess that's an affinity with women too. But when I think of Herbert now, that association certainly has to do with heroin.

Not everyone gave Huncke good character references. Especially if they found themselves at the short end of one of his con jobs.

ELLIS DUNCAN

Herbert was one of the most disingenuous and bitter people I ever met. At one point, Huncke once ripped me off on a deal. I had given him fifty dollars or a hundred dollars for something I thought was going to be equal in value, and what he gave me turned out to be worth five or ten dollars. Two days later, he called back, wanting to know if I wanted more! Huncke had delusions of grandeur. He ripped everybody off. He thought that just because he was Herbert Huncke, even being ripped off by him would be flattering.

I don't think there were any people that Stanley Bard actually turned down when they wanted to move into the Chelsea, unless Stanley had a bad experience with them. But one person who did lose his right to be there was Herbert Huncke. He had a slide toward the end when he would have sent his mother down the river.

He was credited with turning Jack Kerouac onto heroin. That was Herbert's claim to fame. He wrote the book *Guilty of Everything.* Who knows, there *may* even be some truth in that book somewhere!

Clothes Make the Con Man

DIMITRI MUGIANIS

Raymond Foye[40] wrote in the introduction to a book he published that Huncke was a natural nobleman. The dignity of Huncke—he would wear an ascot! It might be a stolen ascot, but he would wear it! And there was a way of carrying himself and presenting himself—he was always clean and well-groomed.

DAVID LAWTON

I always wondered, "How is he doing it? He's an old man, he's a junkie, and sometimes he's sleeping on somebody's couch!" It was incredible, really, how he kept himself up.

Yet, you always wondered—is this nicely dressed, well-mannered gentleman going to rip me off?

Hustler with a Heart of Gold

ROBERT CAMPBELL

Huncke was a hustler. He had this one scam he would do often. I would run into him on the sidewalk in front of the Chelsea.

"Hey, Huncke, how are you doing?"

"Well I'm doing pretty good," he would say, "There's this magazine that's going to publish one of my stories, but I've got to send them nineteen dollars to get it published." And he'd show me an envelope with two or three dollars in it.

"Okay, no problem, Huncke."

I pulled out the money I had, a few dollars, ten dollars or whatever, and gave it to him. He would keep it up on the street for a couple of hours with anyone who would pay attention to him. But he got me that time! I mean, what kind of magazine *charges* its writer to publish his work? It tends to work the other way around. Huncke would take that money and use it however he wanted, probably to buy dope. He was truly a scammer. That's one thing that discouraged me about living that way. Huncke's attitude was like "Live for the moment—don't worry about tomorrow." When you live like that, you just have to scam every day. It gets incredibly old.

Another time, Huncke came over to my room.

"Hey," he said. "You want some dope?" He had some DOA, this kind of heroin that would barely get you high—very weak stuff.

I said, "No, no Huncke."

But Huncke knew I was a wild, partying guy. So he would say okay and leave my room. Then an hour later, he'd call me on the telephone.

"Hey Robert, this is Huncke. You want anything?" He meant the heroin.

"No, Huncke. Thanks a lot, man." And he kept on calling, hour after hour. Finally, at about eleven o'clock at night, he wore out my resistance.

"Yeah, Huncke," I told him when he called again. "How fast can you get over here?"

PAUL VOLMER

Huncke was more than just a hustler. He hustled as a means to an end. There's also a code among hustlers, a code of honor that says you won't hustle one of your friends. Let's put it this way: among the brotherhood of Bohemians, you're not going to rip off your Bohemian friends. Plus, a good hustler's skills work out for anyone's benefit. He'll get you the drugs you want, and maybe you'll profit from them. That was Huncke's mixture—he showed Kerouac and Ginsberg the other side—but also he had charm.

JAMES RASIN

One day I stopped in at a rare book room called Horatio, and that was when I first met Huncke and Gregory Corso. We stayed up late drinking, and Huncke spent the night in my apartment.

When I woke up the next morning, I said, "I'm going out to go get some coffee and a bagel. Do you want me to get you something?"

"You just met me yesterday and you're going to leave me alone in your apartment?" he asked. "Don't you know who I am?"

Once Huncke stole a record player from Allen Ginsberg's place. According to biographer Ted Morgan, Huncke apologized to Ginsberg but warned him not to squeal. Squealing would brand Ginsberg as a "sucker," and no one respected a sucker.

Huncke's attitude was that if you wanted to be his friend, you had to get used to being ripped off once in a while. If you couldn't deal with that, then—no hard feelings—you shouldn't be his friend.

"Such was Huncke," writes Morgan, "Advising his victims on the correct reaction to his stealing while hoping to remain on friendly terms with them."[41]

TIM SULLIVAN

Herbert was a very poor guy. He didn't have any money. When he published *Guilty of Everything*, they gave him a boxful of his books. Whenever he needed some money, he would come to me and sell me a couple of his books.

"Okay, Herbert," I said. "I'll give you twenty dollars. Give me a couple of books."

"I'll give you one book for twenty bucks," he would answer. He would start to haggle over my donations to him!

"No," I said, "give me two books for ten dollars each and autograph them for me."

I would give the books as gifts to my friends. He would always leave my place with about twenty dollars. But he always gave me something in return—it was always a swap. He would never ask for an out-and-out donation. All this when he was in his early eighties!

JAMES RASIN

Everyone would say, "Huncke takes, takes, takes." But he was a real street guy. He would size you up and take you in any way he could, almost as a test. But if he thought you were smart, and you wouldn't let him get away with that much, or you didn't want too much out of him, he never took without returning, one way or another. Sometimes you'd help him out with some cash, and he wouldn't necessarily give you something material in return, but if you listened, he had a lot to give.

Huncke and I once went to Lowell, Massachusetts, where Huncke and Patti Smith did this event at the annual Kerouac event they have there.[42] We stayed at the same hotel as Patti Smith, and the two did their readings. Afterward, Patti complimented Herbert on this sweater he was wearing.

So when we got back to New York, Herbert said, "Patti complimented me on this sweater. I'm going to send her this sweater." And he did! He took it out, he put it in a box, and he sent it to Patti in Detroit. He was good at doing stuff like that.

Later, when I saw her, she said, "Yes, Herbert sent me his sweater. I was very touched!"

DIMITRI MUGIANIS

Someone on the street would ask him for some money, some old black dude would go, "Hey, I haven't seen you since Riker's Island[43] in 1955." And we were headed to a party with a bunch of rich kids, so Huncke knew there would be money at the other end. He had hustled this money all day, and then the last thing he did was give two bucks to the homeless guy he knew standing out in front. He gave it all away.

Once, Huncke and I were trying to get hold of some money. We managed to get twenty or thirty bucks somewhere on 23rd Street, and we were walking down to Greenwich Avenue, probably sixteen blocks. Huncke had twenty or thirty bucks. On the way down, Huncke proceeded to give all of the money away.

There were times when I was dope-sick, lying in my bed, and that old man got up and came back with money for me. He believed in family. He had a code, and he never took money from people who he thought couldn't afford it. No, he *gave*! It's a real middle-class perspective that Allen Ginsberg gave off about Huncke, calling him "The Holy Creep." No, *Ginsberg* was a creep! Huncke was a saint! As a matter of fact, there was a painting of him as a saint, a painting done by Richard Bernstein,[44] but the painting is lost now. It was absolutely gorgeous.

If someone needed something, Huncke would give it to him. He would make a gift of his shirt. He would steal *your* clothes, because you weren't in the family, and he'd give it to somebody else! You'd walk up to somebody and say, "Hey man, you're wearing my shirt!"

Where Art and Crime Intersect

DIMITRI MUGIANIS

There was this Puerto Rican dope dealer, Ramón [name changed], who got introduced into our whole scene there at the Chelsea. He became a peer of these Beat writers like Huncke and Marty Matz, and he didn't even realize who they were. He was a really smart guy, but he probably didn't have more than an eighth grade education.

So I'd tell him, "Ramón, that's Herbert Huncke the writer there, and over there is Gregory Corso, the poet."

"Get the hell out of here!" he'd say.

But the fascination went both ways. When Huncke was living on 7th Street and I was living at the Chelsea, Ramón left a bunch of guns at Huncke's place.

"Come here," he said to me, and he strutted over with his chest puffed out—and Huncke was a very little man—and he opened this big trunk. It was just filled with guns. And Huncke was so excited. He just loved to have his fingers in crime! He had this beautiful smile on his face, as if he'd just done something really, really great!

JAMES RASIN

Huncke could instantly recognize anyone else who was into that criminal scene, and they'd let each other in on their kind of drug and criminality lifestyle. But one time Huncke got beat up pretty badly here at the hotel. He had a pretty terrible bruise on his elbow. When he was unlocking his door, somebody pushed him into his room and beat him up.

DIMITRI MUGIANIS

You don't see much anymore of the place where art and criminality meet, which happened a lot in the Chelsea Hotel, and also happened in the Lower East Side. These old guys like Huncke all represented that mixture. They all did time in prison, and they all read books! They could hang out with someone like Ramón, a drug dealer, who was completely at home with these writers and artists because they were also part of his underground scene. Or they could hang out with someone who had five postgraduate degrees.

Linda Twigg, The Gangster Hippie Chick

DIMITRI MUGIANIS

The whole Linda Twigg scene was fascinating. In fact it was insane! Linda ran a gambling parlor. She's dead now, but when she was alive, she was very, very dangerous! She was this little blonde woman, five-feet-two and with blue eyes, cute and petite and pretty, but scary. She took care of people. Huncke lived with her for a while. But she was also one of the scariest people on the planet. If you knew her, you should be scared of her. If you crossed her, you had your jaw broken.[45]

Her gambling parlor on the Chelsea's second floor was a small room with poker tables set up, and Herbert lived there for quite a while. Linda had her fingers in all kinds of shit, drugs and gambling. She was such a character! You'd walk in there and she'd say, "Get to work!" and she'd be dealing out pounds of weed.

ROBERT CAMPBELL

Once I told Huncke's partner, Louis Cartwright, that I thought Linda Twigg was hot in her hippie dress. He said—and his voice sounded the way you would think Captain Ahab's voice would sound—"Robert, stay away from her. She's a *gangsterette*." I was too stupid to realize that he was dead serious. "She's a *gangsterette*, Robert."

This woman was attractive, smart, and very fucking dangerous.

JEROME POYNTON

There are beautiful shots of Linda's room in Francois Bernardi's documentary called *Original Beats*. Linda Twigg was the only woman who had a licensed poker chip, called the Doubling Cube. Poker chips are licensed as currency and she had one of the licenses and sold chips to casinos that used her brand.

Journalist Mark Kramer describes the Doubling Cubes as "gold poker chips—embossed with a marijuana leaf."[46]

He also describes Linda Twigg's Chelsea room as follows: "Mounted on the wall were photo portraits of William Burroughs, Candy Darling, Allen Ginsberg and other doomed souls who'd visited this room down through the years. Strewn haphazardly about were Ziploc bags of marijuana and envelopes stuffed with cash. Lurking just beyond Linda's preternatural perkiness and the fragrant oils that signified her presence, there was an aura of undifferentiated menace that kept Room 215's delicate behavior homeopathy intact."

Apparently she was also fond of the movie *Dirty Dancing*.

JEROME POYNTON

Linda knew the music scene. She was friendly with the Catholic Worker people. And she was often armed and was not afraid of putting someone in the hospital if they fell out of line.

Huncke lived at her place for a while, managing the casino. I remember nights when Ginsberg, Corso, a rabbinical student, Lawrence Pitkethly—a film producer for the New York Center for Visual History—James Rasin, Roger Richards, and Al Aronowitz[47]—would all be sitting around the same table gambling and drinks would be served.

JAMES RASIN

The Pope of Pot[48] used to hang out at Linda's. Linda loved the Pope. But I thought he was kind of a jerk, a screwed-up jerk. He considered his thing The Church of Marijuana. He was sort of like the Timothy Leary of marijuana. He was very open about it and got a lot of publicity out of it. And he got away with it for a long time! But then, he was caught distributing weed somehow, and it got him into trouble. They put him in jail, and he died there of cancer.

According to Kramer, another poker player who showed up at Linda Twigg's parlor was Bernard Goetz, the notorious "Subway Vigilante" who shot four muggers attempting to rob him on the New York subway. None of them died, and Goetz, now an engineer and politician, was found guilty only of possessing an illegal weapon.[49]

JEROME POYNTON

Herbert Huncke was robbed at Linda's place once—tied up and left on the floor. Another time, I was there with Herbert waiting for Linda's contacts to come over. When they did, we gave them a briefcase they were looking for. They opened it up and counted out so much money and they said it was five thousand short. Neither Herbert nor I knew anything about it, and we had to get Linda on the phone. She patched things up with the thugs. From the beginning, she knew the money was short, which is why she was not around and why she left the near-eighty-year-old man—Huncke—there to hand it off. It worked out, but it was typical Linda. Somehow you were always protected *with* her but never protected *from* her. She was a good scary friend.

DAVID LAWTON

If I ended up in Linda Twigg's room, in the poker room, I tried to melt into the background.

JAMES RASIN

She was very artist-friendly, always interested in and taking good care of Herbert Huncke, and she was good friends with Richard Bernstein. She was really intrigued and enamored of the whole literary-artistic world, very well read and interesting.

Jerry [Poynton] and I had a party there because we had written a screenplay after we did *The Burning Ghat.* We based the script on Huncke, but in the script we turned him into an American Indian conman. We were trying to draw attention to the script, so we had a party at the Chelsea in Linda's room during the Independent Film Project. We had Linda make a bunch of poker chips up with the name of the screenplay on it: "Chicago Ghost Dance." We handed them around at the Angelika to try to get people to show up for the party and get them interested in the script.

And it was a good party! Huncke was there, and Harry

Smith. Robert Frank[50] came, and Richard Linklater was there. He was a big fan of the Beats. And it was kind of fun to have Linda Twigg's poker chips.

Linda really knew how to make people feel very special and welcome. She was a real hostess! Especially if you had this funky, underground fame or notoriety. She loved that.

All Good Bad Must Come to an End

TIM SULLIVAN

Linda ended up leaving the Chelsea when the hotel came down on her about the gambling table. The police had known it for a long time— they had probably been following her around. There are a couple of things they'll really come down on you here for, and those are gambling and prostitution.

JEROME POYNTON

Her gambling room got broken up after her boyfriend shot and killed a cop.

It was 1993 when Linda Twigg's drug-dealing boyfriend, David Degondea, 22, got involved in his last drug deal. He planned to sell his customer ten pounds of weed and some illegal guns. When the customer showed up at the Screen Printing Company on East First Street, Degondea said he only had four pounds. The customer left to get the right amount of money.

The whole deal was a set-up. His customer was an undercover police officer named Louis Lopez, 35, who had actually left the Screen Printing Company to get back-up officers to help with the bust. When they returned, Degondea sensed they were cops and fired shots at them, hitting Lopez in the chest. Lopez later died at Bellevue Hospital.

Degondea suffered a minor injury when a bullet grazed his hip. He was convicted and sentenced to 55 years to life in prison at Great Meadow Correctional Facility. He later busied himself with a lawsuit against the NYPD, claiming his hip injury prevented him from working (his only job was drug dealer). This was declined. Later, he appealed his conviction

based on the fact that the judge had frequently dozed off during jury selection. At first a judge granted him a retrial, but the decision was later
reversed.

According to Chelsea resident Frank Meyer, Degondea was just a
punk kid who got himself involved with Linda Twigg and her seamy underworld. Twigg had made it her project to mold Degondea into a gang-
ster, pumping up his ego by telling him what a tough guy he was.

JEROME POYNTON

Her room became ancient history when the police knocked
down the doors and tore the place apart.

JERRY WEINSTEIN

They had a no-knock warrant, and they arrested her for possession of narcotics.

TIM SULLIVAN

After Linda Twigg was kicked out of the Chelsea, she moved
down to the Lower East Side. She ended up getting killed as well,
but I don't know the circumstances.

According to Al Aronowitz, Linda Twigg died from overdosing on a designer drug she herself had designed.[51]

The Party at Marty's

It wasn't always violence and crime with Huncke and his friends. It was
usually just innocent debauchery.

DIMITRI MUGIANIS

Once there was an insane party at Marty Matz's house for Herbert Huncke, and I knocked on the door. Johnny Thunders[52] answered the door!

Queens-born Johnny Thunders, stage name for Johnny Genzale, played
lead guitar for the New York Dolls. Formed in 1970, the Dolls, with their
coiffed hair, thigh-high, high-heel boots and androgynous makeup,

looked like glam rockers but their sound was garage rock. In fact the Dolls—who named themselves after a toy repair shop called the New York Doll Hospital—deserve credit for helping launch both punk rock and metal. Their sound marked a return to old-fashioned rock and roll, yet was also influenced by bands like the Stooges and T-Rex. The band's core comprised of Thunders, equally deft at piercing guitar solos and power chords, and lead singer David Johansson, whose jellyfish lips and prancing charisma recalled Mick Jagger.

By the time Johnny Thunders opened the door to Marty Matz's room for Dimitri Mugianis, Thunders' substance abuse and self-sabotage had taken their toll.

DIMITRI MUGIANIS

Thunders was half dead. He was carrying around a carton of Haagen Dazs™ like it was a drink. His pancake makeup was smeared on his shirt collar, and he had these two Eurotrash chicks following him everywhere and cleaning up after him. Gregory Corso *loved* Thunders. He loved that Thunders always had these girls with him. I remember Corso calling over to Thunders:

"Hey, Thunders, do you get a lot of pussy?"

ROBERT CAMPBELL

When I saw Johnny Thunders at Herbert Huncke's party, it must have been just weeks before he died, and he did look like death with a couple of rich bitches following him around.

The party was in a Chelsea apartment that belonged to this couple—the husband was the old beat writer Marty Matz. His wife, Barbara, was a concert pianist. On the walls, they had this amazing collection of beetles from Africa. There were three or four hundred of them. Man, these beetles looked like reindeers with their big horns—they were the creepiest things I ever saw in my life, as big as a beer can. If there were one on my bed, I would sleep standing up!

There were other people at the party who looked like people you'd see at Lincoln Center. One woman looked like a librarian and wore expensive clothes. She had just gotten back from Thailand, and she had these photos that showed them smoking opium with a Thai cook who had cooked it up for them.

It was at this party, I believe, where we snorted a bunch of coke off this girl's leather mini-skirt. Also, Huncke's partner Louis Cartwright had some coke with him.

"Louis, give me some coke," I said. "Front it to me and you know I'll pay you back." At the time, I was making money like this and that, but I didn't have any cash on me right at the moment. But Louis wouldn't give me any coke. There were these rich girls there at the party—I think they might have been the same girls that had come with Johnny Thunders—and they were sitting around at the party gawking as if they were watching animals in the zoo.

One of the rich girls asked me, "Need some money?"

"No, no, no. I don't need money," I said, and turned back to Louis. "Louis, give me some coke, man. I've fronted money for you before." So finally, after he wouldn't give me any, I just looked at one of the rich girls and said, "Yeah, give Louis fifty dollars." Without even blinking, she gave him fifty dollars and Louis gave me my coke.

In the meantime, Johnny Thunders had crust on his eyelashes and he looked horrible. He had a sharkskin suit on, and he was sitting there eating chocolate ice cream on the couch. And suddenly, he just rolled off the couch, spilling all this melted chocolate ice cream all over himself and the floor. They picked him back up and propped him up like a dummy.

DAVID LAWTON

I happen to be the guy who cleaned up the ice cream! Johnny Thunders was half-dead. Somehow, he fell into this table, and the table flipped over and the ice cream went flying. I'm not usually that type, the guy who cleans things up, but I thought, "Well, I guess, in *this* crowd, I'm the most responsible person!" I was already irritated because Johnny Thunders was just a mess! And of course everyone was fawning all over him. Sometimes junkies, you just wanna kill them!

There was more to Thunders' catatonia than heroin. Beneath it all was the secret he had been hiding from most of his friends: he had leukemia.

DIMITRI MUGIANIS

Ramón, the Puerto Rican drug dealer, was at the party too. Ramón and Huncke loved each other. Ramón had all of this gold on. He was wearing a nice suit, and he had a camera with him because he was on his way to a Puerto Rican baptism somewhere. He was having Ginsberg and all these major American literary figures pose for pictures.

"Get down in front!" Ramón was ordering them. "Get down in front!"

And these writers, these world-renowned literary luminaries, were like sheepish little kids obeying Ramón's orders, standing closer to each other, like *they* were at a Puerto Rican baptism!

The Month-Long Party

DIMITRI MUGIANIS

Once Huncke fell and dislocated his shoulder. He was seventy-eight years old, and he had been going to cop some coke! And then he refused to go to the hospital! At the time, I was back visiting my parents in Detroit. He phoned me and made me come back to New York before he would go to the hospital. James Rasin had to come in from someplace else. Huncke wanted to walk into the hospital surrounded by a bunch of young men. Pretty young men! He wanted to be taken care of!

When we arrived, we took him to the hospital, and it became another big scene. At least the doctor who examined him had a sense of humor. The doctor asked him what medication he was on at the time. Huncke answered the doctor with this proud smile on his face. "I'm on a hundred milligrams of Methadone!"[53]

The doctor smiled. "How's it working for you?"

Then Hunke's broken shoulder turned into a freaking party

in his hospital room! There were people in there getting high and drinking. His hospital roommate named Frenchie, this old Puerto Rican dude, loved it because he was dying of cancer and at this party he wanted cigarettes. We said, "Well, he *is* dying of cancer! Here's a carton of cigarettes, Frenchie! Smoke your ass off!"

There were pretty girls coming in who drank wine with us. There was good music playing, there was weed, the works! This was the broken shoulder party at the hospital that lasted for months.

There's Methadone to His Madness

DAVID LAWTON

In *The Herbert Huncke Reader*,[54] there's a story about the last time he went in to see his methadone counselor. They'd done the pee test, and everything showed up. *Everything*! There might have been Ecstasy in his blood, who knows? So the methadone counselor was almost breaking down crying, saying, "How can you do all this?"

Herbert was nonchalant. "This is what I've done all my life. You can't expect me to change."

ROBERT CAMPBELL

Once, when I ran into Huncke, he had just failed a piss test. Here he was, a seventy-eight-year-old man. He was on a hundred milligrams of Methadone a day, enough to kill a horse. Most junkies in New York were on thirty or forty milligrams of methadone a day, or fifty if they were really bad off. But Huncke was on a hundred milligrams a day. This guy had been doing junk all of his life.

So he failed a piss test. Cocaine showed up in his urine, and when you do the coke, it cancels out the Methadone. So the Social Services, or whoever was giving him his Methadone, decided to punish him. They started making him walk every day all the way to the clinic to get his Methadone. This was a seventy-eight-year-old man!

PAUL VOLMER

Dimitri asked me if I would do a favor for Huncke. Herbert Huncke had to take a drug test every month in order to get his Methadone prescription. So Huncke had to have clean urine, which he obviously did not. So because I was not a heroin user, I would provide clean urine for Herbert Huncke. Once a month, he would come to my door for urine, which I would supply for him in a mayonnaise jar. It was quite an honor!

DAVID LAWTON

The one thing that Huncke was willing to do was make little testimonial messages, little advertisements, for the Methadone clinic, such as, "I wouldn't be here without the methadone program!" And yet the whole time he was on the methadone program, he never stopped doing heroin, coke, everything! He was incredible! He was up in his late 70s! When he said, "Thank God for the methadone program," what he meant was, "Now, with methadone, I don't have to buy as much heroin as I would have had to buy without it! It gives me a good base so then I can go do more drugs!"

Louie Out to Lunch

There's an inspiring documentary, *Huncke and Louis*, by Laki Vazakis. It's about Herbert Huncke's long-term relationship with Louis Cartwright. It's not only a moving testimony to love in the face of adversity, but it leaves the viewer with a sense of the bright-eyed spiritual *freedom* that a couple of old nonconformists can embody once they've abandoned hidebound social conventions for good. At least that's why I thought they were bright-eyed until someone corrected me. They said it was the heroin.

DIMITRI MUGIANIS

Huncke introduced me to his partner, Louis Cartwright. He used the term "partner" differently than it's used now. If you read

Huncke's writing, a partner is a drug-running buddy. They may or may not have had sex with each other. They often did, but with Huncke, I don't think he identified himself as gay or even bisexual. It was just sexual.

Louie Cartwright was an incredible trip, one of the most unique and frustrating people I've ever met, an incredible guy. He was from Ohio, and he talked really nasally. When I met him, he was very jealous of my hanging out with Huncke. In fact, once we were trying to score some money with Louie, and Louie was trying to shock me. If he said something outrageous, like, "I love to fuck babies," I would say, "I love to fuck *armless* babies." I was trying to get across to him that there was no way he was going to shock me. After that, we kind of hit it off.

ROBERT CAMPBELL

Louis was a no bullshit kind of guy, and sort of humorous. Of course Louis already knew all of Huncke's stories inside out and backwards. So when Huncke was in storytelling mode, Louis would always be amusing.

Huncke would be telling a story, dragging it out, and Louis would keep saying, "Get to the *punchline*, Huncke! Get to the *punchline!*"

Louis was out to lunch. Once, in my room, there was this woman named Anne with us all. She was a nurse for AIDS patients and she had been a friend of Elvis Presley. She was all dressed up really nicely, and her hair was done up in the "blue-haired" lady's hairstyle. She seemed totally out of place here with us at the Chelsea. And on this particular day in my room, Louis Cartwright happened to be standing back behind her, chopping up stuff with a razor blade on my Fender amplifier.

She turned around and asked him, "What are you doing?"

He said, "Chopping up some smack!"

"Oh," she said.

"You want some? I'll give *you* some, but nobody else can have any." Maybe he wanted to freak her out a little because she seemed so straight. And then he rubbed her head like Colonel Parker[55] does Eddy Murphy's. It was the craziest thing. Cartwright was out to lunch.

Louis had a photograph of himself that showed off his pecker. He had a big old pecker and he had a big nail, a ten-penny nail, sticking through it. It was taken well before all the people started putting rings through their eyebrows, etc.

DAVID LAWTON

Louie was always trying to kiss us. All of us.

JAMES RASIN

Louis was a handful. He liked to push peoples' buttons and see if he could get away with things. He was pretty hyper and out there, kind of like an idiot savant in a way, not that he could do incredible mathematical problems. But he could burst into song, perform—he liked to be in the spotlight.

Timur, one of the hotel's desk clerks, got thrown out of Herbert and Louie's room one night because he attacked Louie. Louie was being his typical, button-pushing, obnoxious funny guy, and Timur just finally snapped. I think he punched Louie in the back of the head. That was just not tolerated there. But Timur had been hanging out a lot up there. Louie got what he wanted, ultimately. Timur fell for it, and Louie got rid of him!

Louis Cartwright, R.I.P.

JAMES RASIN

I was phoned right away. We were pretty hung over—we'd been out the night before with a bunch of people. The phone rang and rang and rang, an old phone with a rotary dial. It would not stop ringing, and there was no answering machine. Finally, Laki got up off the sofa. I was in the bedroom.

He answered the phone and it was Roger Richards' wife, Ervine, saying, "Louie was killed." I guess Ervine's phone number had been in Louie's wallet. So the police called Ervine, and she called us, and we called Dimitri.

Laki Vazakis and Jeremiah Newton[56] and I went down to the precinct house. It was odd because when we were walking over to the precinct, we happened to see a shoe in the gutter. When we were walking by it, Jeremiah said, "That's Louie's shoe." Later, we found out that Louie *had* been stabbed right *there*, in the doorway of the church across from the Kiev restaurant, and that Louie *had* lost one of his shoes.

We were the first ones to arrive at the precinct house. The police were being really suspicious of everybody, kind of being dicks. Jeremiah was in his late forties then, but to me he seemed a lot older. He gave the cops a hard time right back, saying, "Look, quit dicking us around and tell us what happened. Or why else are we here?" He wasn't going to take any shit from these cops.

So then we had to go back and tell Herbert. At the time, Herbert was living with Dimitri on Avenue A and around Ninth Street. Herbert slept late every day, and this was all going on fairly early in the morning, relatively speaking. And Laki was making his film *Huncke and Louie*[57] at the time—he had been shooting Huncke constantly. So we were walking from the precinct house over to Avenue A and 9th Street, thinking about who was going to tell Herbert and how we were going to break it to him. And I asked Laki, "Are you going to have the camera on him when we wake him up and tell this news to him?" It was kind of a big decision. He chose not to shoot it. We were all there and decided to have Dimitri break it to him. He and Herbert were really tight.

It was pretty straightforward. We woke Herbert up and said, "We've got really bad news. Louie was murdered last night."

Herbert was just crushed. He really loved Louie a lot. Like everybody, he had a lot of ups and downs with Louie, who would drive him crazy, and Louie had turned their 7th Street place into a real crack den, which had finally prompted Herbert to leave and move into the Chelsea.

I don't think they ever caught the guy who killed Louie. I think the murderer must have been somebody whom Louie pissed off in the neighborhood when he was running his little crack den down there. That's what I think, anyway. But who knows?

Huncke in the Pictures

JAMES RASIN

When I first got to know Herbert Huncke, I was taking a filmmaking seminar at NYU, and we were doing our thesis films. So I adapted William Burroughs' novel *Exterminator*.

I said to Huncke, "I've made this into a short screenplay, and I want you to play the exterminator. I've kind of bastardized the story, taken the dialogue and the idea. You're going to go from room to room—to Vali's room, to Linda's room—and you'll spray for bugs and have this exchange with each one of these characters living in the Chelsea."

So I asked Vali and Linda Twigg and a couple of other people. I thought, "Gee, we're going to bring a small film crew, a few people in the hotel, so I guess I'd better ask for Stanley's permission."

"Don't do that!" said Herbert. "Are you out of your mind? He'll never let you do this. He's going to want money!"

But I was young, and thought I had to do things the right way, and Stanley had always been nice to me, so I went down and said, "Stanley, I want to make this little film with Herbert."

Stanley was aghast. "What!?! What do you think this *is!*"

I wasn't ballsy enough to do it the way Herbert told me. Stanley would never have known, and I would still have this very interesting documentary of the Chelsea and its people, embroidered around this Burroughs story.

I know Huncke had very mixed feelings about Stanley. Herbert could act rather diva-like, and I think he enjoyed sauntering in and out of the Chelsea, and living here. Stanley would sometimes come wagging after him, and Herbert would remind him just who he was talking to!

Star Power

JAMES RASIN

Sometimes I would go visit Huncke during the late afternoon. Herbert loved visitors.

He would say, "Guess who was sitting right there where you're sitting yesterday! Tatum O'Neal[58] was sitting right there!" Our friend Edgar Oliver[59] had brought Tatum over.

Or when I showed up, Huncke would be sitting there and watching *Saved by the Bell!* He'd sit there goofing or getting stoned with a big smile on his face, "Oh those kids, they're so clean cut and well-dressed!" Here's this old Beat guy sitting in this basement apartment watching this horrible show on late afternoon TV, this show about plastic kids in California. "Oh, they're so great!"

PAUL VOLMER

In her memoir *A Paper Life*, Tatum O'Neal makes it sound like Herbert Huncke was an evil guy, the worst drug loser ever. Her portrayal of him was so negative. But I knew Huncke, and he was such a sweet guy. I mean Tatum went and hung out with Huncke on her own volition—it's a free country, right? But she makes believe that it was his evil that sucked her into her own bad ways.

DIMITRI MUGIANIS

Once Herbert Huncke and I spent a half hour with Julian Schnabel, and we had no idea who he was. He kept dropping all these names on us, and we had no idea who *those* people were either!

The 7:00 a.m. Pow Wow

JAMES RASIN

Toward the end of his life, Herbert was so sick, and had so little control over his bowels that he was shitting in the wastebasket. In his room there was no toilet. He had to walk down the hall.

I said to Stanley Bard, "Can't you just give him a room with a bathroom?" And Stanley just growled and wouldn't do it.

When Herbert was in the hospital, he was in a lot of pain. I'd go visit him, and I remember once I held his hand. He was squeezing it so tight and said, "James, I never thought dying would be so painful!" He was in a lot of pain! We were there—me and Jerry and Raymond Foye—Raymond was taking charge of these decisions to be made, like whether Herbert should be force-fed through a tube.

There was a huge battle to try to get Herbert enough meds to relieve the pain. He had such a high tolerance level for opiates. The doctors' thinking was, "We can't give him too much pain killer because it'll trigger his addiction again and he's in the methadone program." I mean, he was *dying*! But they were saying, "No, if he's in the methadone program, he can only be given such and such amount." It was inhumane! Fortunately, there was a doctor from Thailand who was much more empathic and willing to bend the rules a little bit. He upped the dosage a little bit.

DIMITRI MUGIANIS

The last time I saw Herbert Huncke, he was living in a back room, a very small room with a bathroom down the hall. It was Huncke's birthday, and he was doing a reading with Gregory Corso at St. Mark's (Church). It might have been Huncke's last reading. It was a great reading, incredible, and it's shown in the movie *The Original Beats*. In front of everyone, a jam-packed crowd at St. Mark's, Huncke ends up getting in an argument with Corso. Those two were always arguing about one thing or another.

After the reading, the actor Richard Gere came up to talk to

Huncke, and he sort of had Huncke cornered. In the meantime, I knew Huncke wanted to get high, and I wanted to get high. But Richard Gere was talking and talking and talking while Huncke nodded and remained very patient and gracious. This was *Richard Gere*, who was everywhere on TV and in the movies!

They finally said goodbye, and Huncke turned to me. He asked me, "Who *was* that guy?"

So after the reading, Huncke and I were waiting for Huncke to get paid. He had said he was going to give me some of the money. Huncke ended up making five hundred dollars for the reading. He gave me two-hundred-fifty, which was incredible of him.

"Go have fun," he said.

"I'll be back at the place at five-thirty tomorrow morning," I said. It was winter, and I had been staying with Huncke in his apartment. "Be dressed at five-thirty because we have to get you to the clinic on time."

The next morning, Huncke had to be at Beth Israel's Bernstein Methadone Clinic for a six a.m. check-in. No one got in after six a.m. Huncke, at age eighty, was forced to go into rehab, or the government was going to throw him off the methadone program, because he had coke and heroin and weed and everything else you could imagine in his bloodstream. So if he wanted to stay on the methadone program, and keep getting his methadone supplied to him, he had to show up for this week-long daily rehab session, supposedly to get him off cocaine.

Now whenever Huncke had to *be* somewhere on time, had to meet an appointment, this was when Huncke would get into his queen prima donna mode.

I rolled back in at the apartment after a night of doing God knows what, and Jerry Poynton answered Huncke's door. Jerry was already rolling his eyes, because it was five-thirty and Huncke was still in his pajamas. And there was a snowstorm outside.

"Come on, Huncke! Get dressed! Get dressed!"

Huncke was all grouchy and making demands. "I need some

breakfast! I want you to get *apricot* yogurt. I don't want any kind but apricot. And I want toast, but I want the butter on the side."

Now I'm staring daggers at him. But I run down to get his breakfast, and when I come back, the coffee isn't right. And he's still not dressed! He's taking his time, he's doing one more line, or he can't find the line, and he's really disgusted with both of us. Then he starts to get dressed in front of the mirror, trying on different ascots.

I told Jerry, "I've taken people in for detox before. I know that if he arrives after 6:00, they will not let him in."

Finally, we load him into a cab and we're riding over there in the snow.

"I've always done well in institutions," he said proudly.

I was joking around, "Do you think the rehab's going to work this time?" But in reality I knew they weren't going to let him in this late, and I didn't know what we were going to do.

So when we got to the door, Huncke asked me for five dollars, for tips. Even when Huncke was in the hospital, he tipped everybody!

So Huncke walked through the clinic's door like royalty. He went up to some African-American guy, knowing that this was the guy in charge. When Huncke came inside, the guy smiled and said, "What's up, Pops!"

"I wanna go upstairs," Huncke said, slapping a bill into the guy's hand. "Here's a fiver."

The black guy's looking at Huncke like, "No one tips to get into rehab!"

But the door leading upstairs opened up, and Huncke turned around and gave me a wink, a smile, a thumb's up, and sure enough, they let him in! Huncke started walking up the stairs!

That was the last time I ever saw Herbert Huncke.

Around the end of his life, Herbert had really been questioning his talents. There was a nurse who attended him, and she said one of the last things he asked her was, "What do you think a writer is?" He said this to a nurse!

Gregory Corso actually came around, and he and Huncke

would argue bitterly because they had ripped each other off sometime in the 1950s! Every time they'd get together, they would bitch about that! But Corso finally figured out that Huncke was a writer. And Corso was a total egomaniac, so for him to admit that Huncke was a real writer was exceptional.

DAVID LAWTON

There's the great story about when Huncke was in the hospital, and he got somebody to bring him some coke. He was very frail, but he climbed out of bed and went off into the bathroom by himself. "Let *me* do it!" He was snorting away in the bathroom, and all a sudden, you hear this loud crash coming from the bathroom. And then you hear a gigantic fart, and hear him shout out, "*Yeah!!!*" The coke had opened him right up. There's no doubt about it—Herbert Huncke died in the saddle!

JAMES RASIN

Huncke was very happy that, when he was dying, he was a resident at the Chelsea Hotel.

One night, Laki and I and Wiley, my girlfriend at the time, left the hotel and went to the hospital and gathered around Herbert's bed. Herbert was kind of in a goofy haze. He was in good spirits, though.

"I want you to call all of our friends," he said, "and I want you to come back here tomorrow morning at seven. We're going to have a big, old-fashioned powwow!"

We all said, "Sure, Herbert! A powwow sounds good!" And then we had to leave.

And Herbert died the next morning, right around seven!

On August 8, 1996, two years after Louis Cartwright, Huncke's "Get to the punch line" partner had been murdered, Herbert Huncke died at the age of eighty-one. Not a bad lifespan for someone who had systematically abused his body since he was twelve years old, when he first ran away from his banker father and their upper middle-class Chicago home.

Huncke deserves to be remembered as a prime influence upon the Beats, and as a talented writer who was subject to moments of real literary vision. For his ability to combine a high literary prose style with street jargon, he has been compared to Celine.

DAVID LAWTON

The memorial service that they did for Huncke was awesome. It happened at the Friends Meeting House in the East Village. Marty Matz read fantastically, and Corso read. Ginsberg was there taking pictures. He might have started things out with a blessing. John Wieners[60] came in.

We did contributions too. I read a piece, sort of a journal entry of Huncke's that was written in a stream-of-consciousness style. Paul Romero did some singing, and he and I together sang the Woody Guthrie song, "Go to Sleep you Weary Hobo." Patti Smith ended up coming too.

At that event, you kind of knew that the era was over. So many of us were out of the Chelsea by then, and now Huncke was dead, and Corso's health was starting to worsen not too long after. And after that, Marty Matz died.

Jerry Poynton made sure that Huncke had written out his will, which is an amazing document. It consists of, "So and so gets this little box. So and so gets that little table."

JAMES RASIN

In the recognition department, Herbert did all right at the end of his life. He would have been very happy with the positive obituary he got in the *New York Times.*

JERRY WEINSTEIN

He died owing me money. He was the greatest hustler ever, and for a hustler, he was a pretty decent guy. Very, very likeable.

DAVID LAWTON

I grew up in the very Catholic suburbs of Boston. When the people where I'm from found out that I was running around with some of these people like Huncke, they would say, "Ugh! What are you *doing*?"

And yet, to me, Huncke was one of the most elegant, graceful, classy people I have ever met.

Their *example* is what teaches you. It's not like, "See my writing routine here." It's your manner, the way that you see the world, the way you take things in and respond to situations, the way you respond to people when they want to be petty, when they want to be dicks.

The way he responded to life's curve balls showed us younger people, "Yeah, calm down! This kind of stuff is going to happen to you." Huncke would respond with grace under pressure.

People of all strata—whether they were cops or Rastafarian drug dealers—there's a code they respect: to remain cool under pressure. Huncke got this respect everywhere he went. Did these cops, these dealers, know that he was *the* Herbert Huncke, who said, "I'm beat!" Not necessarily. They just knew this guy was the real deal. He deserved respect.

DIMITRI MUGIANIS

I was in the company of guys who changed American culture—and who also made it completely fucked up! And it continues to influence people. Huncke was a real sweet guy. Huncke was a guy who would find the most dejected person in the room and pull up a chair and start talking to him.

A friend of mine, Bob Ross, once talked to Huncke, and afterward Huncke told me, "You know, that guy is so hurt." And he was right. Huncke knew that by talking to him just one time.

You know what Huncke was? He was the coolest white man that ever lived. Huncke was not even thinking about being the "White Negro."[61] And he went out of his way to be kind to people you normally wouldn't look at twice. Huncke was a good man. I think he was actually a great man.

DAVID LAWTON

I wrote a spoken word poem about Huncke. One of the lines says, "He owes me sixty dollars for the rest of eternity." One day in the lobby, Herbert had approached me and said, "Hey, can you help me out?" I thought, well, of course. I think it was the only time he ever asked me for money, other then ten bucks here or a beer there.

It's a simple little poem:

Inspiration to the Beats
Patron saint of the streets
Turned Burroughs onto smack
Once did the nasty with Jack
Huncke the Junkie.
I would have described him as elfin
But he would have slapped me silly
He was the consummate hustler
But he counseled me to be more trusting
Europeans lined up to kiss his ass
While he said he was "No big deal."
Huncke the Junkie.
He did whatever shit he wanted until the end
I couldn't have been prouder to call him my friend
Street people showed him respect
When he walked around the city
He owes me sixty dollars for the rest of eternity
Huncke the Junkie![62]

Gregory Corso: Poet of the Streets

If the first string of the Beat writers featured Jack Kerouac, Allen Ginsberg, and William Burroughs, then Gregory Corso was the number one second stringer, an apt metaphor because he loved baseball and wrote about it. When young, in the 1960s, he was a handsome devil, which helped him befriend Allen Ginsberg, who claimed he seduced Corso. Corso denied it. Corso's smooth good looks were belied by his aggressive personality forged from growing up in eight different foster families and fending for himself on the streets. He met Ginsberg at age 20, right after finishing three years in upstate New York's Clinton prison for several robberies.

Corso's best-known collection of poetry was *Gasoline*, published by City Lights, but he authored something like seventeen books. Probably his most famous poem was "Bomb," which appeared on the page in the shape of a mushroom cloud and argued that we must learn to love the bomb. Haven't we heard that somewhere, say, in *Dr. Strangelove*, Stanley Kubrick's 1964 satire of the Cold War? Corso beat Kubrick to the punch, publishing "Bomb" in 1958.[63]

DIMITRI MUGIANIS

I was on my way with Robert Campbell on 23rd Street, and we saw this crazy old drunk standing on the corner, sort of ranting at people on the street. He looked homeless. He was holding this huge picture of Hitler before Hitler became Chancellor. Hitler was dressed in mourning clothes, those ties that are folded over, and his shoes had spats on them.

So this drunk guy on 23rd had this picture of Hitler and he was screaming, "Ya wanna buy a pitchah of Hitlah?" Naturally, I was immediately attracted to this guy. I went up and talked to him about his picture of Hitler.

When he turned to look at us, I realized he was Gregory Corso! Corso on the street selling this picture! We started talking to him.

ROBERT CAMPBELL

There was this drunk, unshaven guy screaming about Hitler, and it looked like he was holding up a protest sign, but it was this picture of Hitler. I thought this was in really bad taste!

DIMITRI MUGIANIS

So I asked this guy, "Are you Gregory Corso?"

"Yeah of course. That's Corso, yeah," he said, referring to himself in the third person.

So we started walking down 23rd street with Corso, talking with him, and he was grabbing at people as he staggered down the street. At one point, he stopped right in front of the Chelsea Hotel, and he pointed at his picture of Hitler. "*Look* at him! He coulda done so many good things, the motherfucker! The broads *loved* him! Look at his shoes! Those spats!"

And then he walked into the Chelsea. I found out later that he was going up to Marty Matz's room.

ROBERT CAMPBELl

As soon as that guy said "Hitler," I thought the guy was a crazy fucker. I couldn't believe anyone would say that.

James Rasin, who later made a film about Andy Warhol's drag queen associate Candy Darling, eventually befriended Corso as well.

JAMES RASIN

Once Gregory told me, "I'm going to Atlantic City. You wanna come with me? Let's go to the Port Authority and catch the bus."

I had just gotten paid—I had about three hundred bucks in my pocket, so I said, "Sure, let's go!"

So we're walking through the Port Authority, and I was thinking this was pretty cool, doing this with him. But then this homeless guy behind us starts saying "Excuse me," and starts chasing after us.

I thought, "Well, I'm going to ignore this guy!"

But he came up to me. He tapped me on the shoulder and then he started shaking me. He said, "This fell out of your pocket!" He was holding my wad of money—it had fallen out of my pocket.

Corso was ecstatic. "You are the luckiest person in the world. I've never seen anything like it! I'm so glad we're going out—you're gonna be good luck in Atlantic City!"

To have a homeless guy chase you down with your three hundred dollars! I felt like kind of a jackass, so I gave the guy some money and we went on and had fun.

Corso had just gotten the galley proofs of his book *Minefield*. The whole bus ride out, he was reading aloud to me from the galleys as he proofread it. Gregory was a great teacher.

He was a very, very smart guy, different from Huncke in a lot of different ways. He knew so much about the Greek classics and poetry. He knew Greek mythology backwards and forwards.

But sometimes I'd just go over to his place and we'd watch football.

DIMITRI MUGIANIS

One time, Corso was kidding around with me.

"Hey Dimitri, you're Greek. You're supposed to know something about the ancient Greeks! You don't know crap about the ancient Greeks, and you're Greek!"

So Ramón, the Puerto Rican drug dealer, asks Corso, "What's that mean? He's Greek, so what? What's that mean?"

"You don't know?" Corso asks Ramón. "You don't know the ancient Greeks?"

"Nah," Ramón says, irritated, as if it was obvious he wouldn't know such things.

Now Corso's shtick was that there's not much to know, that there were only about five things about the world that everyone should know. And one of them was the ancient Greeks.

"I'm going to break it down for you, Ramón," Corso said. So Corso went home and wrote Ramón a history book! It's got an inscription in it.

Corso was an intimidatingly brilliant man, and all self-educated.

Later, I told Ramón, "Listen Ramón, you hold onto that book. That book's worth all the gold you own."

"Really?" Ramón was incredulous. "From *this* guy?" Ramón just stumbled onto these Beat guys. He had no idea who they were.

"Yeah, bro," I said. "Really."

According to Ginsberg's biographer Barry Miles, Corso—who had next to no formal education—learned everything he knew about ancient Greek and Roman literature by reading the classics in prison. The old convicts advised him about prison life: "Don't serve time, let time serve you."

But being an impressive autodidact doesn't mean you're not sometimes a jerk.

ROBERT CAMPBELL
Gregory Corso used to hit on my girlfriend, Carol, and be really abusive in a verbal way.

DIMITRI MUGIANIS
My wife at the time was absolutely beautiful, and one time Corso

was being rude to her in my apartment. I wanted to kill him. But later on, I got to know him more, and he said to me that my relationship to her was a blessed thing. I had to beat Corso's ass—metaphorically of course—but after I did, he started to be decent to me.

Marty Matz: Poet/Smuggler

The third Chelsea Beat writer, the poet Marty Matz, published the books *Pipe Dreams, Time Waits*, and *In the Seasons of My Eye*. An issue of the Beat journal *Goodie Magazine* was devoted to Matz. Aside from his writing, Matz was well-known for his bad luck, some of which earned him a couple of years in a notorious Mexican prison. But just as heartbreaking, his wanderlust spoiled his chance at fame. After hanging out in San Francisco's Little Italy (now North Beach) with the Beat writers before they had made their names, Matz left town. His timing couldn't have been worse. He departed the day before the now legendary reading at 6 Gallery on Fillmore Street, where Ginsberg read "Howl" and Kerouac shouted encouragement from the corner, the single reading that brought attention to the young poets and launched the writing careers of Ginsberg, Gary Snyder, Phillip Whalen, and Michael McClure. Matz could have been part of it all, but the day before, he had left for Mexico.

Matz was an enormous man with big appetites, one of which was for drugs. This proclivity, combined with his being an inveterate world-traveler, often led him to the opium fields of Thailand or Burma. His poem "The Alchemist's Song," included in his book *Pipe Dreams* is an ode to opium. Matz hobnobbed with shamans and medicine men from cultures worldwide. According to writer John Major Jenkins, another visionary and interpreter of ancient sacred texts, "In 1961 an unknown Aztec codex was revealed to Beat poet and explorer Marty Matz by a Mazatec shaman in the mountains of Oaxaca, Mexico. This codex presents a profound metaphysical teaching describing how the end of time will bring about a visionary ascent. At the behest of his Mazatec teacher, Matz transcribed this pictorial codex into a literary form that would preserve its initiatory teachings and reveal its secret meanings to a wider audience." The book is now called *The Pyramid of Fire: The Lost Aztec Codex.*

The Beached Elephant

DIMITRI MUGIANIS

Marty Matz was a huge, fat dude. He lived in 319 for a little while—and he was an incredible poet. Normally, Marty was one of the brokest motherfuckers you would ever meet. But at one point, his wife inherited some money from her family, so now Marty had money. This turned him into Santa Claus for junkies!

When he got money, he would travel to Thailand. He lived with the Hill Tribe people, smoking opium all day long. He would always tell us stories about this. Then he would come back to New York from Thailand for the pro football season! But he always brought an opium habit back with him, too. This meant that I was the one who had to start copping heroin for him.

Because I was copping for him, we became friends. Marty was an amazing guy, a great writer, and a big baby. It was great for me, a guy in his twenties, because these older guys were taking me in and saying, "Yeah, we're all together on this."

At the time, I was struggling to get a job. I'd been selling weed, but finally I got a job as a bike messenger. Back before cell phones, bike messengers carried beepers around that would instruct us when to phone the office.

One day I was riding my bike on the job and I got a beep on my pager. I went over to some payphone and called the office, and the dispatcher told me in this thick Brooklyn accent, "Your uncle Marty is very sick. He wants you to come home." So I raced back to the Chelsea and rushed up there to his room. Herbert Huncke answered the door, all nervous and irritated. Marty's wife Barbara was inside the room.

Huncke was pacing around the room, disgusted, swinging his arms. He pointed his finger inside Marty's room. "Go on in there! He's in there like a beached elephant!"

Now Marty weighed over three hundred pounds. He was lying—completely naked—on his chaise longue and moaning like a whale. "OoooooaaaaAH!" Marty's arms were like a web. I've never seen tracks like that—he had shot every place in his arms, and because he was so fat, he had to snort his heroin.

He gave me three hundred dollars. "Get me straight, kid. Keep a hundred for yourself." I ran out and purchased three bundles of heroin. When I brought it back to him, Marty snorted up two hundred dollars of the heroin, right then and there.

He did that so many times, "Your Uncle Marty's calling!" I finally lost my bike messenger's job.

Now earlier, I had once told Marty, "Man, I would love to try opium." Everyone else, it seemed, had been going to visit Marty in Thailand, and he was turning them on to opium there. But I was so broke and so strung out that I couldn't go.

So I said, "If you ever get hold of some opium, I would love to try it."

So one day, when I was living over on the East Side with this guy Jerrod from the band Chem Lab, I got a phone call. It was Marty.

"I'm at the Chelsea," he said. "I've got a business proposition."

I was thinking he had gotten a bunch of heroin. He wanted help selling it all, and we could both make a lot of money. So I went over there, and he was in his room with Gregory Corso and Herbert Huncke. The three wise men of dope!

I walked into Marty's room, and he announced, "I've got opium!"

"Opium!" I said. He remembered that I had gotten that amount of heroin for him, that I had once done him a favor.

He very judiciously poured me out some opium mixed with cognac, in a little glass.

Herbert Huncke was with him, and he warned Marty, "Be careful with these kids. It's very potent. They could OD really easily."

So I drank it down and I started to feel it a little bit. Then I asked for some more. After a few times, I eventually got a really great buzz. Then some more people started showing up. This tiny room was filling up with everyone, from homeless people to fashion models. They let everyone in!

Huncke said, "Let's go get some coke!" Huncke had been doing this opium, and he was already wanting coke. Despite all the people partying in the room, we got out and got some coke, which took us about an hour and a half.

When we got back to Marty's room, I saw that Marty was now wasted. He was pouring tumblers of this opium and cognac and handing it out to people who had never done opiates in their lives!

JAMES RASIN

Marty had made laudanum by dissolving the opium in his cognac. He made it very strong because he had a big habit, and he kept it in a flask for this very long flight.

Now back when I had visited him in Thailand, I had smoked some opium with him, and it was no big deal. But now, back in New York, he and I and a couple of others drank almost a whole big bottle of cognac, and then he said, "Now let's have some of this opiated cognac while we're waiting for everyone else to arrive."

I said, "Sure!"

So after I'd shared this bottle of cognac with Marty and a couple of others, I drank too much of this opiated cognac. That's not a good combination, especially for me because I don't do opiates. I didn't have any resistance to it.

DIMITRI MUGIANIS

And all of the sudden, Jerry Poynton came running up to me. "James is in the bathroom. He's turning blue!"

Huncke and Corso and Marty were nonchalant, like "Ahhh, don't *worry* about it. The kid will be *fine!*"

"No, he *won't* be fine!" Jerry said. "I've read these guys' books, and everyone *dies!*"

JAMES RASIN

Herbert, who usually doesn't get too high, was pretty high right now, and a friend of mine who was with us that night asked Huncke, "Herbert is everyone going to be okay? Is this something we should worry about?"

Because in the meantime I was turning blue.

Herbert was indignant. "*Don't* ruin Marty's night," he said. "Do *not* ruin Marty's night!"

DAVID LAWTON

Marty and Huncke were sitting there laughing at them, these two vets who had built up such a tolerance to heroin. They were laughing and saying, "Oh, *this* is good!"

JERRY POYNTON

Then James was out cold. Dimitri came over, and I said, "Dimitri, I don't want to be the one who has to tell Mr. Rasin that his son died."

Dimitri sprang into rescue action with a vengeance. Then Francois showed up with these two French girls. They had never been to the Chelsea. They were just visiting New York. Right away, I told them, "Oh, you girls, you've got to help me. This guy is dying!"

JAMES RASIN

They put me down in my boxer shorts in the shower, and this French girl was putting ice on my balls!

DIMITRI MUGIANIS

I started doing all this stuff, all the junkie lore, putting ice on Jamie, breathing into his mouth, slapping his face.

JEROME POYNTON

Dimitri was slapping him around. Dimitri loves to slap them around.

JAMES RASIN

So I came back to consciousness on the floor of Marty's room, sopping wet in my boxers with these two French girls massaging me! I'd never seen them before. I didn't know what had happened, but I thought, "This is great!"

DIMITRI MUGIANIS
Eventually, James came out of it. Marty came in and said, "Whoa, uh, I guess it *was* a little serious." He turned to me, "Well you're going to have to tell his father that James passed out. If he had died, James' father would have made us pay some *serious* consequences!"

"Yeah?" I asked. "Who is James's father? What does he do?"

"James's father," Marty said, with all pomp and self-importance, "is the man who invented capitalism!"

JAMES RASIN
The fact was, Dimitri saved my life.

Shoe Polish, Ping Pong, and Chocolate

DIMITRI MUGIANIS
Marty traveled the world and he was a master smuggler. Once, he had smuggled all this opium from Thailand, and he had put it in ping pong paddles.

JERRY POYNTON
He took the rubber surfaces off the paddles and smeared the paddles with opium where the glue used to be and put the rubber pads back on. The opium was the new adhesive.

DIMITRI MUGIANIS
He also put opium in shoe polish.

JAMES RASIN
He would take a Bocci chocolate box and make balls of opium and then dip them in chocolate, put them back into the Bocci chocolate box and reseal the box. He made a box of opium chocolates!

DIMITRI MUGIANIS

He was a genius at smuggling—but not a great business mind!

So anyway he had all this opium in the chocolates, but if we were going to sell it, we had to know how to get it out. If someone handled it, it melted. At one point, we found ourselves sitting in the walk-in refrigerator of some restaurant, so the chocolate wouldn't melt and make a mess of everything. We were cutting the opium, but eventually the opium slowly but surely dwindled away into our bloodstreams. So by that time, we ourselves had huge opium habits!

Everyone we went to, like these Puerto Rican guys, said, "We don't need no opium." We went to Italians, blacks, Israelis, all these different crime groups who told us the same thing: "First, we don't believe you have opium. Even if you did, what would we do with *opium*?"

JAMES RASIN

Here in the States, people don't really know what opium is. It was raw opium, like black putty. To smoke it, you'd have to have a special pipe, and you have to have a special chef who cooks it. It's kind of complicated, not an easy thing to cook up properly. I wasn't really into it. No one knew how to do it. You can't really do it in the right surroundings, without a pipe and an opium den in a Hill Tribe village. I don't think too many people in New York sit around with an opium pipe. So there wasn't a big market of people who were curious.

DIMITRI MUGIANIS

I would try to sell it on the street, and people thought I was full of shit. We actually ended up selling a bunch of it to a rock band, whose name I won't mention. Then we only had a quarter of the opium remaining.

Poor Marty had thought we would make a couple hundred thousand dollars out of his smuggling enterprise. But we just went through the opium and ended up totally broke. It was sad. If it had been heroin, we probably would have gotten killed. I was really worried that we were going to get killed.

JAMES RASIN

Because Marty couldn't sell the opium, he ended up giving a lot of it away. So he would mix it with alcohol and drink it, or people would just eat it. And for the people who were junkies, opium wasn't strong enough to satisfy them. If they were desperate, Marty might give them a chunk and it would keep them from getting sick.

Dee Dee Ramone was living next door to Marty. When Marty got the opium, Dee Dee came around a lot! He knew that Marty was pretty cool, and Dee Dee especially enjoyed the times when he and Marty were alone together. Dee Dee didn't really like to hang out with a bigger group of people. But Marty had no idea who Dee Dee Ramone was! He had never even heard of the Ramones—he just knew that this guy Dee Dee lived next door, and he liked him.

The very first time Dee Dee came to visit Marty's, they were hanging out and they got high, and Dee Dee finally left. A bunch of other people had dropped by too, and the next morning when Marty woke up, he saw that someone had left their leather jacket at his place. He said, "Wow, who left that jacket here? Maybe it was Dee Dee." He got on the phone and called Dee Dee's room.

"Dee Dee, this is Marty. You left your leather jacket here."

Dee Dee said, "You have my leather jacket and you're actually going to give it back to me?" Dee Dee was so shocked that someone wouldn't rip off a leather jacket that had belonged to one of the Ramones!

"Well of course!" Marty said. "What else would I do with your leather jacket?"

Dee Dee was so blown away by this, and Marty felt so bad for Dee Dee.

"What kind of friends does this guy have?" Marty wanted to know. "What kind of life is that?"

After that, Dee Dee and Marty became closer friends.

When Marty was in Peru, he got into cocaine. Thinking he was going to make money, he would take some of the local pots they would make in Peru, that they didn't fire, but you would just see them lying out to dry in the sun. Marty was also pretty good at chemistry. So he was thinking, "Well, if they don't have to fire those in a kiln, there must be some way to put the cocaine in the clay syrup, and then get it back out when you get it to the States."

He figured out a way to impregnate these clay pots with cocaine, and he also figured out a way to reverse it and extract the cocaine back out! When he finally got the method down, he made this huge cache of pots he was going to ship to the U.S., and no one would ever think of it in a million years. In celebration, Marty gave some money to this local guy who was working for him, his assistant. Unfortunately for him, in typical Marty fashion, this assistant guy took the money down to a local village bar, got really drunk, and started telling people in the bar about this ingenious, crazy plan they had going. Just by chance, it turned out there was a DEA agent sitting in the bar. So Marty had to take off, leaving all his pots behind. But according to Marty, there was a big article about it in *National Geographic*, something like "Busted Right at the Last Moment, an Ingenious Smuggling Scheme..." Marty was always screwing up somewhere, or getting himself screwed up by others.

But he was a pretty good smuggler.

DAVID LAWTON

Marty talked about being in the Mexican prison. He had a lot of stories about them trying to get out, using a spoon to dig himself out.

According to Laki Vazakis, Matz and an accomplice "hid for days" in the tunnel under the prison before the Mexican police finally discovered them. The story was covered profusely in Mexico's sensationalist newspapers.[64]

DAVID LAWTON

He talked about the brutality of the Mexican prisons. Marty was fluent in Spanish, which I think helped him out. And he knew how to cut the deals in order to not get brutalized himself. But he saw many people killed in those prisons—many people.

During the period he was down there, President Nixon made a deal with the Mexican prisons that said, "If these Americans do try to smuggle drugs out, they're yours. Screw with them as you will."

Matz was in there for something like four or six years. And he felt *lucky*! There were people who had been in there much longer.

JERRY POYNTON

Marty always liked President Carter because Carter had gotten him out of the Mexican prison. It was a prisoner exchange between Mexico and America.

JAMES RASIN

Once Marty and Barbara went back to Chiang Mai, Thailand, and they cooked up this scheme where they bought up a bunch of Burmese lacquered boxes, Burmese puppets, etc. I remember he was waiting so expectantly for his shipment of Burmese goodies. It finally arrived, and he took a machete—he was all screwed up on something—and he started slashing through the paper and the tape. He had this beautiful, big lacquer box that held a scroll, and he scratched the thing right down the front. He was so out of his mind—his eyes would bulge out and he'd be frothing at the mouth. He was so exuberant! And they brought all these beetles and spiders with them. So then they had all this stuff in their room, and they were going to try to sell it. It was another one of Marty's schemes, just like his opium disaster. I think they ended up selling a few pieces, but I don't know what happened to all that stuff.

Marty was notorious for having smuggling schemes collapse. He always said, "I have the best bad timing. I always leave the scene right about when everything's about to take off."

Toward the end of his life, around 2001, Marty wanted to kill himself at the Chelsea Hotel. He was very sick, and he did not tolerate pain well. He had heart problems, and apparently leukemia. He just abused his body, and there were all kinds of things going wrong. So he went to the doctor, and had been to the VA Hospital. He couldn't stand being in the hospital, couldn't stand being poked and tested and needled. So he just checked himself out. That began this long journey from place to place, while he was sick. In all that pain, he was not happy. I tried to take him down to the hospital—he had been staying at lawyer Bobby Yarra's apartment down on Grand Street—and get him to check himself in. But within a half an hour waiting in the emergency room, he said "Screw this, man. I can't do this."

On the one hand, I could see his point. He said, "Look, I've had a long life, and I'm really sick. I don't have the energy or the desire to go through whatever's going to cure me, if it's even going to work. I'd rather just die."

Then 9/11 happened, and Bobby's place, down on Grand and Essex, had a terrace that looked south. And Marty was there, watching the towers coming down. Afterwards, he said, "This is it. After this attack, the government's going to go totally berserk, and this is going to become a country that I don't really want to be around in."

It didn't take too much longer after that before he died. But it wasn't fast enough for Marty. So in his very self-indulgent way, he announced, "I'm going to kill myself." Of course it's not that simple with Marty! We went to the Cedar Tavern,[65] which Marty loved, in the middle of the afternoon one day. Marty was going to talk to me about his suicide plans. He said, "Yeah, I need some money, because I'm going to have a party in a room at the Chelsea. I'll have all my friends there, and I'll get the best booze and food from the Second Avenue Deli. Then I'm going to have a really good bottle of cognac and a bag of heroin. People are going to leave the party, and then I'm going to take my combination of cognac and heroin, and that's going to be the end."

He popped this idea on me, and I was, you know, *ambivalent*! Then he invited everyone at the Cedar, "You've got to come to my suicide party!" He became very into this idea. He went back to Bobby's apartment—he was obsessed with the idea.

At first I said, "I'll give you some money." But then I thought about it and told him, "You know, I don't want to give you money for that. That's going to lay a trip on me, and I don't even know if it's legal. If you want to kill yourself, just jump out the window! Why do you have to involve everybody in your trip? It's kind of sucking everybody into something that should be just your own thing."

I think some people did agree to give him money for it, but I think he just spent it on whatever he spent it on. So it never happened. He did want to go out in this grand flourish at the Chelsea, but he ended up just dying in a hospice.

It was October 28, 2001 when Marty Matz died at the Cabrini hospital hospice. He was sixty-seven.[66]

DIMITRI MUGIANIS

There was a time when Marty helped me out big time. I remember I was with this guy Jerry Agony, who played with James White and the Blacks. I have no idea what happened to Jerry. He and I went out to cop dope. Jerry spoke Spanish—he was Puerto Rican Cuban. We went and got some coke from some Spanish guys. He went and got his dope, and I was doing something else. And then the police came around and we had be cool and wait. When the cops were gone, I went back and got the dope. I came back downtown and I was sick. I had to shoot up, and I had mixed the heroin with the coke. And the heroin was bunk. Jerry Agony got good heroin and I got bullshit because I didn't speak Spanish. You'd have to be a junkie to understand, but when you're sick on heroin, and then you shoot up coke by itself while you're going through heroin withdrawal, it's the worst thing you could possibly imagine. It was snowing outside, it was miserable, I didn't know what to do, I was out of money, I was sick, I was paranoid, my heart was racing, and I went up and knocked on Marty Matz's door. I never did that sort of thing—I never made a habit of going to other people to cop. And Marty said, "No problem." He gave me a hundred bucks. This is the kind of thing you remember! He was such a good man.

JAMES RASIN

Lately, I noticed they put the plaque out there on the front of the Chelsea for the filmmaker Shirley Clarke, and I noticed there aren't too many spots left for plaques! But there should be a group plaque for all the Beat people who lived here—you could knock off ten or fifteen people on one plaque. Some friends of mine who've been living here for a long time said, "Just go talk to Stanley. If you can raise the money to do it, he'd probably put it up." But I'm surprised someone hasn't done it.

Dee Dee Ramone (facing) rehearses with Robert Campbell (foreground, back to camera) in Campbell's Chelsea room.

CHAPTER 4

Three Chords and a Grudge:
Dee Dee Ramone and the Chelsea Hotel Blues

I wanted to play the blues, because I felt the blues.

—DEE DEE RAMONE, *Surviving the Ramones*

To get off heroin and alcohol, Dee Dee Ramone took a room at the Chelsea, of all places. So when Robert Campbell met him, the ex-Ramone was straight edge. Maybe a beer now and then, maybe an occasional joint, but no powders, and forget about heroin.

Dee Dee had left the Ramones by then, but at the Chelsea, his reputation made him a god.

JOHN ZINSSER

Dee Dee's look was incredible at the time. He had remade himself, being divorced from the Ramones. He had this peroxide hair, and his look was so strong—his facial expression borderline psychotic, and this incredible hair. He seemed like a walking disaster waiting to happen, but in a kind of romantic, dangerous way. He was like royalty. He was someone who had lived a whole, entire life and was completely used up.

PAUL VOLMER

He was a person who lived the authentic Bohemian rock and roll life. He just exuded rock and roll, with his rock and roll look and his rock and roll lifestyle. He wasn't the type of rock star to settle down in New Jersey in a big house. He lived in Manhattan and stayed rockin'.

Dee Dee had been rocking since 1974, when the Ramones were pioneers of punk and truly unique. Despite the band's identical hairstyles and outfits that made them look like botched clones, the Ramones were four unrelated middle-class kids from Queens: Douglas Colvin (Dee Dee Ramone, bass and songwriter); Joey Hyman (Joey Ramone, singer); Tommy Erdelyi (Tommy Ramone, drums), and John Cummings (Johnny Ramone, guitar). They named themselves after Paul Ramon, a pseudonym Paul McCartney had adopted when the Beatles were touring.[67]

While the band inherited some of their raw, primitive power from the New York Dolls and Iggy and the Stooges, and while their sound harkened back to rock and roll's simple roots, the Ramones took these influences and forged them into something entirely their own. First, they sped it up. Pedal to the metal, they drove their songs like drag racers, forging their brand of punk rock as we know it. Unlike the heartfelt lyrics found in many rock songs of the early '70s, their lyrics were tongue-in-cheek with ironic titles like "Blitzkrieg Bop" and "Beat on the Brat." And their cartoony look, the goofball black bangs, boots, and leather jackets—the staged, choreographed uniformity of it—put them in a class by themselves. They may have only played four chords, but they played the hell out of them. And because of their famously militaristic rehearsals (no one drinks during rehearsal, always tape everything and listen to it later) their playing was tight as a fist.

Dee Dee was "the cute one" in the Ramones, the one the girls most wanted to be with. He was the band's creative brains, its artistic director and songwriter who kept their songs simple and tight, honest and funny. In his personal life he often played dumb, but he was smart and sensitive.

He wrote most of the Ramones' best songs, which is why, even after he left the band, they kept him on the payroll as songwriter.

In addition to the songs, Dee Dee trademarked the fast 1-2-3-4 count that launched each song (and now the songs of many bands). His personality was irascible and volatile—he could be a handful. But no one could deny his talent.

The Birth of an Unlikely Blues Band

What follows is the story of Dee Dee Ramone at the Chelsea, when he was trying to clean up and do something creative again. He wanted to return to rock and roll's roots and start a blues band, one that would include, as luck would have it, my brother-in-law Robert Campbell from Hickory, North Carolina on guitar.

ROBERT CAMPBELL

When I first saw Dee Dee Ramone, he was on the phone in the lobby of the Chelsea Hotel. At the Chelsea, you could get incoming phone calls in your own room for free. But if you had to make an outgoing call, it cost a shitload. Even the rock star Dee Dee Ramone would use the lobby phone for outgoing calls. He had these pants on that looked like Levis jeans that had been tailored. They were so tight and so thin, I couldn't see how he got them on. And he was skinny as a rail.

On the phone he was saying, "But I *love* her!" He kept repeating, "But I *love* her! But I *love* her!"

Now this was around the same time Herbert Huncke had been telling me "Stay away from Dee Dee." Huncke was warning me because recently my friend Patrick, a harmonica player, had come down to my room at the Chelsea and told me, "Man, Dee Dee Ramone wants to jam with us!" Huncke got word of this. But because Huncke had told me more than once to stay away from Dee Dee, I refused to let him come down to my room! I wouldn't answer the phone, either. Dee Dee kept calling me and leaving me messages. So at this time, I knew about Dee Dee's interest in playing with Patrick and me, but I had minimal contact with him.

I don't know why Herbert Huncke didn't like Dee Dee.

Huncke himself had a spotted history and some pretty heavy-duty friends.

A year or so later, after I had ignored Huncke's advice and become Dee Dee's friend, Dee Dee and I happened to drop by Huncke's room. A woman in Huncke's room at the time said, "Hey Robert, how's it going?"

"Hey," I said.

Dee Dee gave me a deep glare, like "How do *you* know these people?" As if Dee Dee thought Huncke's associates were bad people who I shouldn't know.

So there was a mirror image thing going on. For Dee Dee, the distrust was mutual. Huncke's acquaintances were bad people that I shouldn't hang out with.

But this is how I first actually met and made contact with Dee Dee. Down the hall, there was this spiritual guru ashram. The guru had his disciples coming in there and working on his house all the time. I thought the whole thing a total scam, and the guru and his followers knew I thought so. Not to mention he was cheating on his wife.

JOHN ZINSSER

We would hear this chanting through the door every day. I know that it was probably some kind of Buddhist chanting or something, but the sound of these chants really had this feeling of Satanists chanting in the room! It gave this spooky vibe. We heard it through that boarded up door, which made it especially spooky.

There was a guy who definitely looked like one of these ashram holy men, a bearded guy with this intense gaze. I think they ran a center there—I think it was their business. Like a lot of people at the Chelsea, they never seemed to go anywhere or work or do anything. I think it was a couple, a man and a wife. The guy looked like one of these Jewish mystics. He had a kind of magnetic presence.

ROBERT CAMPBELL

You could hear the chanting and the cymbals clapping and all this, and in the background I heard this electric guitar playing. I knew the guitar couldn't possibly be coming from the ashram, but the guitar music did sort of flow together nicely with the chanting and the cymbals. So I went out, followed the guitar sound down the hall, and knocked on the door of the room the guitar sounds were coming from. And who should open the door but Dee Dee Ramone!

I played it cool, pretending I didn't know who he was, and to be honest, I really didn't know much except that he was somebody famous. I knew the Ramones were kind of important.

"Hey," I said. "That guitar sounded pretty cool. Do you want to jam?"

"Yeah, what do you have?"

I told him I had two basses and a Telecaster, a Stratocaster and a Squire. And I had all these little amplifiers, which were useful in a place like the Chelsea because I would always be having people come over to my place to jam. Musicians didn't have to bring any of their own instruments or equipment. I had everything we needed to jam, unless you were a drummer.

So Dee Dee came over to my room. He checked out all of my equipment and said, "Yeah, I'd like to jam."

Sure enough, early that evening, he called me up. "Hey, so you want to come over at eight o'clock?"

I said okay.

But at the time, I didn't know much about the Ramones. I didn't know that the Ramones had kept a really strict routine, like the Army. You had to arrive right on time and ready to play. I guess I was a little more laid back type. I always went by the feel of things. If I didn't feel quite lubricated enough by beer, I wasn't going to go yet.

I was just tickled pink to be playing with somebody famous. I was a little nervous about it, but I just decided, "I am what I am. I'm not going to try to do anything special on the guitar or whatever." I wasn't going to be out to impress anybody.

When eight o'clock came along, I was still drinking beers to loosen up. I didn't learn until later that Dee Dee was really against alcohol at that time, which was another mark against me. I even took a quart of beer over to his room!

So Dee Dee called me again about ten minutes later. His voice was impatient. "You coming over?"

"Okay, yeah, yeah, yeah. Sorry I'm late!"

When I finally got to his place, Dee Dee said, "Well, what do you want to play?"

"Let's just play what you want to play."

Dee Dee wanted to play Motorhead's "Ace of Spades."

"Okay," I agreed, "but I've never heard it."

He started playing "Ace of Spades" and somehow I just kicked right in on it. So despite my nervousness at first, we played a bunch of songs and it was a nice time.

The following day, Dee Dee came over to my room. "Last night you weren't smiling or hamming it up or doing any stupid stuff. Would you like to start a band?"

I couldn't believe my ears. I had next to nothing going on in my life at the time. All I was doing was selling pot small time and hiding from Stanley Bard, who was always badgering me for the rent.

I honestly feel that one of the reasons Dee Dee chose to play with me was because I didn't have any idea how big the Ramones were. I knew nothing about Johnny Thunders, the New York Dolls, or G.G. Allin or any other guys that Dee Dee associated with.

But some people weren't thrilled by our playing together. For some reason, the Ramones people felt threatened by me. They kept saying "Keep it in the family, Dee Dee. Don't play with people who aren't in the family." The same policy went for some other people who might have wanted to play with Dee Dee, like Richard Hell or somebody in the punk rock world.

I guess that was how the Ramones held onto their money. By now, they were past their heyday in the late 70s when their material was new. "Keep it in the family" was a financial thing. Making music was just a job to them.

To the Ramones, it was like this—if you had been a Ramone, for the rest of your life you had to be 100% Ramone. You couldn't record solo albums and you couldn't do your own work. But Dee Dee had quit the band like five years ago! By that time, Dee Dee hated all of the Ramones except for Joey, and he only liked Joey on good days. He hated Marky Ramone, and he hated their drummer Tommy really bad.

Dee Dee told me that he finally decided to quit the Ramones this one time when they were driving in the van. Dee Dee wanted to listen to a Reba McIntire tape but Johnny wanted to listen to a baseball game instead, and Johnny angrily threw the Reba McIntire tape at Dee Dee. That was the last straw for Dee Dee.

Dee Dee also said that, when he and Johnny Ramone had been getting along, they would try and see who could look at the audience with the most hateful face possible. Dee Dee said Johnny was pretty damned good at it.

When Dee Dee and I had first started rehearsing together, it was really fun. We'd play for a while using these little battery-powered amplifiers. He had a Fender Twin, this little amp about as big as three packs of cigarettes. So we'd be playing for a while, and after some time he'd say "Let's talk for a while." He'd sit there on the couch and tell me these stories about the Ramones, what it was like being on the road with them and all this crazy stuff. He also told me about other rockers that he knew.

Among these were two of punk rock's most controversial provocateurs: Lydia Lunch and G.G. Allin.[68] As it turns out, their stage antics were too provocative for even Dee Dee, who reveals himself to be something of a punk prude.

ROBERT CAMPBELL
G.G. Allin!!! Aaagh! That guy's crazy. He's out of jail now?

DEE DEE RAMONE
Yeah, he got out. I saw him in Chicago. He got out. He was in Jackson County Jail, in Michigan.

ROBERT CAMPBELL
Does he really like to eat shit?

DEE DEE RAMONE

I don't know, you know. I think he's a very disturbed person. But I've always tried to not judge him, even though dealing with him was too much trouble. I met him when he was a little kid. He's from either Providence or Boston or something. And I never forgot him. He's so different! Back then, he loved the Ramones, and he was trying to make it—he was like a David Cassidy type. You should see his first album cover! He was so trite! He came up to me after a show and he gave me his album. He had made it himself. He was a real poor kid.

Then like three years later, he came in and I saw him again, and he had *changed*! He wasn't David Cassidy anymore! He gave me another album he made. He ended up lying on the floor, giving everybody the finger and all. I never listened to the album. But he corresponded with me all that time. I knew his brother, Merle, but at the time I didn't know he was G.G.'s brother!

Once I went to Merle's house, and Merle asked me, "Would you like to do a session with G.G.?" This was like two years ago. I said, "Oh sure. He's such a nice kid. And then Merle showed me a video of G.G.'s band doing stuff in a van. And I was shocked! "Merle," I said, "I can't do this! What am I gonna do? Stand with a can of Lysol and spray it away from me?" It was awful!

ROBERT CAMPBELL

What were they doing in the van?

DEE DEE RAMONE

I could never go in there and do that!

ROBERT CAMPBELL

What were they doing? Eating shit?

DEE DEE RAMONE

I can't talk about it! I couldn't believe it! But okay, so despite everything, to help G.G. out, what I would do was this. The last time G.G. got out of jail, I tried to show him a different side of life. I said, "Now don't be G.G. Allin for a while." I would take him to a nice place, inside a nice restaurant, and say, "Look, do you want to be part of this world? Get yourself a little apartment, and change your life." I tried to help him, but then I couldn't take it much more.

G.G. is just going to go to jail again. I know it. But I tried. I said to myself, "No one likes him, and I know what that's like because no one liked me." But the last time I went to one of his shows, he just went too far. He started making all these anti-Semitic remarks, and I walked out.

Later I told him, "You know, G.G., I'm not a prejudiced person. That's why I'm hanging out with *you*, man. But you gotta think this stuff over. You've got this hard-line jail attitude."

ROBERT CAMPBELL
Hey, what did they do in that van video?

DEE DEE RAMONE
I can't even *say* what they did. Their drummer is a big fan of the Lunachicks, an all-girl band, and on their album cover, they're all messing around naked. But I can't talk about that stuff! It's not my thing.

Now you know something about me: Dee Dee Ramone is very—*conservative*! People don't believe this about me, and they think I'm a nut when I get embarrassed about everything. But I'm only a human being!

ROBERT CAMPBELL
G.G.'s stuff sounds as wild as Lydia Lunch.

Lydia Lunch was a seminal screamer in New York's early punk and No Wave scene. She first performed with Teenage Jesus and the Jerks, as well as providing background vocals (as "Stella Rico") for James White's two bands—The Blacks and The Contortions. The compilation album *No New York* featuring both Lunch and White is a collector's item documenting the music during this brief but energetic time.

DEE DEE RAMONE
Oh, Lydia Lunch is offensive! I never knew her well—I met her

around 1976 when she came backstage at Max's Kansas City. I knew who she was, and she came up to me. I don't know how she got backstage. She looked at me and said, "Oh, man, I'm really disappointed in you. You're nothing like I thought you'd be."

So then all these years later, I went to a Blitzkrieg concert, and she was reading before they went on. I had to leave. I couldn't listen to what she was reading—it was going too far. I mean, what was that supposed to mean, what was she saying? What's that have to do with getting famous? Shock value? The thing about shock value is that it's *very sleazy*!

Now, Lydia Lunch and all these people want to be my *friends*. Because they know I've also had a lot of difficult times in my life. And then what I try to do is set a good example, and say, "Look, I can be anything I want. You can go take all the drugs that you want right now. But I'm not doing it! Just go home and think it over." I tell them, "I guarantee you—I may be miserable, but I'm not as miserable as you." I try to tell that to G.G. all the time to not make it worse. I don't want him to go to jail.

Not many people really know his story, and it's not a pretty one. No one ends up like that because they're bored, exactly. Maybe the people who abused him were ignorant, but they were still abusive. He's had a very abusive life. And now he doesn't know any better.

ROBERT CAMPBELL
How does G.G.'s brother cope, then?

DEE DEE RAMONE
Merle? Merle is like a total Johnny Ramone type. He said, "Fuck! To get over the system is my God." That's it. Merle is *business*. He's into the business thing, and that's his way of getting over it. He won't take drugs, won't waste his life. That's his thing— looking good and making the money!

ROBERT CAMPBELL
Dee Pop said he played for G.G. Allin, and he said he wouldn't even tell G.G. where he lived. He said, "You don't want to bring

G.G. home with you."

DEE DEE RAMONE

No, no.

The rehearsals commenced, but their progress, to Campbell, seemed slow.

ROBERT CAMPBELL

Even though it was fun, I knew I was over my head with Dee Dee, a rock star. So I tried to take it one day at a time. I wondered if we were wasting our time trying to start the Dee Dee Ramone Group. In fact, I felt more comfortable just playing my old soul records for him, like Aretha Franklin, Tina Turner, and Stax/Volt[69] stuff. I was turning him on to some music from the past that he knew very little about. Dee Dee wanted a blues band, and I think playing with me was the closest he ever got to having a blues band. Dee Dee and I played blues, not rock or punk. What we had together was blues.

The honest fact was, when I first worked with Dee Dee, I thought he was stupid. He always came across as being ignorant, like, "Oh, I don't know." He acted like everything was new and fresh and a wonderment to him. So in the beginning, I didn't realize how smart he really was. He *acted* just like a child, but the fact is, he was actually very street smart. He really had a grasp of the big picture. I think the dumb behavior was play-acting. It was his protection. If someone was getting too close, and he didn't want to be around them, he would act really dumb. He could have been a circus hustler.[70]

At the outset, Dee Dee was only occasionally difficult with Campbell, but they did have issues. Often the issues concerned alcohol and drugs, but just as often they were about old-fashioned work ethic. Dee Dee knew drugs and work were at odds.

ROBERT CAMPBELL

In the beginning, it was just me and him, and each of us had a

115

tape recorder. I'd teach the songs to him and he would sing them. Now I was supposed to go back home and listen to the tapes, but I didn't know that. I didn't understand why he wanted me to tape everything at our rehearsals. It turns out, the Ramones always tape-recorded their rehearsals and took the tapes home to listen to them and try to improve.

Dee Dee was always on this Ramones kick.

"The Ramones were always on time," he said, so I had to be on time. "The Ramones don't get high or drunk during rehearsals or during their gigs." Even if I had drunk one beer walking home from work, he wouldn't play that night. He said I could only drink *after* rehearsal. We'd rehearse until ten or ten-thirty at night because we were in the Chelsea and we couldn't keep people awake by playing any later than that. So that meant I couldn't start drinking until ten or ten-thirty. But then I had to go to work the next morning.

We played every single day, these little get-together jams, but that was all that he had in his life.

Dee Dee's eccentric behavior filled Campbell with anxiety. He was always tiptoeing around Dee Dee's moods.

ROBERT CAMPBELL

It was weird because he'd say, "Let's take tomorrow off." Then tomorrow would come, and since we weren't rehearsing, I would have a drink after work. Then he'd phone me and say "We need to jam." Since I'd been drinking, I couldn't play well, and then he'd act as if *he* was the one being so professional. But just the day before, he had given me the day off!

Dee Dee's lifestyle could be just as impulsive. He used to pack up and change rooms in the Chelsea—he lived in a total of about five different rooms while I was there.

For some reason, he would decide he didn't like a certain room. He would say, "Meet you after school," and I'd come home that day from work and he'd call me and tell me his new room number for rehearsal. Or if he was going to do dope—as long as we weren't rehearsing, he would occasionally allow himself some drugs—he would rent an entirely different room to do the drugs in, and then afterward he'd go back to his own room. It was weird.

Also weird was the fact that you could set Dee Dee off and not even know why. And then rehearsal would be over—he would just call it off. Or he'd have a temper tantrum. Being around him could be really demanding.

TIM SULLIVAN

Dee Dee had been a heroin addict all of his life, since he was a teenager. So he never really had the chance to develop emotionally, to be able to handle these stressful situations. As I got to know him, I understood that about him. He couldn't control this rage that he had, and it would just burst out. Because of all those years of pushing the anger down with the heroin, repressing it. So he really had a tough time dealing with the pain of being alive. Because of that, he was never able to develop the tools to deal with it.

One day he came down to Chelsea Music guitar store, where I worked. That day his face was on the cover of the *New York Post*[71] for getting busted smoking a joint in Washington Square Park. In the photo, he kind of looked like a criminal.

I was kidding him, "Hey man, try to stay off the cover of the *Post*!" And he got so mad that he threw a temper tantrum in the store. He started yelling at me! About two hours later, he came in and apologized.

"Man, I'm really sorry. I get crazy sometimes."

We became very good friends after that. He used to come up to my room and we'd hang out here or go out to dinner. At that point, he was in a very good place in his life. He was clean.

ROBERT CAMPBELL

Once I went over to Dee Dee's room at the Chelsea and he was jumping on the bed like a little child. He had these nunchucks and he was slamming them around like he was Bruce Lee. He was really good at it, jamming on these nunchucks!

Dee Dee told me, "When I was a kid in Queens, all of us kids

117

had these nunchucks. But cops were finding all these kids lying around on the sidewalk dead from blows to the head! So they outlawed nunchucks."

And man, Dee Dee did the most screwed up stuff I ever saw. He had this really cute girlfriend with gorgeous long blonde hair who he didn't give a damn about. And for some reason, he once told her that if she cut off all her hair, he would stay with her. She had flown all the way in from Chicago to stay with him. Once I went over to his room to do something, and I could tell she was not happy. She looked good as hell, sitting there with her shirt not all buttoned up. She was bad to the bone. And he did get her to cut her hair off, and then he dumped her ass. He could be such a jerk! So he had some bad stuff in his life, and I think he was confused, but I also think that deep down inside he had a good heart.

Dee Dee's volatile personality is well-chronicled in punk lore. Once he destroyed Johnny Thunders' guitar in an act of revenge, the story goes, after Thunders had stolen a few of Dee Dee's personal belongings. It was not, in fact, about a few personal items.

ROBERT CAMPBELL

Most people think Dee Dee got revenge on Johnny because he thought Johnny had stolen his sunglasses and his leather coat. The real reason was that Dee Dee thought Thunders and Stiv Bators[72] stole his song "Poison Heart," which he said was the greatest song he ever wrote. They recorded a version of "Poison Heart" and Dee Dee found out about it.

Dee Dee was so mad about their stealing "Poison Heart" that he took a bottle of drain cleaner into Johnny Thunders' room and poured it all over Johnny Thunders' stage clothes. And then he took Thunders' guitar, which was his trademark, like Eric Clapton's black guitar, or B.B. King's guitar Lucille. If you thought of Johnny Thunders, you thought of his Les Paul Junior with a sticker on it—and Dee Dee smashed it to bits. But it wasn't about a jacket and a pair of sunglasses—it was about stealing a song.

Dee Dee also said that Richard Hell[73] wrote *one line* of the song "Chinese Rock" but only one line, and that Johnny wrote none of it. Then Johnny's people said that Hell wrote the whole song. But listen to the song! "Chinese Rock" is definitely a Dee Dee Ramone song.

Dee Dee also told me that Johnny Thunders had hated LSD, but there was some rumor that he'd been taking acid on the last night of his life—he'd hooked up with these freaks in New Orleans. When Johnny Thunders died, it turns out he had leukemia. He would have died anyway, whether he'd OD'd or not.

Dee Dee would talk about living in Paris with Johnny Thunders and Stiv Bators, and he told me that they would be sitting there having dinner with Stiv Bators, and Bators would have one glass of wine and pass out with his face in the dish. Stiv Bators had a really bad liver, but nobody knew that before he died. Later on, one night Bators got hit by a car, and that night he died in his sleep.

Enter Drummer

ROBERT CAMPBELL

As our band practices kept going, we got this drummer named Michael who lived up the street from us. He was an all right drummer, about as good as I was a guitar player.

I was still never listening to the tapes like Dee Dee said we were supposed to. So we got the drummer, and that's when we started practicing at the drummer's house, which was only about a block away from the Chelsea. So we would just walk down the street carrying our amps and guitars and go to his place. At the new drummer's house, he had every type of drum you could imagine. He had this practice room that had no windows and it was painted black. It was a great room until we started playing, because we found out that if we left the air conditioner running while we played, it would blow all the fuses. So when we started playing, we had to turn off the air conditioner. We would play as long as we could until we couldn't stand it anymore because the room got hot and humid as hell. Then we would stop playing and turn the air conditioning back on for a while.

Sometimes, it was kind of hard playing with Dee Dee. To be honest, it seemed like he wasn't really that good a guitarist. I could play better than he could. But he told me once that Johnny Ramone had told him, "You are what you are, so you should just go out and play now, and the tight playing will come later."

Stepping Out

It wasn't long before the friendship between Dee Dee and Robert expanded beyond their rehearsals and they would hang out, wandering Manhattan's streets together.

ROBERT CAMPBELL

Sometimes, Dee Dee and I would go to guitar stores. We'd go walking down in the city, walking a long way to Matt Umanov Guitars, or Mojo Guitars, to look at the old antique guitars.

Another time, Dee Dee and I were trying to go see Junior Walker[74] at the club Tramps.[75] So I said to Dee Dee, "I'll call Steve. He'll get us in." I called Steve Weitzman and asked, "Can you get me and Dee Dee Ramone in and get us a table?"

Steve said, "Robert, I'll do it for you, but I'm not going to do it for Dee Dee. His ex-girlfriend works here, and she says he used to beat her up."

"Okay, Steve, I'm sorry." I hung up and went and told Dee Dee.

Dee Dee got serious as hell. He called up Steve Weitzman and started cussing him out. So long story short, we got to go up there to Tramps to see Junior Walker and the All Stars. Junior Walker was really cool, playing saxophone.

Another time, we went to Tower Records and Dee Dee bought the first Ramones album on cassette. When he got up to the cash register, the guy at the register, of course, knew who he was.

"What? *You* don't have that record at home?"

Dee Dee just looked at the guy and said, "How many of *your* records do you have at home?"

Dee Dee Ramone: Writer

Writing a good pop song isn't as easy as you might think. The best songs are simple and filled with feeling, and that kind of deceptively simple writing actually takes skill. Dee Dee had little trouble infusing his songs with feeling—punk rock was a perfect medium for expressing his frustration and rage in words. And like many writers, he had his own odd rituals.

ROBERT CAMPBELL

One thing that was really cool about Dee Dee was that when he would write songs—I only saw him write once or twice—he would lie down on the floor like he was trying to crawl into the floor or something. He was like one of those dead guys after he's jumped out of a building, all sprawled out with arms akimbo. He'd put his cheek right down on the floor, and the piece of paper on the floor, and he'd write the lyrics right there. Dee Dee never said why he did that.

He *did* used to say, "All you need for a good punk rock song is three chords and a grudge."

TIM SULLIVAN

Dee Dee wrote all their best songs, all the lyrics for them. He wanted me to work on some song lyrics with him, but I knew better. I didn't want to get involved in that Ramones circle. Dee Dee was really weird about writing music, which was why I didn't want to write any music with him. He got very possessive. He had a hard time with his emotions anyway, and he thought people were always going to rip him off.

So I thought, "Okay, write your *own* songs." I wouldn't deal with him.

ROBERT CAMPBELL

One of the things that really surprised me about Dee Dee was that he had this book he had written. And here I was, a wheeler-dealer type, always trying to say, "Well, I know this guy and that guy, and I'll try to hook you up. Let me help you out trying to get your book published." And I gave him a fictional idea—why don't you write a fictional story where some event happens, and every character in the story reacts to the same event in their own way, the way they normally react to things in any given real situation?

So he came up with this story in which the band's van wrecks, and Monte Melnick's [the Ramones' manager] head goes through the windshield and gets cut off. And Joey's standing there at the edge of the road, twiddling his hair and saying, "What a drag!"

Dee Dee didn't have any numbers on the pages of his manuscript, so when you tried to add in any material, it became a big pain in the ass. It wasn't inputted on a computer. I remarked about this.

This made him mad. "Don't tell me how to do my job!" And he threw the pages up in the air, like a hundred and fifty pages. So I just picked them up and went out. It took me a while to get them all straightened out.

JOHN ZINSSER

Robert Campbell gave us this manuscript. He told me, "I'm working on this book with Dee Dee Ramone, where he tells the *real* story."

I was very curious about Dee Dee's book, but I couldn't believe it—Robert gave a copy of it to us! I've always considered it like I own a copy of the Codex Bible or something, this unknown manuscript. This version is rough and raw and more naïve than what eventually got published. When I tell people I have this secret manuscript, *My Right to Survive*,[76] it's always funny!

Straight Edge Gets Dull

Even though Dee Dee was cleaning up from drugs and alcohol, he occasionally backslid and bought some heroin.

ROBERT CAMPBELL

I only did dope with Dee Dee once. He took my guitar cord, wrapped it around his arm and shot up. He said, "I guess you want to share my needle with me, don't you?" He had a bottle of bleach.

"No," I said. "I don't." So I snorted a bag, and then I went over to visit these three women, Nancy and her friends. I was supposed to go back and hang out with Dee Dee when we were high, but I didn't return, and I think he really held that against me. But, man, it was hard to do that. I had so much going on—I had my girlfriend giving me pressure, and I had a stressful job with Harry Fox because I owed all this money—like thousands of dollars for my room at the Chelsea—and I was hustling all I could. Always on my mind was "Let's make some money!"

Every now and then, Dee Dee would get hold of a quarter-pound of weed. And I had the scales, and I knew people. So he would supply it, I would sell it, and we'd split the profit. We didn't smoke any of the weed we were selling—it was a business kind of thing.

But one day, Dee Dee came by my room at the Chelsea and knocked on my door. He had this *beautiful* chick with him, Laura Allen.[77] I mean she was knockdown gorgeous. Dee Dee told me she used to be a runway model. But she was crazy. She was a bad girl.

I just looked at her.

Dee Dee said, "Lucky me, huh, Robert?"

"Yeah," I said.

"How about giving me a joint?"

So I rolled a joint and gave it to him.

Two or three days later, I didn't have any weed. So I called

123

him up, "Hey Dee Dee, will you lemme get a joint off you?"

He just went ballistic. "We're just not going to do this any-more! This isn't music! We're just not going to do this!" He freaked out so badly that he brought my scales and the weed back to my place, and he was all pissed off. Of course two or three days later, everything was back to normal. Dee Dee was like a child. Of course, this incident was the flip side of the time I hysterically accused him of stealing my guitar.

Dee Dee and I had been partying once after rehearsal. I had drunk a bunch of forty ouncers. We were just sitting around talk-ing. I said, "I'll go buy a dime bag and we'll smoke some joints." So I went over to this guy's room and got the weed. The guy who was selling the pot was really into music, so I brought along this really nice guitar to his room, a 1969 Fender Mustang Competi-tion. I said, "Here man, you can play my guitar for a while." He said "Cool, cool." So he borrowed my guitar, and I went back to Dee Dee's room with the pot.

The next morning, hung over, I didn't remember anything about lending my guitar to the pot dealer. I went to Dee Dee and told him I wanted my guitar back. Dee Dee said he didn't have my guitar, and I started accusing him of stealing my guitar. I fig-ured Dee Dee must have been a closet crackhead or something.

"I can't believe it! You've got all this money," I said, mad as hell. "And you're going to steal my guitar!"

But when I realized my mistake, Dee Dee still played with me. He must have thought I was an idiot, and I guess I was. And then a month later, the guy I loaned the guitar to said "Oh, here's your guitar back, Robert."

Down to Business

ROBERT CAMPBELL

The next stage of the Dee Dee Ramone Group started when Dee Dee got a bass player to play with us. His name was John Carco. He had been with this band called D Generation.[78] They were getting ready to put out their first album. So he came in and joined us. At first, when it was just Dee Dee and me, it was fun. But as soon as we got John Carco, it got to be work.

Once, when we were rehearsing, John Carco asked Dee Dee, "How does this song begin?" He was asking what key to begin the song in.

Dee Dee looked at him flatly and said, "One two three four." It was a pretty low blow.

I think the tendency of most guitarists trying to play like the Ramones is to put fat strings on, and beat the hell out of your guitar. But Dee Dee told me that Johnny Ramone found he could play the fastest and with better tone by using light strings and picking as lightly as possible. Face it, he had four Marshall stacks, so he didn't need to beat the hell out of his guitar. Dee Dee said that he and Johnny would try and see who could pick the fastest and the lightest.

One thing I couldn't understand about Dee Dee was why he couldn't or wouldn't play fast for us. We were, after all, The *Dee Dee Ramone Group.* I remember one time we were playing too fast to suit Dee Dee. He threw one of his many temper tantrums and yelled at us, "I can play faster than any of you fuckers so don't try to get playing fast 'cause I can shut you fuckers down. I *invented* fast."

When we played "I Just Wanna Make Love to You," which of course is not a punk song, we made it even more minimalist than three chords. We used a classic Dee Dee *one* chord arrangement. If there is one thing I learned from Dee Dee, it was how to play a whole song with just one chord. On the rehearsal tape, at the end of this one-chord song, you can hear Dee Dee say, "That was a nice structure! What do *you* think?"

But not long after John Carco joined the band, Carco suddenly announced that he had gotten us a gig. In five or six weeks' time.

I was not into it *at all.* We just weren't ready. I would have been satisfied not playing any shows. I knew that all of New York would come to see Dee Dee play, and I couldn't stand the thought of it. We just weren't good enough yet.

The six weeks passed far too quickly for Campbell, and time came for the Dee Dee Ramone Group's first gig at the Continental Divide.

NANCY ROGERS

The Continental Divide was the bar I went to when I first moved to New York. Now it's just called the Divide. But when they called it the Continental Divide, they used to put little plastic dinosaurs in your drink. It had to do with paleontology and all that. They really made strong cocktails. After just a few of those, everybody was best friends.

ROBERT CAMPBELL

Playing with Dee Dee Ramone on stage at the Continental Divide was the worst time I ever had in my life. We weren't prepared, and as far as I was concerned, we sucked. And suddenly I was chosen to be the lead singer!

Some people in the crowd were recording it, other people were acting like they were shooting up. It seemed like they were getting into the music. I wish I hadn't tried to sing lead because it made us too pedestrian. I was not ready. We opened our only gig with "Somebody Help Me" by the Spencer Davis Group. Instead of singing the right lyrics, "When I was just a little boy of seventeen, I had a girl" I blew it and sang "When I was just a little *girl* of seventeen." This embarrassed me so bad that I hated every millisecond of the gig after that.

I hated every second of it and wanted to stop it instantly. It felt like being in church when I was a kid—I wanted nothing more than to just get the hell out of there. Now that I look back on it, I should've just gone with the flow. It didn't matter what we played, people were freaking out on it because it was Dee Dee.

JOHN ZINSSER

When we went to see Dee Dee's band with Robert at the Continental Divide, Robert was wearing button-down Brooks Brothers shirts with blue jeans. That was his look, with the long hair and wire-rimmed glasses. He looked like an unlikely rock star. And they earnestly tried to get it together, but I don't think they had practiced that much. Dee Dee did, however, play "Chinese Rock," and it was incredibly poignant because that's his story. He was still stuck on a rock. After all this time, it was his song.

Campbell may have been mortified about The Dee Dee Ramone Group's performance at the Continental Divide, and John Zinsser may have thought they needed more practice. But when I listened to the tapes of their rehearsals, they were often quite tight, rocking hard enough to get people up and dancing.

The show also attracted a coterie of CBGB's veterans.

ROBERT CAMPBELL

Joey Ramone came to the show with Clem Burke, from Blondie. But Dee Dee acted really rude to Joey. After the show was over, my girlfriend Carol happened to be sitting at the bar. Dee Dee was about to leave, and he walked up to the bar to say goodbye to Carol. Joey was already at the bar, talking to Carol, and Joey said, "Hey, Dee Dee!"

Dee Dee didn't even say "hello" to Joey, who had gone to the trouble to show up at our gig. Dee Dee totally snubbed him.

Carol told me, "Man, Dee Dee was really mean to that guy. He walked right out on him."

I thought it was strange too. But at the time, the Ramones had been trying to get Dee Dee not to use the name Dee Dee Ramone. He had been forced to go to court and spend money just to use the name Dee Dee Ramone. I remember the day they agreed to let him use his name. He was thrilled about the fact that he could use the Dee Dee Ramone name, but it really didn't mean anything to me at the time. I guess if you look back on it, it would have been pretty wild if the Ramones had made him go out on stage as Douglas Colvin.

After their experience playing with each other in the Dee Dee Ramone Group, Robert Campbell's final statements about Dee Dee aren't about his musical talent, and they aren't about his impulsive personality. They're about his work ethic. Lots of people have talent, but talent only goes so far.

Not everyone has a work ethic, though. Not everyone has self-discipline. Young artists need to remember that the tortoise wins the race. Dee Dee forged his work ethic by playing with the Ramones, by practicing hard, always with an eye toward improving his skills. He humbled himself to his craft. And, like a mentor to a pupil, he passed his work ethic on to Campbell.

ROBERT CAMPBELL

I learned a lot about playing from Dee Dee. For one, I later realized that making those tapes during rehearsals really helps you out. You can go back and hear where you're messing up or whether you're sounding good. And I also learned, when I played with him, to go in there and play the entire time. We'd stop a song, and might take a minute, maybe two minutes, for a break between songs, and then we'd be off playing again, no time for fooling around. That's how I do it now, too. So I learned about that.

So that is how I hooked up with Dee Dee, a real rock star. People think that rock stars just lie around on their ass all day, but that's not true. Anyone who's a creative person has to work their ass off. Somebody in a major band can tell you what they're going to do on July 4th three years from now. They know exactly what they're going to do. Now what kind of freedom is that? They owe people their time. Real freedom is when you don't owe anybody anything. That's why it's true, in that Janis Joplin song, "Freedom's just another word for nothing left to lose."

Dee Dee had all his money and everything, but he didn't live like a rich man, even though if he wanted to buy anything, he had the money for it. Plus his rent at the Chelsea was all paid up—he didn't have to hustle like the rest of us.

The Chelsea's front desk manager Jerry Weinstein had a somewhat different take on Dee Dee's wealth and spending habits. And Weinstein may well have had a better line on it all, since he was the person who collected Dee Dee's rent every month.

JERRY WEINSTEIN

Dee Dee went through money so quickly that he was not allowed to keep his own money. He had an agent who paid all his bills. He was always paid up at the hotel because whenever he owed us any money, we would send the bill to his account and his agent would write a check for it right away. But Dee Dee went through money like water. Now, since he's dead, there's more money in his account than when he was alive. Barbara, [Zampini, Dee Dee Ramone's widow] came back recently to the hotel, last month or so. They make a lot of money off of Dee Dee Ramone.

TIM SULLIVAN

Dee Dee ended up moving to California, getting inducted into the Rock and Roll Hall of Fame, and then dying of a heroin overdose. I know that he hated being a junkie. With a lot of junkies, it's not so much that they're junkies and want to stay high all the time—it's a matter of being able to get their fix so they'll simply feel okay. If they cannot get it, they get very sick. I'm not sure if Dee Dee was a full-on daily junkie, or if he was a binger, who would do heroin, say, once a month for four or five days. And then feel bad about it.

The stereotype of the suffering poet may be a tired one, but the fact is, Dee Dee lived the stereotype. When his childhood wasn't brutal, it was lonely. He had a hard time being happy.

ROBERT CAMPBELL

According to Dee Dee, everyone was always screwing him over. Somebody had always betrayed him or done him wrong.

His suffering no doubt led to his heroin addiction, which ultimately took his life. Campbell swears it must have been suicide.

ROBERT CAMPBELL

Dee Dee had been doing heroin all of his life, since he was thirteen. When you're that experienced with heroin, you *know* exactly how much you're taking. You know what's not enough, what's too much, and what's just right. An experienced heroin user rarely overdoses, and the only explanation I can think of is Dee Dee wanted to die.

TIM SULLIVAN

I do believe he wanted to die. He had a lot of pain, and it was obvious. And in West Hollywood, where he was, there's a lot of heroin. I was always lucky and smart enough to stay away from that kind of stuff. I saw what it did to other people, and said, "I don't want any part of it." It destroys your soul.

A re-invented Dee Dee Ramone (left) and Robert Campbell, with the Dee Dee Ramone group on their debut gig at the Continental Divide.

CHAPTER 5

Getting By

Perhaps I would have to take a job—
a most depressing thought.

—HENRY MILLER, *The Air-Conditioned Nightmare*

The thorny predicament of making a living has always dogged Bohemian artists. The Beat poet–turned-affluent-entrepreneur Lawrence Ferlinghetti defined Bohemians as "nonconformists who don't lead a nine-to-five life."[79] Some Bohemians don't want the nine-to-five life because they find it too constricting, others because they're lazy, and still others because they haven't the confidence to enter the mainstream life of working for a living. This is why Stanley Bard was such a godsend to artists. But Ferlinghetti failed to mention the main reason why Bohemian artists don't want a full-time job: they already have one.

For artists to improve at their craft and be successful, they have to work at their art for hours every day. Having a full-time job, then, means having two jobs, not a life many would relish. Most of us average full-time drones come home tired from our full day's work. To begin our second job with a pen, a paintbrush, a guitar or a camera requires concentration and energy, two resources that day jobs have a way of devouring. It's hard enough to keep on top of life's quotidian routines: laundry, groceries and housework. And the fact that most aspiring artists make little or no money from their creative work runs them through a mill of self-doubt, frustration and depression. After a hard day at the job, it's easier to crack a beer and watch TV than inspire yourself to make art.

One option for artists is to work half-time at their day jobs and half-time at their real vocations, their art. This is also easier said than done. Most half-time work pays peanuts, relegating artists to poverty, and here they are again, back to being starving Bohemian artists. This is why the Chelsea Hotel, with Stanley Bard at the helm, proved so invaluable. He kept his rooms affordable enough for artists who had committed themselves to Mistress Poverty, for a while at least, as they worked at making it big.

Even the more well-known and accomplished artists like the painter and printmaker Bernard Childs didn't have much money.

JUDITH CHILDS

It was a funny thing, because my husband Bernard was a really distinguished artist—certainly known to the *cognoscenti*—but we never made a whole lot of money. We survived—we lived on what he made—but it takes years for this stuff to fall together. Suddenly, it becomes the time when something catches on. We sold a lot of work, obviously. We couldn't have lived on it otherwise. But we lived by it, so when we had money, we would buy a good bottle of wine or go to Puerto Rico, and we paid attention and lived quite meagerly, except for expensive paints. I don't know how we did it! I *still* do it.

The less successful artists, or those just setting off down the path to find their creative voices, had it at least as hard.

PAUL VOLMER

We were all basically poor and hustling money for our hotel rooms. It was a little hard to make the rent, so we were always broke. Some days we would be living on only a few dollars. Your friends would help you out with a few dollars if they had it. Everyone was on the edge.

DIMITRI MUGIANIS

The Chelsea was sort of a fallback place. You could still come here and grab a room. It wasn't cheap, but it wasn't expensive, either, and you didn't need a down payment. You didn't need a month's security deposit! And all the reference checks—you didn't need any of that.

Prior to being hired as the Chelsea's bellman and night watchman, Paul Volmer had taken a job as a waiter.

TIM SULLIVAN

Paul couldn't keep his waiter clothes clean. He'd wait until just before he had to go to work, and he would wash his shirt in the sink, and then iron it right away, soaking wet.

"You can't do that!" I said. "You'll burn the shirt!"

He'd get the shirt all brown in spots from burning it with the iron!

PAUL VOLMER

During the first few years I lived there, I was always just slightly behind on the rent, and Stanley Bard was totally on my case. I liken living there to being in a little boat, a dinghy, and there's a hole in the dinghy, and you have to keep bailing water to keep yourself afloat.

Even after Stanley Bard had hired Paul Volmer as bellman/watchman, Volmer managed to bring a dollar in now and then with little projects on the side.

PAUL VOLMER

Because Nicholas' father, the painter Herbert Gentry, had lived and worked in these different places all over the world, Nicholas was quite cosmopolitan even though he was only nineteen. He taught me how we could always hustle to scrounge up a few dollars, like borrowing a few bucks from this person, and then buying some pot from that one, and then selling it for a few dollars' profit to the other one, and making a few dollars. We always managed.

PETER JOHANSSON

Paul was also dealing a lot of pot at the time. Management knew all about it, but since he was the security dude, he was allowed to. The thing is, he was the worst pot dealer you had ever seen. He smoked most of it up, and he would always be giving people pot on credit. Nothing ever came back!

"Paul," I said, "it's beautiful that you're trusting and all that. But, man, you're spending more money buying pot than you're making yourself! How does that compute?"

"Well," Paul said. "I know where they live."

As mentioned earlier, Robert Campbell also had a weed business going, at a much larger scale than Paul's.

ROBERT CAMPBELL

I was buying weed from a guy who worked at Atlantic Records. He turned me on to a drug dealer who was getting out of the business. So this drug dealer gave me his business, with his phone list, and then people called me on the phone, and they'd come to my room, and I'd sell them the weed. I didn't do much delivery, except at work every now and then. The thing was, I never sold powders. I always did my own powders, but I never sold them. I was scared to death of selling them.

There was this one guy I always sold to. Once I was sitting in his car, and he had a policeman's badge sitting there in his open glove box! Maybe he wasn't a cop —I don't know. I'm lucky I got out of the business.

I have to admit that I myself had a pretty good scam going, selling weed at the hotel. I could make some good money. But then I realized that it wasn't going to last forever. I was either going to have to quit before I got in trouble, or I would wind up selling weed for the rest of my life. Neither alternative seemed that attractive.

But I was paying at least some rent every month—at least something.

Maybe he was paying. Campbell's rent receipts indicate that when rent came due, he paid Stanley a small portion of his overdue rent—about a third of the time. Ultimately, Campbell owed the Chelsea over fourteen thousand dollars in back rent.

Down in Debasement

Interestingly, the basement of the Chelsea played a crucial role in the hotel's economy.

JOHN ZINSSER
It was an unbelievably scary, dungeon-like warren of rooms with these vaulted brick arch doorways.

If you were brave enough to go down into this dark chamber—which had developed a sort of mythology of its own—you were allowed to rummage around, find some old furniture abandoned by previous tenants, and carry it up to your room.

JULIE EAKIN
The basement was kind of ramshackle, but you could go and just pick up tables and dressers, whatever you wanted, and put them in your room. If you felt like something else, you could go next week and trade it off. If you were twenty-four years old and didn't care about elegance, the selection was good.

DIMITRI MUGIANIS
One of my rooms was really sweet, really big, with a working fireplace. Herbert Huncke and I would find old furniture in the basement to build big fires in there. Herbert got this chest of drawers and broke it up and burned it in the fireplace. With the paint and the lacquer, it was emitting all these toxic fumes! It was dangerous.

ROBERT CAMPBELL

Tim Sullivan got himself an upright piano from the basement.

TIM SULLIVAN

The piano had belonged to Bobby Fisher, another friend of mine from Virginia Beach. He put it out, and then I snagged it. Somehow we brought it up here to the seventh floor. So I actually had a piano in my room! When I was a kid, I wanted to be a piano tuner, so I had learned a little about it and I kept it tuned and played it. I used to have the transom window that opened up at the top of my door, because I didn't have air conditioning at the time. The cats would climb up the top of the piano and jump out into the hall, and I'd have to run out there and get them.

When I ran out of room for it, I put it out in the hall. Someone else took it, and it's still somewhere in the hotel!

The Dutch painter Willem Van Es[80] found a piano in the hall. It's likely it was the one Tim had left there.

If ample furniture could be found in the basement, occasionally you found something more colorful.

PETER JOHANSSON

There was this table right in the middle of the boiler room, and that's the table we would go down to in order to snort blow on its surface.

But believe it or not, people actually lived down there! If you walked through a couple of doorways in the dark down there, you found out that this one guy had practically put together a loft in the boiler room! He had bookshelves, he had electrical lights hooked up. He was a homeless person living there. Nobody knew about this guy, not even Stanley Bard! I mean, somebody must have known about it, but it was accepted. But I don't think anyone knew the lengths he had gone to make himself comfortable down there! I was blown away!

It was a beautiful little place there, and I felt like I was invading somebody's space. But then I also thought, "Somebody lives here for free." I told Paul about it, but I never told anyone else.

Why would I rat this dude out? I'd never even met him. But later on, I again ran into the guy who lived in that improvised loft. He was a real wacko, really weird and paranoid. He said he was going to turn me in for invading his privacy.

I asked, "Well why would you do that?"

"You have no right to be here."

"Do you have a right to be here?"

"I've been here forever."

"Okay," I said, "I can't argue with that." And then I just left because it was not a positive scenario.

It was a really weird experience. It was really his place, even though it wasn't! That's the kind of beautiful thing that I saw at the Chelsea.[81]

I Only Work Here: The Staff

Any successful economy depends on its labor. In focusing on the Chelsea's residents, it's easy to forget that many of the people walking the hotel's halls did it for a living—and I don't mean the hookers. The room maids, the bellmen, the switchboard operators and the front-desk clerks had their own milieu at the Chelsea.

PAUL VOLMER

They had a maintenance guy they called the Engineer. If you needed a light fixed, or you had a faucet go out, the Engineer in the basement had tools and would fix things.

There was also a whole staff of bellmen, two on during the day, and one on during second and third shifts. The bellmen would wear green uniforms, sort of like suits, with gold braid. A lot of the bellmen were black and had been there for years. One of the advantages of living in the hotel was, let's say you were having a party or hanging out and drinking beer, and you wanted some more beer or snacks, they had bellman service. You could ask a bellman to run to the deli and get you more beer or sandwiches. For a Bohemian like me, it was a special treat. Then the bellman would come back and you'd party with the bellman. You'd give him a couple of bucks, and then offer him beer or pot and they'd hang out with you. You were friends with him. Some people treated the bellmen like servants, but the more Bohemian people had them as friends. They were good guys.

One bellman, a short black older guy, he had this really young girlfriend. Everybody wondered why he had such a young girlfriend, and then one day he showed me a picture in his wallet. It was him naked. He had a foot-long dick. Now I knew the source of his popularity!

ROBERT CAMPBELL

Later, that bellman died of AIDS. Tim Sullivan told me that he was Long Dong Silver, the porn star.[82]

PAUL VOLMER

You also had the maids who were always cleaning the rooms. If you wanted maid service you could get fresh linen. They were all friendly, mostly women of color. There was a bit of style in living there, to be able to get fresh towels and linen. The permanent residents had to pay extra for it. I only did it when I first lived there, when I was feeling a little extravagant. Once I had settled in there, I didn't use maid service. But some people, those who had money, availed themselves of these added services.

JULIE EAKIN

Theresa was a wonderful maid. She had been there for a long time, and she'd tell you about Janis Joplin and all these people she'd befriended.[83]

JOHN ZINSSER

The maid staff wore peppermint green maids' uniforms. Their job was to take care of the hotel function of the building, which was maybe forty percent of the building. But they also had a laundry room down in the basement that was primarily for washing sheets and towels. This room was run by a woman named Doris, who was a formidable character, an imposing African-American woman who was probably sixty years old. She had been there forever—she was a Chelsea fixture. You could have your laundry done by her. Otherwise, there was no place in the building to do your laundry—your room didn't have a washer and dryer. But you had to sneak your laundry to her because Stanley didn't want her doing this. It was on the sly.

You would put your laundry in the service elevator, a teeny, tiny back elevator, that had its own elevator shaft. You could send your laundry in this little elevator down to the basement where Doris would wash and dry it, and you would pay her for it. But she was very, very particular about when she would take your clothes and what condition you delivered your laundry in. She was very imperious about these things. You had to work out your plan with one of the maids who came by your room and would say, "Okay, you can send your laundry down now."

So with your house phone, you could call Doris about your laundry. "Doris, can you do laundry for us?"

She'd be very gruff. "Okay, twenty minutes," she'd say, as if you were setting up a surreptitious deal.

ROBERT CAMPBELL

At the front desk, there was a desk clerk who once checked in Ginger Baker,[84] the drummer from Eric Clapton's old band Cream. He checked in one night and the desk clerk kept giving him shit.

"What kind of name is Ginger for a man?"

Ginger Baker freaked out. He was furious!

PAUL VOLMER

There was a lot of gossip about the residents at the front desk, and I found that fact interesting because I was both a resident and an employee. In the hotel life, whatever shenanigans you were up to, your life served as entertainment for the people at the front desk. This guy or that woman would burn out or do this crazy thing, and people who worked there would gossip.

But one desk clerk, Herman, wasn't like that. He would always come down on anyone who would gossip at the desk. He would tell me we weren't here at the hotel to gossip, and gossip was beneath us, because *everyone* had something going on. It was better to have a little class and not talk about other people. I always thought that he actually had a good outlook on giving people some privacy.

They also had a few desk clerks who were gay and sort of fastidious, and they did a good job at the hotel. And the Head Desk Clerk was Stanley's brother-in-law. His name was Jerry Weinstein.

JULIE EAKIN

Jerry was amazing—he really made you feel safe and welcome. Having someone give you your mail every day was this gracious thing.

JERRY WEINSTEIN

For years, I used to give tours of the hotel—many, many years. I still do periodically, but only part-time because I'm old and tired. That was my own thing—I was an independent contractor. I worked for the 92nd Street YMCA, giving tours of the hotel. During the tours, we would visit five or six artists' studios, walk through the hotel, go up on the roof, and I'd tell people the whole history of the place.

When we visited the artists' studios, we would talk to the artists about their work. Depending on who lived there at the time, we went through DeKooning's[85] old studio, and John Sloan's old studio. We'd go through Thomas Wolfe's old apartment, and Arthur C. Clarke's.

ROBERT CAMPBELL

On Sunday afternoons, Jerry gave tours of the Chelsea to straights who didn't live in the Chelsea. One time, I was with this artist friend of Jerry's, whose name I don't recall. We were hanging out in his room, and he got this phone call from Jerry. Jerry wanted his friend to pretend he was one of the more famous "artists" featured in his tour that was beginning in twenty minutes!

Not every artist appreciated being "showcased" to tourists at the Chelsea.

JERRY WEINSTEIN

If I had a tour, and I would go past Dee Dee Ramone's room, he would run out and say, "What are you bothering me for?"

We had nothing to do with him—we weren't even looking at his room—but he always felt people were trying to look at him and see him.

Like everyone at the Chelsea, Jerry was just getting by.

Stanley Bard, former co-owner/manager of the Chelsea Hotel

CHAPTER 6:

Stanley Bard:
Steel Fist in a Velvet Glove

"... pain and pleasure are in the power of our Lord and Master."
—SRI GURU GRANTH SAHIB

In the Chelsea's many-floored economic ecosystem, the alpha male was Stanley Bard, its manager and one-third owner for over fifty years. It was Stanley Bard who transformed an old hotel into one of the world's most productive and eccentric artist colonies.

Stanley's father, the Hungarian immigrant David Bard, had always been in the hotel business when, in 1939, he bought the Hotel Chelsea. Soon after, some long-time Hungarian friends of the Bards, Joseph Gross and Julian Kraus, joined Bard as co-owners.

Each had his separate role. Gross took charge of the front desk. Krauss managed the bellmen and the maids and took care of the hotel's repairs. And David Bard, a "people's person," according to his son Stanley, was the hotel's general manager. While the other two busied themselves with their own jobs, Bard dealt with people. The arrangement was a success.

STANLEY BARD

They worked together very happily. They never really got in each others' way, always had great respect for each other, and it worked.

As naturally as water flows downhill, the Chelsea became an artist-friendly hotel. The first reason was architecture. Two factors make a good artist's studio: space and light. Searching for the perfect studios, painters might rent lofts in old factories, but these drafty, cavernous spaces, usually lacking kitchens or bathrooms, weren't ideal for making a home. And the average New York hotels, which catered mainly to tourists or business travelers, had only small, poorly lit rooms that were decidedly not artist-friendly.

The Chelsea was different. Originally built as a luxury co-op (rather like upscale condominiums today) it featured spacious rooms with high ceilings and big windows, perfect for painters. It also had kitchens and bathrooms.

David Bard's personal touch and special interest in the arts also attracted artists to the Chelsea.

STANLEY BARD

He loved the artists and writers in the hotel, and he became very friendly with them. For example, he knew John Sloan[86] very well—they were dear friends.

Young Stanley would tag along as his father perambulated the hotel, so he too had access to the artists and luminaries.

STANLEY BARD

When I was a child, I met these people like [composer and writer] Virgil Thomson. These people were quirky, someone might say. They had their own distinct ideas, and they were interesting people. I loved being around them.

As the years passed, however, young Bard began to march to the beat of his own drum. After graduating from college and, in 1955, serving a stint in the Army, he wanted to forge his own path in the world.

STANLEY BARD

As a child, who thinks that someday he will do exactly what his father did? That was not my intent.

But the elder Bard had a feeling about Stanley.

STANLEY BARD

My father asked me if I wanted to learn management. He said, "You will love this hotel and the people living here."

The younger Bard agreed to give it a try and fell under the spell of the hotel's allure. He started out "doing the accounting work, learning management and learning about the hotel business," he said, while his father worked to convince co-owners Gross and Krauss that his son had what it took. In college, Stanley had received good training in accounting, but he was young. Nevertheless, Stanley and the other owners hit it off.

STANLEY BARD

Joseph Gross and Julius Krauss were very lovely people, and I never had any problem with them.

Once the two elders trusted him at the helm, they retired at around the same time, and before his father died, Stanley had taken over his duties as general manager.

STANLEY BARD

Then, I was left to myself running the hotel.

Stanley Bard not only preserved his father's business, but expanded the artist-friendly policy. Turning a profit was significant, but producing art and nurturing artists became the hotel's *raison d'etre*.

STANLEY BARD

We'd had a few artists at the hotel. I tried to capitalize on those few, and I also happened to know a lot of artists who weren't living here yet. I befriended these artists, and drew them to the hotel. A lot of them were global, internationally known.

As a result, the Chelsea became famous worldwide for its hospitality to artists and for providing a safe haven in which to live and work. Bard's management style was unconventional, to say the least, and some have called his methods into question. But he was thinking long-term. For example, out of his genuine love for art and artists, he often let them move in on a dime.

PAUL VOLMER

If you were an artist, or if Stanley Bard thought you had potential, he would allow you to slide for a while with your rent, because if you came up with a big painting and you sold it, Stanley would expect a piece of that money. A lot of people paid their rent that way.

Chelsea Time

Tolerance has its perils. Desperate artists, or unprincipled ones, could take advantage of Bard's generosity. But being an adept businessman, he adopted a strategy for squeezing as much money out of poor artists as he reasonably could. It was a complex strategy befitting his complex artistic clientele.

If you zoomed back to see the big picture, his approach had a certain logic and consistency. Its foundation was the Five-Year Plan.

ROBERT CAMPBELL

Stanley would let people who weren't properly paying their rent stay at the hotel for about five years. In the long run, it was good for business. The hotel had all these tourists that came there from all over the world, and the tourists wanted to see some freaks living at the Chelsea. So Stanley picked out these people, these artists, and if he felt like they were creative, he gave them five years to get on their feet and get going. After five years, if you didn't get there, you were out the door. He would call you up and razz you a little bit first.

Long-term artist residents paid $500 to $750 a month for a small room on the lower floors. Tourists, on the other hand, paid at least a hundred dollars a night. To Stanley, the artists were an investment used to attract the higher paying tourists.

Bard's five-year probation grew to be known as *Chelsea time.* To the artist tenants, Chelsea time meant "give yourself five years to show real progress at becoming the artist you dream to become. Don't get all worked up too quickly about results."

Five years were pretty generous terms, better than any artist retreat or colony. Rent was comparatively cheap. Even so, over the years, some "promising" artists—including Robert Campbell—ended up owing over ten thousand dollars.

Chelsea time was akin to tenure in universities: produce or empty out your desk. If an artist made it after five years, or at least made enough money to pay the overdue rent—or pay *most* of it—he got to keep his room. But if five years had passed and an artist had missed a rent payment or a dozen, *and* had not accomplished much as an artist, then Bard began Stage Two of his management strategy.

Stage Two was for more problematic individuals, artists who turned out to have little talent and less money, often the ones who slid into hard partying and general debauchery.

In his observant way, bellman Paul Volmer watched how these problem types cycled in and out of the Chelsea's lower floors with great regularity. Bard knew he could get rent out of them for maybe a few months. He also knew they couldn't party too hard with hard drugs too long before they flamed out. In those cases, the poor degenerates would just evict themselves, dropping away from the Chelsea like leaves off a tree. Bard only had to wait.

PAUL VOLMER

Stanley basically gave everyone enough rope to hang themselves with. It generally worked.

It saved Bard the trouble of filing complicated eviction notices, hiring someone to toss their belongings into the street, or calling the city to haul them out in body bags.

Stanley could wait. But most residents fell somewhere in between the fabulous success stories and the wastrels. Dealing with these in-between rent laggards was trickier and required finesse. It involved those more complicated cases, artists who had lived there for five years, never managed to make it big, but never indulged so deeply in debauchery that they flamed out on their own.

It was in these situations that Bard would develop a "Dr. Jekyll and Mr. Hyde" strategy. When the artist first moved in, the Chelsea was an artist's paradise provided by Bard's kindly Dr. Jekyll figure wearing velvet gloves.

Until you got well behind on rent and showed little promise.

Then, out burst Mr. Hyde, swinging his steel fist. Bard would *hound* you mercilessly. At precisely eight o'clock in the morning, he'd rattle you awake with a phone call, demanding you pay up or else! He'd slip threatening notes under your door. Every time you passed the front desk, he'd call you over and give you a scolding. It was Chinese water torture. Bard seemed to enjoy exercising his lordly right to swing between permissiveness and harassment. It energized him.

As a result of Bard's split personality, tenants developed their own divided psyches. It was not unlike a dysfunctional family. Tenants loved him for loving artists, but after fending off his aggressive rent collection methods, they were deathly afraid of him.

PAUL VOLMER

Stanley Bard was always after everyone for rent like an annoying little dog that would grab your pant leg and pull at you as you were heading out the door and off to work. Sometimes, he'd just sit behind the desk and rush out into the lobby to get you as you were going out. But most of the time, he would catch you when you were coming back later in the day.

Sometimes, if you were behind on your rent, you would try to look through the window from outside and see if Stanley was behind the desk. If he was, say, talking to the desk clerk, you might be able to walk behind someone and shoot up the stairs.

ROBERT CAMPBELL

Stanley always let you know he was on to you. He told me I was a deadbeat. I was so naïve, I didn't even know what that meant!

When you started hiding out from Stanley, you almost never

left your room for fear of Stanley finding you, you'd stay in your room so long. You'd sort of lose track of which day was which. You knew nothing about what was going on in the outside world.

We'd always be wanting to know if Stanley was down in the lobby, and what kind of mood he was in. Because he would just stand there at the front desk. When he happened to be out of town, it was the greatest. You would just come and go as you pleased, and you could go down into the lobby during the day.

PAUL VOLMER

What was amusing was that when I first moved in, I worked as a waiter, and I would come home and generally take my tip money and give it to the desk to pay part of my rent. But I was always a little behind—sometimes I owed like sixty or seventy dollars. Later on, I learned there were people that owed him thousands of dollars. But I guess he thought I was vulnerable, and he would always harass me as I went through the lobby. For just this little money, he would never miss an opportunity to harangue me.

One night we stayed up all night partying in the hotel, and then we left the hotel to go out for breakfast. When we came back into the lobby, Stanley was there, and here we were, the four biggest rent slackers walking in there together. Stanley was totally steamed! We were a thorn in his side, especially me, because I hung out with all these so-called worst people and yet I was also working for him as a bellman.

ROBERT CAMPBELL

Just about everybody owed money there. They'd finally pay in chunks of three thousand or five thousand dollars. Stanley wouldn't accost you in the lobby too often, in public, in front of other people. Only if he didn't have anything else to do and he was in a really bad mood would he say something to you in the lobby.

Instead of stopping you in the lobby, he might phone you up in your room and say, "Uh, Mr. Campbell, this is Stanley Bard down in the office. The management is really upset with you. You owe them so much money." He never acted like *he* was the manager

151

and owner of the hotel. He acted like he just worked there, which was a total scam.

PAUL VOLMER

After calling on the phone and seeing if he could get somebody out of bed to pay some rent, if he did get some money, he would get right on the phone to his stockbroker. Whatever rent he could juice out of the people, he'd be playing the stock market with it that very *morning*.

ROBERT CAMPBELL

Sometimes, as you came into the lobby from outside, if you saw the elevator doors just starting to open, you could just jump right into the elevator. By the time Stanley looked over in your direction, the elevator doors had shut and you were gone.

Or you would make it look like you were going over to the telephone, but you'd go to the service elevator instead, which was hard for Stanley to see. If it was pretty far up, then instead you could walk up the back stairs, the service stairs.

Also, there's a restaurant on one side of the Chelsea called El Quijote. It has a back way you can take out, which exits out into the other side of the lobby, so you can avoid Stanley that way too.

But usually, to avoid Stanley I just became an entirely nocturnal person. I would go to bed at around seven in the morning and get up about four-thirty or five in the afternoon, maybe three-thirty if I was feeling healthy. And Stanley would leave work at about five-thirty or six p.m. We'd always call down at the front desk and see if Stanley was still there. If he had gone home, then we could cruise!

Nobody ever knew where Stanley lived, not even Paul, the bellman. And Timur, another bellman, didn't know where Stanley lived. Nobody knew.

PAUL VOLMER

Stanley lived in New Jersey. I believe he has a very nice home there. People tell me that when he went home to New Jersey, he definitely left the Chelsea all behind. He was a family man.

The World-Famous Waiter

Stanley Bard wouldn't even let the presence of a major celebrity distract him from the business of rent collection. One occasion involved the Pulitzer Prize-winning playwright Arthur Miller.

PAUL VOLMER

Once, Stanley and the staff were celebrating the hundredth anniversary of the hotel.

JULIE EAKIN

Smithsonian magazine did a huge article about the one-hundredth Anniversary when it happened. It was really fun—they did an extensive photo shoot. I think they even hired a dance troupe to move through that central stairwell and took photographs of them doing it. It was wonderful!

PAUL VOLMER

At the anniversary, they were putting up a plaque for Arthur Miller. The Chelsea has these plaques out in front to commemorate the hotel's eminent residents: O. Henry, Dylan Thomas, Thomas Wolfe and others.

So I'm walking through the lobby, coming back exhausted from my waiter's job. They're having this media event in the lobby. All the newspapers were there—the *New York Times,* the *Daily News* and others. Stanley Bard was talking to Arthur Miller.[87] As I was walking into the lobby, Stanley made a point to dramatically turn and glare daggers at me as I walked past. This prompted Arthur Miller to turn and see what famous or illustrious person was coming into the Chelsea. And it was just little old me, whose money Stanley wanted!

His personality was very odd because he would let some people slack on the rent, but if you were chosen, he'd give you the worst business. Stanley was very greedy. Money was the only thing he cared about. He would let known drug dealers live there as long as they paid their rent.[88]

DAVID LAWTON

You hear about people leaving the Chelsea owing thousands or whatever. I myself probably got away with one month's rent unpaid, and I was thinking, "Oooh! I really got *away* with something here!" They used to send a monthly bill. When I first moved there, there was one month when the bill never arrived. I was never charged for that month. I waited, and nothing happened. They never caught it! I thought, "Jesus, does one of those guys down there at the front desk like me more than I know?"

DIMITRI MUGIANIS

You know what's funny? I ended up owing money on every single apartment I lived in at the Chelsea. And Stanley never said anything about it. I moved in and out of the Chelsea several times, and each apartment I moved into was smaller than the previous one. The last place I lived in was like a shoebox, one of these rooms where you shared a bathroom down the hall. When I had no money and nothing left, that's the room that Stanley finally decided to come down on me with.

DAVID LAWTON

Even before I actually moved in, I would come walking in the front door to visit friends, and I would see Stanley in the lobby looking up to see who was coming in. I could see the wheels turning in his mind as he desperately sized up the data banks.

"Does this guy owe me money?"

Viva la Viva!

Probably the Chelsea's most historic battle over unpaid rent occurred between Bard and a counterculture celebrity named Viva, one of the Warhol superstars and star of *Chelsea Girls*. Born Janet Susan Mary Hoffman, the daughter of a well-known attorney, Viva grew up in Syracuse

THIS AIN'T NO HOLIDAY INN

in a repressive Catholic family that worshipped Joseph McCarthy. It's no wonder she rebelled hard. After she asserted her way into a prominent position in Warhol's scene, she was featured in his films *Lonesome Cowboy; Ciao, Manhattan;* and *The Loves of Ondine.*

ROBERT CAMPBELL

Now Viva had a great big, beautiful apartment, which only cost her seven-hundred-fifty dollars a month, and she *still* wasn't paying her rent! She owed many thousands. I guess she felt entitled because she had all the history with the Chelsea and the Warhol scene.

DAVID LAWTON

Those people who did have a little touch of celebrity got away with paying no rent. It was so bizarre!

JOHN ZINSSER

Viva, who was known for her fights with Stanley, would argue, "*I* made this hotel famous!"

TIM SULLIVAN

Viva was always in your face—that was her personality.

Finally, in the early 90s, Stanley had had it with Viva's freeloading, and started demanding payment.

ROBERT CAMPBELL

Stanley told me that, after decades living there, she had only just recently started paying any rent. He wouldn't kick her out, but for some reason, *she* was mad as hell at *Stanley*!

Stanley said to Viva, "Listen, if you just pay your rent every month, you can stay here. Don't even worry about what you owed me for decades." And for some reason, Viva just had it in her mind that she hated Stanley so badly and he was trying to take advantage of her.

Once Stanley called me and said, "The management wants to talk to you in the office about your rent." So I went downstairs. But Viva was first in line. She was getting her ass chewed by Stanley, but she was chewing out Stanley back just as fast as he could give it to her.

So I had to wait in line to get my ass chewed by Stanley. But once she had left, and before he started on me, he said, "That's a bitch on wheels! She's just a bitch on wheels!" He was very proud of that excellent little quip.

PAUL VOLMER

When Stanley got on her case, Viva would bring up all of the disreputable characters he was allowing to stay there, the pimps and hookers and drug dealers.

JOHN ZINSSER

Stanley loved to fight! You would think, "This man is going to have a heart attack!" He would be apoplectic, just over-the-top screaming at somebody in the lobby at a quarter past ten in the morning! If that didn't happen once a day, it wasn't a good day for Stanley.

The Velvet Glove

But some of the more successful artists, at least the ones who paid their rent on time, have a very different story to tell about Stanley Bard. If you had earned a place on his good side, his purely benevolent Dr. Jekyll side, he would do most anything to help you out. And let's not forget the big picture—in the history of the world, how many landlords have bent over backward to help struggling artists have a place to live and create? How many landlords looked the other way when a month's rent check never made it to his office? How many landlords accepted artworks— sometimes of questionable value—in lieu of rent?

DAVID LAWTON

I mean, we made fun of Stanley a lot, but obviously there's something very, very unusual about the Chelsea Hotel and what he did with it.

JUDITH CHILDS

Once, when one of Bernard's exhibits was coming along, we didn't have enough room at the Chelsea. At that time, we were thinking that we should buy a loft in SoHo and fix it up, because they were very cheap. So we went to Stanley Bard, our leader, and we told him of our plight with space. Stanley didn't want us to leave.

He said, "No, no. We'll fix it up. You can have the room next door. We'll cut a hole in the wall between them."

He really adored Bernard. Finally, there was a space available upstairs, and Bernard mentioned that if he could have it permanently, it would be great. So he took it, fixed it up, brought in a licensed electrician with the help of Julius Krauss, who was one of the partners at the time, and who was fascinated by what Bernard was doing mechanically, technically. He wasn't an aesthete, but he loved the way Bernard worked with his hands.

Then we needed more space for the paintings, so we rented the room across the hall. We had three places here—going and coming, going and coming—at the same time. This was how Stanley got us to stay instead of leaving for SoHo. He made it affordable. The rooms were in terrible shape, but that didn't matter. Bernard got what he needed and we never complained because everybody was so nice.

Those were the kinds of things that Stanley Bard did. We always paid our rent on time—that was never an issue. But he made it possible for creative people to create. He's a kind of genius himself. He got along very well with the artists because they're also mad geniuses.

JOHN ZINNSER

Stanley had a genuine love and admiration of artists. He wanted artists to be there. When they redid the lobby, they wanted a painting of mine. He sent his son David down to my studio, and David picked something out. It was a great episode for me. At this time, Stanley managed to get paintings from me, from Phillip Taaffe, Joe Andoe,[89] —a whole new generation of artists in there.

One time I was there when there was some event downstairs in the lobby. Edward Albee[90] was at the event, and he said to Stanley, "Isn't that a John Zinsser painting?"

Stanley came up to me and said, "Edward Albee just noticed your painting! He knows your work!" For him it was great, and it was a huge thrill for me.

When I first moved into the Chelsea, they had that famous Larry Rivers "Dutch Masters" cigar painting in the lobby. I recently saw it at the Guggenheim: "Gift of Stanley Bard."

Here's another story about Stanley and his generosity. The art dealer who first showed my work in New York was a gallery owner named Julian Pretto. He gave lots of people their first shows, people who subsequently became important artists. But he also had these strong ties to a generation of artists from the 70s, which included Sol LeWitt and particularly Carl Andre.[91] Pretto was a very good friend of Carl Andre, an American minimalist sculptor.

Carl Andre, by the time I met him, was obviously a deeply considerate, serious artist, very important in the 60s and 70s. He was also very loyal to Julian Pretto. When Pretto started to get sick with AIDS, he had no health insurance. He had nowhere to live—he basically lived out of his galleries. So Carl Andre came to visit my apartment, 622. His sculptures, by the way, are these geometric floor pieces set out in grids. So I was very concerned about laying out the tea crackers on the platter in the right way!

But he had come to talk to me about whether we could actually get Julian Pretto a room at the Chelsea when he was dying. I talked to Stanley on Andre's behalf. I played to Stanley's art appreciation and love of famous people. I told him who Pretto was, his whole history, and who he had worked with, and that he was dying of AIDS. He needed a place to stay.

"Is it possible to get him in here?"

Stanley said yes, which meant he was opening himself up to all kinds of problems. I believe Carl Andre paid for the room—the full daily price as a hotel room, which is high. He paid for it without telling anybody. It was a private act of friendship and charity. So we were able to get Julian Pretto into the Chelsea for his final days, the final days of someone who had already lived nine lives and knew the importance of the Chelsea.

People would come visit Pretto as he was dying at the Chelsea. I would come visit him. He'd be up in his room, making Campbell's soup and watching terrible TV shows. It was kind of a sad final destination, one of these crappy Chelsea rooms, totally depressing and overpriced. Nonetheless, it was a safe haven.

I remember Andre went down to the Capitol Fish & Tackle[92] store below the Chelsea and bought this funny little piece of tackle. It was a metal box that had these regularly spaced perforations in it, and it was so true as a Carl Andre. It was like a ready-made Carl Andre that he gave to Pretto, like, "This *is* a Carl Andre because I say it is." And yet it was something he bought down at the fishing store!

We had a party after my opening at Stark Gallery, and Pretto appeared in a wheelchair at the party. He was this hollow-cheeked specter—he looked like Dorian Gray.

People were saying, "Oh my God! Is *that* Julian Pretto?" because everyone had known him as this beautiful, youthful, charismatic guy.

Stanley Bard's Amazing Revolving Rooms

Bard was also famous for another of his management tactics. He employed it when a tenant had to leave, whether by choice, by Stanley Bard's decree, or to answer the Grim Reaper's call. Bard was expert at instantly getting house painters and carpet guys in the room and prepping it for the next person in line with a checkbook. But some rooms took more work than others. Rooms that had seen a lot of parties might take a little longer, or rooms occupied by eccentrics who hoarded animals.

One of the most challenging tasks was to take a room where a dead body had lain for a week or two. How did one make such a room as fresh as a daisy?

ROBERT CAMPBELL

This is what Stanley would do. If somebody was found dead and rotten in their room for a week, he would clean the room out and rent it the next day. If somebody slit their throat and there was blood all over the walls, he would paint it and rent it the next day. So one day, for some reason, he got mad at my friend Umberto. This was during a really busy weekend, when Stanley was making a lot of money. But the hotel was full and Stanley needed one more room to make even more money. And here's Umberto, the Italian count with the wife Schizo, who had two rooms. One room he owed thousands on, and on the other room he owed about the same. Stanley decided that he wanted to rent out the second room. And remember, there wasn't ever a room in the Chelsea Hotel that Stanley couldn't rehabilitate pronto.

Stanley told Umberto, "You're going to have to get out of that room right now because I have to rent it out."

Umberto said, "I think you better look at the room, Stanley. I don't think you can rent this room out right away."

"Bullshit!" Stanley said. "Any room can be turned over fast. Take me up there now."

They went up to the room, and Stanley walked in and looked at it. Umberto had painted one wall blue, another one gold, and another red. Then the last wall he painted this wimpy whitish green that didn't go at all with the other bold colors. Then Umberto had taken a paint roller and painted the carpet turquoise blue, the same color he had painted his shoes. Then he took this mirror that he had broken, and shaped a Phoenix out of the broken pieces. It started down in the carpet. Into the carpet he had cut holes the shapes of the broken pieces of mirror so they could be inlaid into it. The phoenix stretched all the way up the wall to the ceiling.

Then he had this box spring mattress and a bed that he had painted turquoise just like the carpet. He called that his "water bed." And on top of that, one night there had been a fire in his room. He had once caught his couch on fire, and he wouldn't let the firemen take his couch with them. It ended up having this foot-long burn hole in it, and his whole room smelled like wet smoke.

Here was the landlord who could repaint and re-carpet any room in one day so somebody else could move in and keep the money coming. But this time Stanley just shook his head at Umberto.

"You better have this room clean in a week."

But one time Stanley did accomplish an amazing room turn-around. It had been the room of this person Christine, a drag queen. I had read about Christine in James St. James's book *Disco Bloodbath* about Michael Alig. Christine was very, very tall and had very dark hair. You know how with some drag queens, you think, "Wow, that's really a *guy*?" Christine was not like that. She looked like a guy. Evidently she was some rich kid, and at one time, she was big in the New York party scene, a pretty happening dude, or woman, or whatever. When I saw her, she'd be in the Chelsea lobby with these long, lace gloves on that went up past her elbows. She was always smoking a cigarette, and she looked very unhealthy.

I swear to God, every time she lifted her cigarette hand from her lap, it must've taken thirty seconds to get the cigarette up to her mouth. She would take a hit off that cigarette, and then she'd lower the cigarette and that would take her another thirty seconds to bring her arm down. It was like she moved in very slow motion.

I remember thinking, "Man, that person's not long for this world."

Now we had this friend named Alan Cohen. For some reason, Christine the drag queen got a crush on Alan. Christine lived right around the corner from him. One day, Alan started hearing all these weird noises outside his door, so he went up to his door and looked through the peephole. And what did he see but this big eyeball staring right back at him! He knew it was Christine peering into his room. Then Alan and Christine got into some kind of conflict because Alan told Christine to leave him alone.

Then after a while, we realized all of the sudden that we

hadn't seen Christine around for a long time. We used to see her around all the time. I went over to Alan's room, and something in the vicinity of Alan's room smelled really, really bad.

"Man!" Alan said. "I don't know *what* that smell is!"

After about two weeks, I guess the hotel finally went and checked Christine's room, because the smell seemed like it had been coming from there. It turned out that Christine had died in her bathtub. The tub, of course, had been full of water, and Christine had been soaking in there dead for all this time, like two weeks! Parked out in front of the hotel for that entire day was this old red van that said "Coroner" on the side. It took the coroner's people a whole day to get Christine out of the bathtub.

Now here's Stanley for you. The *very next day,* after Christine's body was found, I was over at Alan's place. Here came Stanley walking around the corner. He was showing Christine's room to these two college-looking girls.

Stanley said, with a flourish, like he's showing them the finest apartment in New York, "And yes, *this* room here has its own private bathroom!"

Stanley had Christine's room ready to rent *the very next day*! I remember thinking, "Man, that room has got to sit for a month or so before the smell goes away." And on top of that, he was using the bathroom as a *selling* point! The same bathroom Christine had been steeping in for who knows how long!

That's what Stanley would do. Another time, a girl rented 923. When she checked in, she had cancer. They used to call it "checking in to check out." So she paid her bill and went back up to her room and phoned her mother. She didn't have to pay for that phone call! But then she slit her wrists and got blood all over the room, the walls and the carpet. Then she jumped out the window from the ninth floor. She landed right in front of the hotel's awning. Dee Dee Ramone told me that he was walking out the front door right when it happened. Slam! She hit a taxi cab and then bounced onto the street. I guess Tim Sullivan said she hit a manhole cover instead of a taxi cab, but either way, she

162

was flat as a pancake. They left her there for hours.

On the *Living with Legends* blog, this story was confirmed by Bruno Wizard, singer for the punk bands The Rejects and The Homosexuals. Said Wizard, "At that moment I ran into Dee Dee coming back into the hotel, his face white as a ghost. This was right at the time he was trying to quit using drugs, and he had just worked up the courage to go out after staying locked in his room for several days. What had happened was that a woman had thrown herself from a window on the 9th floor. The operator had called her and said she had to check out, and she had said, 'I'll be right down.' And it was right at that moment that Dee Dee stepped out of the hotel."[93]

ROBERT CAMPBELL

And Stanley rented *that* woman's room out the very next day! He got his guys in there, pulled out the bloody carpet and threw some paint on the bloody walls. It seemed like it got the mojo off the room really fast, exorcised the demons. I think that was Stanley's way of saying, "Okay, life goes on." He made a point of renting those rooms out right away. He'd probably tell you I'm full of it, but that's my opinion about why he turned those rooms over as quickly as possible.

JERRY WEINSTEIN

It depended on the condition of the room. If it was really destroyed, you couldn't do that. But if it was just moderately turmoiled, so to speak, we could do it. We would turn rooms over in one day. But if someone killed themselves, the room would be sealed by the police. We couldn't go in there.

*Stormé DeLarverié, the legendary male impersonator,
and longtime Chelsea resident, who allegedly threw the first
punch at the Stonewall Riot of 1969.*

CHAPTER 7

Chelsea Portraits

*"[Bohemia] should ... be the preserve of—in no special order—
insomniacs and restaurants and bars that never close; bibliophiles
and the little stores and stalls that cater to them; alcoholics and
addicts and deviants and the proprietors who understand them;
aspirant painters and musicians and the modest studios that can
accommodate them; ladies of easy virtue and the men who require
them; misfits and poets from foreign shores and exiles from remote
and cruel dictatorships"*—CHRISTOPHER HITCHENS, *Vanity Fair*

During these years, a person wandering the halls of the Chelsea could encounter every Bohemian personality-type cited above in spades. Some were world famous, like Tom Waits, Virgil Thomson, Dee Dee Ramone, and Jaco Pastorius. Others were famous in smaller circles, such as Johnny Thunders in punk rock, Kinky Friedman in mystery novels, and Harry Smith in music history and the dark arts of black magic.

Some were known only to a small coterie of specialists. Suzanne Bartsch, for example, the imperious Austrian queen bee of event planning, with her thick Transylvanian accent, who threw parties with the notorious "Club Kids" including Michael Alig, now in prison. That sordid scene, which ended in a particularly vile murder, was memorialized in James St. James's book, *Disco Bloodbath*.

And other Chelsea Bohemians were famous to no one. But the more obscure Chelsea Bohemians could actually be more colorful than the superstars, freed from caring about their public images. They didn't have to be suitable for prime-time. What follows is a catalogue of people who were creative, those who were crazy and creative, and those who were merely crazy.

Chelsea Royalty: Virgil Thomson

In her book *At the Chelsea*, Florence Turner remarks that Virgil Thomson, who hung out in Paris in the 1920s, had nothing but disdain for his contemporaries in the Lost Generation: Hemingway, Fitzgerald and the like.

"The Lost Generation was silly," Thomson said. "War made lost generations, because the people involved had no jobs to go to."

Chelsea fixture Virgil Thomson was a heavyweight, a giant of twentieth-century music. His film score for *Louisiana Story* won a Pulitzer Prize. With his close friend Gertrude Stein, he composed the opera *Four Saints in Three Acts* based on her libretto.

Thomson was also a prize-winning music critic for the *New York Herald Tribune*. He wrote eight books, one of which won the prestigious National Book Critics Circle Award.

DAVID LAWTON

With all the Beats and the Warhol superstars, sometimes you forget that we loved holding the door for Virgil Thomson. At that time, there had been people up in his apartment for years cataloguing his belongings. I think he had a triplex up there, gorgeous and refinished. It's interesting, when you're on those lower floors with the stench and you realize that upstairs there is unbelievable splendor.

Old Virgil Thomson would be coming out of a cab, and I'd run and hold the hotel door for him. He liked the attention.

JULIE EAKIN

Working on my undergraduate thesis was exciting because it was about the first photograph show at MOMA, the Walker Evans show in 1935. During my research, I found out that Virgil Thomson, the composer, had actually attended that very show. He lived on the Chelsea's tenth floor. I would send questions to him through his secretary—I actually never talked to him directly—and then she would get answers back to me, and I was able to supplement my work by finding someone who actually attended the Evans show. Virgil Thomson had a very keen memory. It was very exciting to feel like you had access to so much, which we did feel when we lived there.

JOHN ZINSSER

Before I even moved in to the Chelsea, the first time I visited it was around 1984. I had just gotten out of college. I'm from New York originally, so I was always familiar with the Chelsea Hotel. But my father, who is William Zinsser, a writer and journalist, had been an editor and movie critic at the New York *Herald Tribune*, this great writers' paper in New York. Because he had been an editor of the arts section, and Virgil Thomson was one of the writers there, he had gotten to know Virgil and really respected him. He thought of Virgil as this grand old man of arts and letters in New York. I was just out of college, and my father, as sort of a rite of passage, wanted me to meet Virgil. So he made an appointment, and we went over to the Chelsea together.

I was just beginning to embark on thinking I wanted to become a painter. And that's how my father introduced me to Virgil: "This is my son. He wants to be a painter." We went up to his apartment, which was the former Chelsea manager's apartment. Because it had been a manager's apartment, it had all this beautiful wooden cabinetry and period Victorian fixtures. There was a grand piano. It was a modestly-scaled apartment, but it had these beautiful trappings and appointments. It had a little Hans Arp wall relief.

Virgil himself must have been in his eighties or nineties

then—a very old man. My father had told me that he was kind of a bridge figure between European Modernism and Post-War American intellectuals. Because, when he was in Paris, he had known Gertrude Stein and Picasso. So in a way, by the time he was the music critic for the *Herald Tribune*, he had already lived one life and brought the experiences of that life with him. My father said that he was the most beautiful writer at the Tribune. He would come back to the Tribune office after a performance and hand write his reviews on legal pads, and tear off the review, page after page, and send it down to Copy. They didn't edit it. He could write absolutely to spec, mellifluously, just in pen and ink.

So when I met him, I said, "Oh, I want to be a painter."

He said to me, "Oh yes, I know well the smell of oil paint."

Now I realize that's just something people say. Like, "I know what the painter's life is." But at the time, I was horrified because I was then working in acrylic. I thought, "Oh, to be a real painter, you have to work in oil!" From then on, I worked in oil. I never worked in acrylic again. It wasn't because he'd given me this great art advice—I just was caught up in the romantic definition of it.

Thomson was kind of old womanish and owlish. He was fond of himself as a raconteur. We had a very formal "tea with your grandmother" visit. He was quite catty and bitchy, which was not what I expected. His general, perfunctory way of addressing us, addressing the world, was catty.

But it was a marvelous glimpse of the Chelsea for me, and this man who had lived there. That was my introduction to Virgil Thomson and the Chelsea Hotel.

PAUL VOLMER

My crazy girlfriend Neicy would sometimes randomly call up people on the hotel phone and just chat with them for her own amusement. With the phone lines in the hotel, you could call from room to room using just a four-digit number, so she would call different rooms randomly to chat with people. One time she had been on the phone for about ten minutes, and she was talking in a very flirty way.

"Who are you talking to?" I asked her.

"Virgil Thomson!"

I was shocked. He was such an eminent person. "Oh, you shouldn't talk to him!" And I got her off the phone. But it was probably the most fun that he had in a long time. I should have let them gab.

ROBERT CAMPBELL

After Thomson died in 1989, the guy who ended up moving into Virgil Thomson's Chelsea apartment was the artist Phillip Taaffe. He went to Sotheby's or Christie's auction house and bought all of Virgil's old furniture back. In his carpet, there were indentations where Virgil's furniture had been sitting. So Taaffe brought every piece of the old furniture back and put everything right back in those same dimples.

The Final Days of Jaco Pastorius

When I first met [Jaco] he was extremely present tense and, I would have to say for lack of a better term, extremely sage. He was so accepting of everything going on around him; at the same time he was arrogant and challenging: "I'm the baddest!" He was so alert, so involved in the moment. When people are in that state they're generally fun to be with. He was very alive[94] —JONI MITCHELL

Jazz musician Jaco Pastorius was the Jimi Hendrix of the electric bass. He's the only bassist in *Down Beat* magazine's Jazz Hall of Fame. He played with Weather Report, Joni Mitchell, and Al Dimeola, and a host of other luminaries. Sadly, he suffered from bipolar disorder, which eventually disintegrated anything resembling an ordinary life.

PAUL VOLMER

Tim Sullivan kept an extra guitar in his room because frequently a friend would drop by his place and want to play. Tim worked in a guitar store downstairs, Chelsea Music, and a lot of times his musician friends would come up. One friend was the famous bass player Jaco Pastorius.[95] He was a genius bass player, but he was also kind of crazy, a schizophrenic. He would totally lose it. He would sort of phase out until he couldn't even function—he was a real drinker too. I think at the time he was hanging out in Washington Square Park, being a bum, begging money for liquor. But he used to come over to our room with a friend of Tim's, and they jammed a little bit.

TIM SULLIVAN

Probably the biggest thing that happened to me when I worked in the guitar store downstairs had to do with Jaco Pastorius, considered the Charlie Parker of the bass. Other than the poet Rene Ricard, he was the only true genius I've ever met. What is a true genius? A true genius is something that, when you see it, you know it. He was staying here in the hotel, and he came into the guitar shop. My friend Rick knew who he was, but I didn't. I had seen him on the cover of *Guitar Player* magazine, and read the interview, but I didn't really know too much about the guy.

He came in, and we started talking. My friend Rick said, "Oh man, you're the best! Where are you playing?"

"I'm playing over at the Lone Star,"[96] he said. "Why don't you guys come down?"

So we went down to the Lone Star and started hanging out with him and his band. But when Jaco would start to swing in the depression mode, he got really self-destructive. Sometimes the depressive valleys would last for years. He had his real high moments, but at the end of his life, he was in a really deep valley. They tried to give him medications for it, but sufferers of this disease at that time were self-medicating. They might drink tons of alcohol, which he was doing.

But he was pretty lucid when I met him in the guitar store. He was doing these gigs, these legendary gigs at the Lone Star. He did four or five shows in a row, advertised only by word of mouth, and they sold out big time. But the jazz musicians were always into cocaine, and when Jaco started doing coke and drinking a lot of booze, that started his decline, the out-of-control wild man thing was common for him.

He was thirty-two when I met him. This was two years before he hit bottom and died at thirty-four. So I witnessed his decline. So we started hanging out, and there was a lot of cocaine and alcohol around. He had his girlfriend, this German-Japanese girl who was just as crazy as he was. He was not doing well financially, and he ended up getting thrown out of his room at the Chelsea and staying in my room, sleeping on the floor!

One night, we went to see Paul Butterfield with Jaco. He got up and played with the Paul Butterfield Blues Band. They played this Hendrix medley. Jaco was better than Hendrix, but had the same kind of strong hands and physicality with the instrument that Hendrix had—only Jaco had it with the electric bass, an even bigger instrument.

When I listened to them play this Hendrix medley, I thought, "My God, *that's* what a genius does!" I gained a wealth of knowledge from being around him and understanding what it is that makes somebody that good.

Once I was giving a guitar lesson in my room, 220, and Jaco burst in, interrupting the lesson. The guy I was giving the lesson to had never been around this kind of whirlwind person. He said, "Listen, I gotta go. I'll talk to you later."

Jaco felt really bad about screwing up the lesson. He'd been drinking and was kind of crazy at the time. "I ruined your lesson. The least I can do is give you a guitar lesson." Not a bass lesson, but a guitar lesson. And he showed me two songs. This is sort of the tradition with other musicians, we exchange songs. You say, "Here's a song I know. You show me a song *you've* learned." You learn a lot about music that way. The two songs he taught me were "Blackbird" and "Changes" by Buddy Miles. His technique and smoothness really had a major impact on me and affected my playing for the rest of my life.

When Jaco taught me how to play those songs, he didn't diagram the notes for me. He didn't say, "Well this is A, and this is

C." He just took the guitar down and *showed* me how to play it. That's why it had an impact on me. Luckily I had the ability to understand the direct language he was using, the language of playing the instrument

Jaco was also a trickster! He would roll up his pant cuffs, pour baby powder in the cuffs and jump around. The powder would go everywhere, all over the floor! This is what he did when he gave me the guitar lesson. You have no idea about how crazy this guy was, but there was a genius behind the curtain! He'd roll his pants up all the way and put Indian makeup on his face and braid his hair. He'd put powder in his hair, or pour beer over his head.

Down around the West Fourth Street basketball courts, all the black guys came from the 'burbs to play basketball, and these semi-pro guys would play too on these asphalt courts. Jaco was about six-foot-four and loved basketball. He would dive into the middle of these basketball matches between two teams, grab their basketball and run away with it down the street. They'd chase him down and *pound* the guy, beat the crap out of him and toss him out onto the street. They didn't know who he was.

PAUL VOLMER
I used to play basketball on a local court, so I had a basketball. I turned my back for a second, and when I turned around again, Jaco had run off with my basketball! Later, I heard that Jaco had been seen enjoying himself in the park with a basketball.

TIM SULLIVAN
But Jaco gradually deteriorated. He ended up losing everything, including his ability to play. He kept drinking. He became homeless. I saw him down at Washington Square Park sitting there begging for money. He had been beat up—his face was all puffy. Then I heard he went down to Florida and somehow got thrown out of a bar down there. The bouncer punched him and killed him.[97] He was thirty-four.

Chelsea Seduces William Eggleston from his own MOMA Opening

ELLIS DUNCAN

I met the photographer William Eggleston through Frank Dogrell. Doggrell was one of the most amazing people I've ever met. He was from Memphis, where the Doggrell family was very well-known. He looked like an old Arrow Shirt model, with dashing good looks, very laid-back speech patterns, bedroom eyes, you might call them.

Frank got a beautiful one-bedroom that had been Dylan Thomas's suite, or at least part of it had. He got the living room and then a little anteroom off to the side which he had a bed in, and a bathroom and a fireplace. It was on the south-east side of the building on the sixth or seventh floor. It was next to the top floor, I think. I was there on many occasions.

He got away with being mysterious. People would say, "Frank, what do you do for a living?"

"I'm in business," he would say.

And people would just blink their eyes, fascinated, as if gee, they wished *they* could be in business. He used very clipped, very allusive descriptions, and gave very short answers. That seemed to work fine because people were fascinated by the mystery surrounding him.

But another instance in Frank Doggrell's apartment involved William Eggleston, from Memphis. Eggleston was a tremendous photographer. His work now sells for quite a bit. He's fascinating, quite a recluse, quite a womanizer. He was in New York for the grand opening of his show at the Museum of Modern Art. It was very exciting because it was the first time a color photographer had ever been admitted in a fine art museum. You had Richard Avedon and Diane Arbus—they're black and white artists. What Eggleston did was travel around the south and take color pictures of, say, the front of a gas station with a rusting Coca-Cola machine with a rake leaned up against it. Or a family in squalor sitting on the front porch of their house with a washing machine. During the era, nobody thought these things were noteworthy or picture-worthy. But he had the genius to do that, and he did it in a very sensitive way with great photographic ability and made it into quite a collection. The first color photo to make it into MOMA was a bare yellow light bulb in the corner of a room. It was barely a color picture because the yellow light bulb was kind of faded. But it was considered an earth-shattering photo.

William Eggleston's pictures revolutionized photography in subject matter and approach. Born in Memphis in 1939, Eggleston spent his childhood with his grandparents in the tiny rural Mississippi town of Sumner. The Delta would later figure in his photographs. As a person, Eggleston is as multi-sided as a disco ball. An innovative artist from a wealthy family in a town that thought art was for sissies, Eggleston managed to keep a "gracious and remote" quasi-aristocratic bearing, at least on the surface, according to journalist Richard Woodward. He smoked and drank and wore jodhpurs. But a wild man was always on the verge of breaking through his patrician skin. He shot off guns in the house, collected DWIs, kept his wife in one house and his mistress—one of them, anyway—in another.[98]

Eggleston's pictures were as original and unpredictable as his personality. He was thirty-seven when The Museum of Modern Art in New York agreed to exhibit his work. It was a momentous exhibit for several reasons, the first being color. Before the 1976 show, photographers and critics considered only black-and-white photos to be artistic—color photos were more suited to family snapshots, fitting for the masses but not for art. Eggleston's second innovation was subject matter. Eggleston photographed the Mississippi of his childhood in full color, but he wasn't interested in the statues for the Confederate dead, the antebellum mansions, the swollen-trunked cypress trees in the bayou. Eggleston's eye was attracted to discarded artifacts and the people associated with them, objects and people so common as to be overlooked. As Eudora Welty described them, "...old tyres, Dr Pepper machines, discarded air-conditioners, vending machines, empty and dirty Coca-Cola bottles, torn posters, power poles and power wires, street barricades, one-way signs, detour signs, No Parking signs, parking meters and palm trees crowding the same curb."[99]

As momentous as the MOMA exhibition was, the night it happened, Eggleston was nowhere to be found. A few of his friends, noticing the conspicuous absence, set out to track him down. They found him at the Chelsea, where, according to Ellis Duncan, a young commodities trader from Alexandria, Virginia, Eggleston had been drawn in by the hotel's dissolute pull.

ELLIS DUNCAN

We were in Dylan Thomas's old room having drinks, and Eggleston just decided not to go to the opening. He had come to New York for the MOMA show, but because he was having such a good time partying at the Chelsea Hotel with Frank Doggrell—having drinks and such—he missed the opening of his own work at the MOMA!

Actually, his friends were able to drag him drunk to the exhibit that launched color photography as a legitimate art. At first, critics were uniformly hostile to the show, one calling it "cracker chic." *The New York Times* dubbed it "the most hated show of the year." There was, they said, nothing to these photographs, just tricycles and road signs. But the banal subjects and off-center framing could create a whole range of effects. His photos—lurid and grotesque, poignant and elegiac, tough and unsentimental—served a larger social purpose. They threw grit in the gears of the south's mythmaking machine—the glittering image of grand aristocratic chivalry more at home in Sir Walter Scott than the post-civil rights South. It took a full generation for color photography to topple the fine art world's black and white dogma. Now Eggleston's work is venerated precisely because of his eye for color.

Eggleston, up to then a frequent visitor to the Chelsea, finally moved in after the 1976 show. There, he met Viva, the strawberry blonde, former top-tier superstar in Andy Warhol's Factory scene. Now the diva, known for her tough personality, was living like Bohemian royalty at the Chelsea.

According to Woodward, Eggleston was drunk and high in his Chel-

sea Room when he met Viva. He vomited and took her by the arm, ex-
claiming, "Honey, you sure are a strong woman." Eggleston was already
married, in the loosest sense of the word. His affair with Viva survived
for a number of years. They drove around the South taking photos to the
car stereo soundtrack of *Gone with the Wind.* After a couple of years of
on-again-off-again, Viva pressed him on marriage. Eggleston responded,
according to Woodward, "Honey, you're a six-part fugue and even Bach
never wrote more than five."

The partnership never led to marriage but it did spark the discovery
of another great photographer at the Chelsea, Louis Faurer. The Phila-
delphian had lived by his magazine work, mostly pastel fashion photographs for *Harper's Bazaar,* where he befriended fellow employee Robert
Frank. But Faurer's artistic work remained unnoticed.

Part of what held Faurer's career back was his tetchy personality,
says videographer David Leonard, who has followed Faurer's career.

DAVID LEONARD

Faurer was not known for many, many years because he was
a difficult character, a little bit crazy. The one opportunity he
had to have an exhibition, Faurer said "Oh, you're hanging it all
wrong," and he would start taking stuff off the wall. He was just
difficult enough that, back when there weren't very many photo
galleries, he made a bad impression.

But Viva found out about his work. The curator Walter Hopps related the story to Leonard.

DAVID LEONARD

Walter told me, "Well, you know, we really have to thank William
Eggleston for the fact that the world knows who Louis Faurer is.
When Eggleston and Viva were living in the Chelsea Hotel, Louis
Faurer was also living in the Chelsea, and he had this chest full
of his photographs. Viva, who had known Faurer for years, now
saw that he had this big chest filled with photographs. She said,
'Bill, you've got to see this guy's stuff!'"

Heaped in the chest were Faurer's candid street photos displaying what

Leonard called an "amazing eye" and a documentary approach similar to Robert Frank's.

DAVID LEONARD

Eggleston introduced Faurer and his work to other people, who began to collect his work, who made sure prints were made, and who invested in his career. His career finally came to fruition in 2002 with a retrospective exhibit at the Museum of Fine Arts in Houston.

Faurer missed his own retrospective show at the Houston Museum of Fine Arts in 2002, dying only months before. But if it hadn't been for Viva and Eggleston's encounter at the Chelsea, Faurer would likely have died a fashion photography footnote.

Harry Smith: Black Magic Music Archivist

If Alan Lomax was the great musicological explorer who ventured into the Mississippi Delta to record this strange, haunting, new music played by blacks called the Blues—thus introducing it to the world—then Harry Smith did the same for Appalachian Folk and Bluegrass. Only, instead of venturing into the mountains of Tennessee or North Carolina, he explored his gargantuan record collection, harvesting songs there. In doing so, he saved a slab of American culture that would have been lost.[100]

Archiving was only one of the wild-haired genius' achievements.

JEROME POYNTON

Harry Smith's *Anthology of American Folk Music*, which was the founding of Folkway Records, is now at the Smithsonian. He was also an experimental filmmaker and ethnologist of sorts. He was so many things, it's hard to describe exactly who he was. People have been trying for years, and I don't think anyone has gotten it right yet. But he was very interesting and a wealth of knowledge.

As an old man—Harry aged very fast—he was awarded a Grammy for his forties' work to archive important American folk music that started the new folk scene in the fifties. His films are extremely important and considered "Essential Cinema" by Jonas Meekas at Anthology Film Archive. With Huncke, Harry Smith is one of the most interesting figures in the beat generation who lived his life as he saw fit and was least impacted by the group mentality around him. He died in his room at the Chelsea. Allen [Ginsberg] was about to relocate him to Naropa, in Boulder.

JAMES RASIN

Harry had moved into a room across the hall from Huncke. There's a famous story—I don't know whether it's true or not—but when he was living here back in the sixties or seventies, he collected all kinds of things. One of the things was Ukrainian eggs, beautiful, intricate, hand-painted eggs. He actually lived with Mary Beach and Claude Pelieu[101] in Cooperstown near Cherry Valley. They lived up there for about a year. Mary would tell stories about when they lived together, such as how he would collect his own urine. The whole house was filled with sealed jars filled with his piss.

Anyway, he had this collection of Ukrainian eggs, and supposedly he was convinced that if he left his room at the Chelsea, someone would steal his eggs. So the story goes, he never left his room for a year! Finally, everyone was worried about him being holed up there, and they convinced him to leave his room. Sure enough, that day, someone broke into his room and stole his eggs! Maybe unconsciously he *made* it happen.

DIMITRI MUGIANIS

Harry Smith died singing in the arms of Paola Igliori.[102] He was a wizard, a black magician. To me, there was something off-putting about his vibe. I think Huncke actually wrote about being put off by Harry Smith's appearance and the whole black magic thing he had going.

DAVID LAWTON

When Harry Smith died, someone asked Herbert Huncke to

write something for his memorial. The piece he wrote is now in the *Herbert Huncke Reader*. The funny thing is, it's all about how Herbert didn't know Harry. It's an interesting reflection of how authentic Huncke was that he didn't want to mislead his readers or listeners.

In the memorial, "Thanksgiving, 1991: Harry Smith," Huncke writes with characteristic candor: "To speak honestly—I didn't respond comfortably to his personality. His appearance made me feel skeptical of his trustworthiness … on the other hand… I did not wish him despair or pain, and certainly not death."

Lady Madonna

Madonna never lived at the Chelsea, but she used it for some shots in her notorious black-and-white photo book, *Sex*, done with photographer Steven Meisel, which featured her scantily clad, if at all. When it was released in 1992, she was at the pinnacle of her career and the sleek book—bound in an aluminum cover—got a lot of press. Much was negative, since the book was provocative and people already either loved Madonna or hated her.

ROBERT CAMPBELL

When Madonna was shooting that *Sex* photo book, my friend Alan Cohen called me on the house phone and said, "Get over here—let's see if Madonna's over here."

I didn't give a rat's ass about Madonna, but I said, "Okay, Alan, cool."

So I was hanging out with Alan, watching Madonna down the hall. Madonna stopped the shoot and came up to us. She had this long, black leather Nazi coat on and a leather Nazi hat. She came up to us and said, "Oh, excuse me. Could you all move? Cause you're going to end up in the shot."

She was just matter of fact about it—she wasn't bitchy at all.

Viva la Viva Redux!

A sure way to earn status as Chelsea royalty came from being part of Andy Warhol's scene in the 60s. Viva, mentioned earlier for her notorious verbal brawls with Stanley Bard, starred in several of Warhol's films, and was lead actress in one.

MARLOWE WEST

Viva had a big, beautiful apartment. She was nice to me—she'd say "Hi" to me in the hall or in the elevator. I went to her place once, it was very nice, with big high ceilings.

STEVE HOUSE

She used to come out of her room in a vodka haze with her paisley bathrobe on, and say in this whispery voice, "Hey. The music's too loud out here." And she'd run back into her apartment. She seemed like she was on acid! She was the trippiest bird I've ever met!

PAUL VOLMER

Viva had a young daughter named Gaby who was so cute. Gaby grew up there ever since she was a baby, and when I knew her, she was a little girl. And there were a few other people who had their Bohemian kids living in the hotel.

ELLIS DUNCAN

Gaby, Viva's daughter, was an interesting little girl.[103] Very, very bright—she was twenty-five at the age of eight. She could be very full of herself. I used to see her playing board games with other children in the lobby, and if it looked like she was going to lose the game, she would suddenly change the rules. The Chelsea Hotel was her babysitter. Her mother evidently never feared for her. Everybody kind of knew Gaby. You'd see her in the elevator, running up and down the steps. The hotel was her playground. She was to the Chelsea what Eloise was to the Plaza. She was precocious, very self-assured. I'm not surprised that she went on to do as well as she did in TV and Hollywood.

Vali Myers: World's Evilest Tattoo Artist?

In his book *Chelsea Horror Hotel*, Dee Dee Ramone wrote kind things about Vali Myers.[104] He was most impressed by her elaborate tattoos, words inscribed in a language that he called "unreadable... part pagan and part paranormal." Vali gave Dee Dee a tattoo of three dots arranged in an equilateral triangle on his hand. Dee Dee said it was the most evil tattoo in the world.

Decades before tattoos had become fashionable, she tattooed a Dali-esque moustache on her own upper lip, forever ruling out a day job. But she adorned more than skin—her paintings and drawings achieved underground renown, appearing in magazines like Penthouse. Born in Australia, she lived a peripatetic life. In 1970, she moved into the Chelsea. She knew Andy Warhol and Abbie Hoffman, Jean Cocteau and Jean Genet. In addition to tattooing Dee Dee Ramone's hand, she tattooed a lightning bolt on Patti Smith's knee in the room Smith shared with Robert Mapplethorpe. Ultimately, Vali moved back to Australia—Melbourne—where she died of cancer at 72. Her life was featured in three films.

Her artwork is trippy, mythic, and baroque, some of it done with airbrush in a way that resembles contemporary graffiti art. Considering her penchant for tattoos and the airbrush art, it wouldn't be a stretch to say she was forty years ahead of her time.

PAUL VOLMER

Vali Myers had thick red hair and curly facial tattoos at the ends of her mouth. I remember going into her room once, and it was very much like an Arabian tent with beaded curtains and lush brocades on the walls. It was definitely otherworldly, like a medieval tent.

MARLOWE WEST

Vali was really beautiful but she had this blue moustache tattooed on her upper lip. She was a Salvador Dali type chick, and she had a crush on Miss Mercy of the GTOs.

JAMES RASIN

Herbert Huncke had told me, "You've got to meet this woman Vali. She's wonderful and wild and exotic." So he took me down there, and she was with Herbie and Irish Johnnie and it was really fantastic! She was holding court while everyone was spread out on the floor. They had weed, and she would command the Irish guys to fix you whatever drink you wanted. She was a really lovely, wild person, not intimidating, just really sweet and friendly.

To me, it seemed like Vali liked to be paid attention to by her little minions, and some of them obviously enjoyed it a lot, but she was very generous with her time and her spirit. She would sing and laugh and tell stories. She made you feel good.

Scary Poet Rene Ricard

The reclusive poet Rene Ricard is another member of Chelsea royalty by virtue of being part of the Warhol scene. Ricard had radar for being in the right scenes at the right time. In the '80s, he was instrumental in launching painters Julian Schnabel and Jean-Michel Basquiat into fame. When Ricard's essay about Basquiat, "The Radiant Child," appeared in *ArtForum* magazine, the young artists' career skyrocketed.

TIM SULLIVAN

When I moved in, the poet Rene Ricard had been here for a while, but he's kind of scary, so I kept my distance. Rene would pass through the lobby, and David Linter and I would be sitting there, and we would say something to Rene, or he would say something to us, a little back and forth and joking here and there. As we got to know him—and Dave's a big reader and writer—he'd be reading a book and Rene would take interest. They'd start a conversation, and as it turned out, Rene is this *heavy* intellectual, a truly knowledgeable guy about just about everything in the arts, from literature to painting to music. He's truly a genius. So, knowing that we all had interests in common, he gradually sat down more often with us in the lobby, conversing about ideas. That's how I became friends with him.

My girlfriend Hillary, also, at first thought Rene was kind of scary. He's high sometimes, and you're not quite sure what he's high on. So you want to give these kinds of people their space. You don't want to get pulled into their circle, that edge of the abyss. Luckily, he doesn't have the abyss that sucks people down and destroys them. If you leave him alone, and he does what he needs to do to maintain his thing every day, he's fine. He's not out to hustle anybody. As long as he keeps creating, he's okay. And once you get beyond that scary façade, you get to know him.

If you're intellectual, Rene Ricard is a blast. It's like sitting with someone like Shelley or Milton. He's that brilliant. I wouldn't say he's shy, but he's kind of vain and self-conscious, so he can be, "Well, I'm going to get out of here," and then he pops off somewhere. But now he and Dave have become very good friends. He'll sit and talk sometimes for hours, which he enjoys. Other people will chime in and sit down, even Stanley Bard.

JAMES RASIN
Rene Ricard could turn a very interesting, witty phrase quickly. He incorporates them into his paintings now, paintings with words.

TIM SULLIVAN
Stanley used to let him slide a little bit, but Rene always paid his way once he sold a painting.

Victor Hugo: Maniacal Window Dresser

Victor Hugo was probably most famous for being the lover of Halston,[105] the first international fashion superstar. According to Salon.com, Victor Hugo (not to be confused with the 19th Century author of *Les Miserables*) was "a bizarre, unintelligible and maniacal Colombian window dresser… who liked to give window mannequins submachine guns and have them act out The Patty Hearst bank robbery scene." He was called Victor Hugo not in honor of the great French novelist, but because of "his physical endowments, his literary ones being undoubtedly few."[106]

ELLIS DUNCAN

Victor Hugo was the last lover of Halston—fashion designer Roy Halston Frowick. Victor lived with the painter Scott Covert off and on at the hotel.

When Halston died, Halston's family paid Victor a million bucks to shut up—not to tell anyone about his relationship with Halston—and get out of everybody's hair. After taxes and a tremendous amount of partying with a lot of everything that could be purchased, that money was quickly running out.

Victor, at that point, was also sick with AIDS. In his desperation toward the end, Victor decided to write the book he had been paid not to write. He had spoken to some publishers to try to figure out how he could write something, because he had agreed in his payoff never to speak of his relationship with Halston. It had me scared to death that if he'd put pen to paper, he would be sued.

I think Halston left a brother or sister as beneficiaries for any residuals from Halston's licensing deals. So they had to make sure that Victor Hugo didn't go out and queer the whole thing—no pun intended—by blabbing.

He didn't die while he was staying with Scott Covert, but it was shortly after moving out of Scott's apartment, a week or two after having failed to find a publisher.

ROBERT CAMPBELL

The first time—and subsequently every time—I did crack cocaine was with Victor Hugo. It was two or three in the morning, and I was looking for my friend Mario to get some more coke. He didn't answer the door, and then all of a sudden, Victor was there. He said, "Come on—I want to show you something." I think he lived in Room 525 then, which later became Dee Dee Ramone's room. He loaded this crack pipe and showed me how to smoke it. Then he gave me a hit, and it hit me like a ton of bricks. I was sitting there wondering why would Victor Hugo give me his last hit of crack? Years later, I realize, he was hoping I would say, "Damn, that stuff is the shit! Can you get me some more now?" I didn't do that. All I could think was, "Fuck, keep me away from this shit because I will get addicted to this, and it will be the end of my life as I know it." I thanked him and got out of there as fast as I could. I felt like I had met the Devil. Thank God, I had the strength to avoid getting into that. Even in those wild days I somehow knew better.

At one point, my friend Mario felt sorry for Victor Hugo, who had lost his apartment, so he let Victor Hugo live with him at the hotel. According to Mario, Victor Hugo was so *glamorous* because he had been a fixture at Studio 54, and he had been Halston's lover. And Andy Warhol had painted a painting of Victor Hugo's dick, so Victor was glamorous. But all of the sudden, Mario started noticing some of his belongings had gone missing from his room. One night, Mario was at a club, and he saw this male prostitute wearing his leather jacket.

Mario walked up to him. "Hey, how you doing? Where'd you get that leather jacket?"

"Oh, yeah, Victor Hugo, Halston's lover," the guy said. "He gave me the jacket."

Mario wanted Victor Hugo out of his apartment. Ellis also told me, "Yeah, Victor Hugo's moving in with Scott."

Scott Covert was my friend, a painter. So I told him, "Be careful of Victor Hugo. He stole some stuff from Mario."

I didn't really have anything against Victor. My girlfriend Carol liked Victor because he would give her constructive criticism on her artwork. He was a knowledgeable, classy guy. But he was at the end of his rope, and instead of dealing with it, he was stealing from his friends.

So the next thing I knew, Victor was angry at me for warning Scott about him. He was telling me how tacky I was, how sophisticated he was, and I was ruining his reputation.

"Well, Victor," I told him, "at least I don't steal from my friends. I don't give a damn where you've been or who you know. Scott's my friend, and if I want to tell him you stole things from Mario, you're not going to stop me."

After that, Victor and I were never friends again. It caused some difficulty between Scott and me, too.

Scott Covert: Graveyard Artist

As far as I am aware, no artist has made it big in grave rubbings except maybe Scott Covert, who does *frottage*, rubbings with a twist—brilliantly colored collages collecting the engraved names from tombstones of famous people. He gathers some rubbings according to theme—like the bright blue country music collage featuring rubbings from the graves of Tammy Wynnette, Patsy Cline, Johnny Cash, and about a hundred other country stars big and small. Other rubbings, like one juxtaposing Fred Astaire, Buster Keaton, and Lenny Bruce, seem to lack an organizational principle other than fame.

Besides his art, Scott Covert had personality in spades.

ROBERT CAMPBELL

One night Scott Covert ended up at Herbert Huncke's place, and this is how I met him. He was carrying a big duffel bag. We hung out for a while, drinking and smoking, and we started talking. He said he was an artist, and then he started pulling these beautiful paintings out of his duffel bag. He had like five hundred of them in there. They all featured grave rubbings of famous people. He had a story he would tell about each one.

He would just stack the paintings up in a pile. It was blowing my mind. Since he was homeless, if he could, he would find a nice warm place to crash for a few hours at the end of the day. But at night he didn't have anything to do.

The night I met him, I had a little bit of money, and I just couldn't believe this guy. I thought he was perfect Chelsea material. We got along, and were talking. So I said, "Man, you gotta come along and talk to Stanley about getting a room." He was just flat broke. So I bought two paintings from him that night. I think they were three-hundred and fifty dollars a piece. One of them was a rubbing of Brian Jones's grave, and it had Andre Breton's rubbing on it too, and the rubbings of some other people. My ex-girlfriend Carol's still got them. Carol also got one of Coco Chanel. They were really cool. So after we talked to Stanley, Scott was admitted into the hotel and moved in.

Scott got this really cool apartment. Stanley really hooked him up nicely. It was on the corner on the fifth floor. Scott and I would hang out drinking on his balcony and watching the world go by. His room, of course, was trashed.

There seems to be some dispute as to who really introduced Scott Covert to the Chelsea.

ELLIS DUNCAN

I brought Scott to the Chelsea Hotel and introduced Scott to Stanley Bard, which helped him get his room. When I first met him, Scott was living in the subways because he had nowhere to live. A lot of homeless people lived on the subways because the trains were somewhere warm to go to, and all you needed to do was bum fifty cents. You could ride them endlessly back and forth, back and forth. They never shooed you off of those old trains. He'd ride it from Harlem to Coney Island and back and make six trips, or ten trips or whatever, in the course of an evening. But he couldn't *sleep* on the train at night for fear of being stabbed or mugged. But then he'd get off in the morning, and during the day he would go and sleep in Central Park.

At that point, he was just using regular paper to do his tombstone rubbings, like a lot of people had been doing for many years. The first one he rubbed was in Detroit, the grave of the dead Supreme, Florence Ballard. She had fallen out with Diana Ross and the Supremes cast her aside, and she died indigent. Covert's from that area in Michigan. He also always wanted to open a pet cemetery. He had this interest in death, not a macabre interest, but also not a fear of it certainly.

Then he started doing tombstone rubbings and went to Pen

Argyl, Pennsylvania and rubbed Jayne Mansfield. It was a big, tombstone carved into the shape of a heart. Then he found out that Moms Mabley and Joan Crawford were buried in the same Ferncliffe cemetery just north of Manhattan, and Malcolm X was also buried there, and a lot of other famous people. So he frequented that cemetery. He also loved going and rubbing the graves of mobsters and of Harry Houdini out in Brooklyn. Not to mention the grave of Jean-Michel Basquiat, who is buried with a very simple gravestone in Green-Wood Cemetery in Brooklyn. Those were some of his favorites.

MARLOWE WEST

I went over to Scott Covert's place two or three times. I was very curious about his work, which turned out to be awesome. Almost like the Plaster Casters[107] or something, these groupie girls who would go to meet rock stars and take plaster impressions of their erections.

ROBERT CAMPBELL

Once, Scott sold a bunch of paintings to Holly Solomon,[108] this really hotshot art dealer on 57th Street. She bought about thirteen of them, I think.

ELLIS DUNCAN

Solomon Gallery was supposed to do a show with Scott, and then Scott and she had a fight and a falling out. Even after the show fell through, a lot of his artwork still had the stickers on it from this woman's galleries, numbered stickers that would have related to the pricing catalogue.

He had these huge paintings, like ten feet by twenty feet on rice paper that he'd gotten at Chinatown. He'd draw these really tiny checkerboards on them. He had these huge canvases, and they'd have these tiny, tiny checkerboards in red ink all over them. And they had grave rubbings on them too, like of Billie Holliday and Harry Houdini and Charlie Christian, and on and on, everybody you could imagine. He'd do the checkerboards and the grave rubbings on the same rice paper. But then he would fold them up. He took no care at all of the paintings. He'd walk on them. If he was telling a story, he'd lay out this canvas, and it'd have all these grave rubbings on it. He'd just lay more and more paintings on top of each other, and then he would walk on them. He didn't really care.

When he first started out, he was trying to be really neat about making his paintings. But once he went to Andy Warhol's grave and the wind started blowing and it started raining, so he went in to get some coffee and said "Screw it." He left all his paintings and things out there in the wind and rain. It screwed up all of his paintings. After he had calmed down a little bit, he went back outside and got all his stuff. He just figured he didn't care. I guess it gave his paintings the weathered look. From then on, the weathered look became his style.

As a person, Scott is a volatile guy, smart but prickly. When I met him, he was full of energy. I guess he was older than I am now, but he was *wide open* and I liked him.

He's got a photographic memory. He's never forgotten the name of anyone he's met, nor any small detail about their lives, and he can be terribly, terribly charming. He's truly interested in people, and people are fascinated by him.

He also felt like his artwork had catapulted him to vaunted levels, levels not everybody agreed he had actually achieved. So he could very easily need you one day and not need you the next. Scott had been a runner and cocktail waiter at Studio 54 when he was young and beautiful. He's gay. He was fascinating to be around, but some people didn't consider his work, his grave rubbings, an art as much as a craft. He was constantly fluctuating between being high and mighty to being knocked down a few pegs by people telling him what they really thought of his work. And he had trouble making the jump.

He did make an alliance with an art supplier by the name of David Davis, who had a famous art supply company by the same name down on Hudson Street in the West Village. He supplied Warhol and Basquiat with most of their paint. Scott used to use little finger-thin pastel crayons—oil crayons—but he found that they would crumble and break, and they were hard to hold onto. So he lamented his problem to David Davis. Davis's handsome son-in-law had taken over the business, and he had taken a real interest in Scott. Together, they came up with a hunk of an oil crayon the size of a bar of soap, that Scott could hold like a bar of soap and do rubbings with. They might throw in some glitter, and they would throw in different mixes until he got what he wanted.

David Davis also sold a wide range of canvases, etc. At one point, he got hold of some paper that was used in Holland as thatching for huts. Each sheet of paper was about the size of a newspaper page opened out. So they would use these things in Holland pre-drywall. It was very rough paper that almost looked as if horsehair and small twigs and old yarn were woven into it. Then they'd nail these sheets or tack them to the sides of their houses, and spackle over them. The paper would prevent drafts in their houses as a form of insulation and windbreak. David Davis called Scott one day and said "I've got fifty sheets of this paper from this old Dutch plant that's been making it the same way for four-hundred years, and they're going out of business."

"I want it," Scott said. They worked out some deal and Scott got the paper and did a whole series of rubbings on it. It was light brown, with scalloped, irregular torn edges. On gravestones with heavily recessed letters, he could rub through all those heavier papers. He later made the jump to canvas. His first canvases were very lonely looking because they were large.

Incidentally, his paper pieces he folded and carried in big duffel bags. Anybody that knew him had a closet with one of the duffel bags in it. Scott would come and retrieve the bag at one time or another when he was going to Paris to Pere Lachaise to get Jim Morrison and Alice B. Toklas, or to England to get Herman Hesse and Oscar Wilde. He also went to Egypt and got Anwar Sadat. He even went to the Wailing Wall in Jerusalem and tried to rub some there. He was all over the place. So he left his duffel bags at a lot of peoples' places, and I don't think he ever got ripped off, because people respected Scott and his artwork.

ROBERT CAMPBELL

When Scott went to Egypt to rub the grave of Anwar Sadat, he had this girl with him who had an art gallery of her own. The Egyptian army soldiers who were guarding Anwar Sadat's grave wouldn't let him do the grave rubbing. So he offered to let the guards play with this girl's breasts for as long as he was rubbing. So he was rubbing the grave and she was getting fondled, yelling at him, "Hurry up, motherfucker!"

Then they went to Greece and stayed at this really chichi resort. There, he ripped this door off the wall. He could be totally, totally nuts. I think he was forty, forty-two at the time.

One time Scott was going to go down to the South and do grave rubbings of the great blues artists. My friend Yves Bevais, a producer at Atlantic, hooked me up with Robert Palmer, who wrote *Deep Blues*,[109] an awesome book. So I called Robert Palmer on the phone and he talked to me for an hour or two, just as nice as he could be. He hooked Scott up and told him where to go and do grave rubbings of all the Blues singers down south. Then, on the same trip, he did Martin Luther King's grave. Evidently, the Martin Luther King monument is on the other side of this huge fountain. So he had to go there in the middle of the night, and wade across this huge pool, and there were overhead lights he had to avoid. It turned out to be a huge, huge rubbing.

I would buy one of Scott's paintings from him for about three-hundred-fifty dollars. And then I had this picture framer who would frame it for me for one-hundred-twenty-five dollars. He would come in from Brooklyn. He did a great job, and then I would turn around and sell them for eleven hundred dollars. But I never really tried to make a whole lot of money that way.

STEVE HOUSE

It was great hanging out with Scott when he was fine. But when people were way too high, it would be awful. People would be yelling at each other, "Get out!" There'd be these weird gay fights. Stuff where I'd take my tall boy and say, "Okay! I'll see ya!"

I was around sometimes when Scott was doing his paintings,

though, which was absolutely great! He did the cover for one of our cassettes, a grave rubbing. He inspired me to do it. I went out to Queens and found Johnny Thunders' gravestone. It took me hours to find the grave. I walked up and down every row and found his situated at the bottom of some other family member. It said 'Johnny Genzale, aka Johnny Thunders,' and it was on the same stone as Bobby Genzale. And I filmed myself rubbing it.

ROBERT CAMPBELL

Somehow through his connections, once Scott got these two silk Donna Karan suits. One of them was off-white, and the other was dark blue—both made of beautiful silk. He would wear them with flip flops on his feet, which back then was unheard of. He'd go to these graves and use these big rock-like pieces of crayon. He would get these crayon marks all over these beautiful jackets.

Toward the end of my friendship with Scott, when he started getting crazy—well, when we all did—right near the Chelsea there was a fish store that sold tropical fish and supplies. Scott said "Come on in here with me!" He had an off-white Donna Karan suit on, and he started shoplifting aquarium plants out of the aquariums! He would just reach his hand down into the tank and steal this whole plant and put it in his suit jacket's pocket! His arm was soaking wet! It was ridiculous! And those guys at the fish store didn't say a word to him! When he was stealing those plants out of the aquarium, I was freaking out. I always had cocaine on me, and weed, and I was thinking, "Oh man, why in the hell are you *doing* this?"

And then he took the plants and put them in the aquarium in his room at the Chelsea.

Once, Scott had said to me, "Man, you need this painting." Pretty much, he had given it to me. It was a grave rubbing of Lizzie Borden, Sharon Tate, and all these other names. It was a huge red painting, and beautiful. So I had one of Scott's big paintings in our room.

But one time, Scott and I had a falling out over something

small, because we didn't get together to meet with him somewhere.

After our falling out, he wanted his big, red Lizzie Borden
painting back. And I was angry. I had a big ego. I said, "Forget it!
I'm not giving you the painting back."

That went on for two or three weeks. A friend of Scott's even
came to me, trying to convince me to give it back, and Ellis Duncan tried. Finally, I just said, "Okay, Scott, you can have the picture
back." And we made up. The last time I heard of Scott, he was on
Entertainment Tonight—they had a segment about Studio 54. He
was on that show talking about it, and he had cut his hair.

Helluva Stormé

Stormé (pronounced "Stormy") DeLarverié attained celebrity in certain circles in the 1940s and '50s as the cross dressing emcee for the Jew-
el Box Revue drag act: a woman in top hat and tails emceeing for a troupe
of men in gowns. But what made her really famous—at least in the gay
community—was a punch she threw at a cop, the punch that launched a
thousand queens.

TIM SULLIVAN

Stormé DeLarverié is eighty-six. She is the person that punched
the policeman at Stonewall in 1969.[110] She was a male impersonator. She dressed like a man, and the police were going to arrest
her for wearing men's pants. She's lived in the hotel for a long
time. Stormé's a real character and a real icon in the gay community in New York City. She worked as a bodyguard. She was
the door person at The Duchess, a famous lesbian bar where
they wouldn't let men in.

She hung with everybody, including Charlie Parker.

To the Manner Born: Suzanne Bartsch

Imperious Suzanne Bartsch is a high-class event planner, known in New York circles for the parties she throws for the most mainstream businesspeople as well as for the fringe-dwelling underworld. Some of her best underground friends were the Club Kids, who have their own sordid story.

ELLIS DUNCAN

Suzanne Bartsh lived in the room across from Robert and Carol's room. She is from Switzerland and has been a mover and shaker for years in New York, was giving some of the finest parties at bars and night clubs. She was the ultimate purveyor of camp. You would often see her leaving the Chelsea with a teddy bear backpack and twelve-inch, layered, stacked tennis shoes, which were her trademark. You wondered how the hell she walked on them.

Suzanne Bartsch's young, nubile boyfriend, was a party boy, a male femme fatale named Ty Basset of the Basset furniture fortune. Ty was a very good looking, nice guy, a mover and shaker on the party scene, just post-Studio 54 and pre-Club Kids[111] scene, the ravers who ran around with lollipops in their mouth, or pacifiers, so you couldn't tell they were on Ecstasy, grinding their teeth.

She left Ty and married David Barton, who owns the David Barton gyms. She lived at the Chelsea then, and there were always a lot of the early drag queens coming and going from her apartment—RuPaul, the Lady Bunny, Lahoma Van Zandt, Her Royal Highness Princess Leila Scheherazade Dovima Stratavaria Zoraya—that whole scene.

But Suzanne Bartsch would throw a party, and then she would show up with all these "freaks," at least by Time-Warner standards. And then corporations would also call her in to throw a "New York" party, a straight party for straight people. She traversed both worlds.

JOHN ZINSSER

When we were in 725, our neighbor was Suzanne Bartsch. She had this corner apartment that was adjacent to ours. She wanted to take over our apartment as a nursery for their child.

She kept phoning me over and over, saying in this vampy voice of hers, "I vahnt your apahtment."

I didn't know what to do. I wanted to stay at the Chelsea. But because she had some influence there, she was able to finagle it with Stanley Bard that maybe we could look at some other apartments elsewhere in the building and make a parallel move. We were pretty friendly with the staff there. We knew the bellman named Timur.

Timur said to me, "You know, the most beautiful apartment is 622. It's a room that they reserve for photoshoots." It's this beautiful period room with a back bay window.

I thought, "Wow, this is interesting!"

So I went to talk to Stanley. He said, "Yeah, yeah, let me try to find you something else."

He starts showing me these awful, awful apartments. At the time the Chelsea's rooms that he might convert to rentals were terrible. They had these horrible stucco walls and wall-to-wall carpeting. Tourists who go stay at the Chelsea are often disappointed because of these horrible rooms. Stanley was showing me these dark rooms with no character.

I said, "What about 622?"

He rolled his eyes and thought about it. He agreed to show it to us. Unlike these other rooms, 622 had the original wood floor, the fireplace with all the original tile. The Chelsea was built as co-op apartments, and this room had been the parlor room of a larger apartment, so it had this kind of yoke between two rooms that you could hang a velvet curtain from in Victorian times. On one end, it had a bay window looking south. On the other end, it had a full-length, floor-to-ceiling, framed mirror, so the light came into the room in this beautiful way and filled it up in a corridor of light. Even though it was a one-room apartment, and the kitchen had been carved out of a closet space, it had a beautiful generosity of scale.

If you look at the map of the rooms on the landings that shows the fire exits, it shows the configurations of the rooms, you see that 622 is the largest single room on any given floor.

Stanley begrudgingly said we could have it. It was a triumph for us because we'd been admitted to the inner sanctum and had this beautiful, beautiful apartment that was protected, secluded, and very special. I could have stayed there forever, but we had children. I subsequently traded a painting for a slight reduction in rent. It was my understanding that if I had stayed in 622, the rent would stay the same into perpetuity. So it was a tough thing to give up.

Umberto and Schizo: Punk Aristocrats

The couple Umberto and Schizo may have reached their pinnacle of fame when they were mentioned in a *New York Times* article, in which journalist Michael T. Kaufman described Schizo, a rock and roll singer/songwriter, as such: "a woman with clouds of red curls, very short shorts and at least four rings stapled between her upper lip and the bridge of her nose."[112] Schizo told Kaufman that the ghosts roaming the Chelsea were the muses that inspired her songwriting.

JERRY WEINSTEIN
Schizo was a punk rock singer who opened for Nina Hagen,[113] a European who specialized in shrieking. It's not my kind of music. So Schizo was the opening act, and Umberto, her boyfriend, was a manager and a rock and roll person. He inherited a lot of money from his father. He was German, but he lived in Italy. That's where he met Schizo.

PAUL VOLMER
Umberto and Schizo were definitely interesting. They were a couple who, the best I could gather, had some money. At least Umberto, an Italian count, had money. They had a very nice room. Schizo's name was pronounced in German like *Skeetzo*,

as in *skeetzo-phrenia.* Umberto had his own band that would perform Iggy Pop covers. He also promoted Schizo and hired different musicians for the band and recorded them with his money. His main work was trying to promote his wife. She had bright red hair and sort of a Nina Hagen look.

ROBERT CAMPBELL

Umberto decided to sell his countship, his nobility. He had his up for sale for $120,000. One time I went out in the hallway and Umberto was spray painting his shoes that looked like they came off the Joe Jackson *Look Sharp* album cover. He was spray painting his shoes turquoise!

"What are you doing, Umberto?"

He said in his thick Italian accent, "Oh, I am getting married tomorrow."

His bride-to-be, Schizo, was really freaky. She had a pocketbook that looked like a cat. And she was wearing these really slutty clothes despite the fact that she was pushing fifty. She was very strange. She would go to CBGBs and have all these great musicians playing in her band. So they were in my room one night partying, and they were talking about how they were going to spend ten thousand dollars on a breast job.

And I said to her, "Well, why don't you just get a new wig?" I said it in total innocence. To me, her wig had looked like it was made out of a broom! Except it was red.

I was later told that after I had made the wig statement to her, she almost jumped out the window. She wouldn't leave their room for two weeks.

TIM SULLIVAN

Schizo idolized Iggy Pop. So she got a bunch of musicians together—including myself—but I only did roadie work for them—and did a bunch of gigs at CBGBs. They were an Iggy Pop cover band. She did all these songs like "Now I Wanna be Your Dog," all of Iggy's worst stuff.

They were trying to write songs, and they even got Dee Dee to work with them on some songs. And I think they actually recorded them—Umberto was going to be their big promoter. Umberto ended up smoking crack and hanging out with some trannie and doing the whole crack scene.

They were also friends with Nina Hagen. Nina Hagen used to come by the hotel all the time and hang out with Dee Dee. They wrote a couple of songs together.

So for about five years, Umberto and Schizo were going to be big rock stars living at the Chelsea Hotel. Then they finally ended up owing Stanley so much money that they had to leave. They went out to West Hollywood, and that's the last I've heard of them.

MARLOWE WEST

Schizo was a crazy chick! She had poodles the same color as her hair. I loved her! I go for that kind of Bohemian thing. She had spirit! One time I crossed paths with her when she and her group were just leaving a recording studio. So we had this little camaraderie because we'd see each other at the Chelsea, and we recorded at the same recording studio. I thought she was pretty neat looking. She sort of had a thing going like Dee Snyder, that guy from Twisted Sister. She looked like him but with henna-colored hair, all curly and frizzy and bushy. She must have hennaed her poodles too. What a sight!

When they were walking down the street, you knew they were going into the Chelsea! She and Umberto had a very serious type vibration. They weren't clowns, even though she looked clownish. And Umberto would have the colored hair and wear neon chartreuse clothes, and just be "Crash!" He'd be a billboard. But I love that! I used to try to encourage her. When I saw her, I'd say "Hey!" rather than saying "What the hell are you?" I like to bring that part out in people.

Marilyn Knew What Crazy Looked Like

Some Chelsea celebrities are celebrities only at the Chelsea. They're not Arthur Miller, Picasso or Dylan, but as someone used to say, "I'm sure they each had their own contribution to the world." The first, Marilyn, contributes a chilling episode in an elevator.

ROBERT CAMPBELL

When I moved into 723, this woman named Marilyn lived next to me. She worked in a mental hospital. She was always saying that Janis Joplin used to come over to her room with a Pepsi can full of Southern Comfort and be saying, "Please don't be mad at my loud music."

PAUL VOLMER

Marilyn knew what crazy looked like, and she said to me, "You know, I rode up the Chelsea elevator with the woman who shot Andy Warhol," she said. 'When I got off the elevator, I said to my friend that's the craziest person I have ever seen, and she's going to try to kill someone.'" And not long after that encounter, this woman she saw in the elevator tried to murder Warhol.

In fact, the woman, Valerie Jean Solanas, was headed up the elevator to the Factory to shoot Warhol. Warhol's health was never the same after the shooting, and it is generally believed that it began the gradual decline of his career.

The General

The unnerving thing about some residents at the Chelsea is you could never be sure they were who they said they were or did what they say they did. One of these was an Irishman known only as "The General."

JOHN ZINSSER

When we were living in 622, there was a guy who would intermittently show up at the Chelsea. He was Irish, and he would stay in one of the transient rooms, or student rooms, these rooms that had no bathroom. You had to use the bathroom down the hall. This guy would wear a dark gray military trench coat with a sash belt and epaulets. On his head, he wore a beret. He was a large man, about two hundred pounds, very imposing, very paramilitary. He would stay for about a month at a time, during which he would get on these incredible drunks.

He would go down to the lobby and fight with the hotel staff, or with Stanley. They would get into these screaming fights with him, and then he would disappear upstairs again. I don't know if they were fighting about rent or whatever.

This guy was like the general who had come to stay, like the Al Pacino character in *Scent of a Woman*. He was this scary, scary guy.

So one time I was in the elevator there. The elevators at the Chelsea are infamously slow and irregular and won't stop on your floor. You would end up trapped with people for an indeterminate amount of time in these fairly small elevators.

This Irish paramilitary guy was in one of his drunks, and he said to me, "I need to show you something."

His whole obsession was that nobody would acknowledge who he really was—nobody understood that he was this important person.

He said to me, "I am in charge of the IRA in America. I'm the liaison between the IRA and the U.S. I want to prove this to you."

"Great," I was thinking. "What is this going to be?"

I don't know why—curiosity, I guess—but I followed him into his student room, with wood floor planking, a bed, a sink in the corner, and a window. Like an eight-by-eight-foot room. But on the floor was this big duffel bag with a zipper down the middle. He opened up the zipper, and the entire bag was filled with paper files in file folders, as if it had been taken out of some file cabinet somewhere.

"All the proof," he said, "is here."

I was mortified.

"Okay, it's great to meet you!" I said, as I backed out the door. "I understand that you're involved in something really important and I respect that!"

For him, this was proof that he was actually the person he said he was. But for me, when I thought about it later, I figured that when this guy sobered up—and if in fact he was telling the truth—he was going to come kill me, in a "Now that I've told you who I really am, I have to kill you" sort of way!

Fuchsia Gold's Mushroom Tea Parties

You may remember Fuchsia Gold from when she chased her male slave Nelson around the lobby with her whip. But Fuchsia was more than a dominatrix, she had a nurturing side, very Italian. For one, she brewed a mean cup of magic mushroom tea.

PAUL VOLMER
Fuchsia was such a unique person—when I met her, she had sort of a Boy George look going on, with that hair cascading down the side, and she used to do her eyes like cat eyes, sort of pointed up at the ends, and of course she wore lots of lipstick.

DAVID LAWTON
Fuchsia was always in black, or maybe shiny stuff, leather or pleather. Heavy makeup. She had that real East Village look.

PAUL VOLMER
When Fuchsia got into the profession of dominatrix, she would tease her hair up with this goop called "Stiff Stuff." Her hair literally stuck two feet up in the air, and then from that high up it would begin to curl down. Sort of like Divine. Fuchsia was only in her early twenties, but she would get herself dressed up in the complete S&M gear, with patent leather thigh boots and leather bustier. She even had a whip she would carry around. She was a pretty good-looking girl, of Italian descent with an Italian nose,

but good looking with a very strong personality, very intelligent and cultured. Some people did find her hot, and she had her sex appeal. But she had this personality that was almost masculine—she was so tough.

She wouldn't take any shit from anyone. She spoke very forthrightly. As a dominatrix, she used to make pretty good money. First she had been staying in a pretty small room, but then she moved up to a bigger room, where she would have these mushroom tea parties all the time. So we would all go up there and drink her mushroom tea and smoke weed and drink booze, and have this completely debauched evening. She would cook, making Italian dishes for her friends. She was a very good cook.

She wouldn't talk about the dominatrix business very much. When she got off work, she would get into casual jeans and a t-shirt and just hang out and be the hostess. But when she went out to rock clubs, she was into pagan symbols and the Goth look.

She had a boyfriend named Drago then, an immigrant from some Eastern European country. I don't believe he was a legal immigrant, so he couldn't really get work very easily. But he had actually come across a job as an actor working in an independent film, playing a cab driver. It was set in New York's meatpacking district. It was a bare-bones independent film. But when we were going through this stage of having these mushroom tea parties, and partying all night, we'd still be there in the complete depths of the night, at two in the morning.

That also happened to be the only time when the streets were clear in the meatpacking district, so you could shoot your film without a lot of traffic around. So Drago would come out in his bathrobe with his toothbrush and tell us in his Eastern European accent, "I've got to go to verk." Then he would do all his toiletries, as if he were getting up at seven a.m. to go to work at a regular job, while the rest of us were just partying with abandon.

Fuchsia also worked as a stripper at this place called Billy's down on Twenty-third and Sixth. She used to cop coke in that bar—there was so much coke there. I went there a couple of times to pick her up after work, but I got embarrassed by the nudity and stuff. But once when I visited Billy's, and she was stripping on stage, she got everyone to sing the songs that accompanied her dancing. As she danced, she had all these degenerate strip bar patrons singing like an old-fashioned sing-along!

Neicy: Edie's Ghost?

Neicy, the pouty punk with whom bellman Paul Volmer shared a complicated relationship, managed to get herself known around the Chelsea. Sometimes she caused trouble indirectly—it was Neicy whom Marlowe tried to date before he fell off the fire escape. Other times she caused trouble straight on. The fact that she was beautiful didn't help.

PAUL VOLMER

A lot of people, the punks, would come to the Chelsea to see Sid Vicious's old room. My ex-girlfriend was one of them. We called her Neicy, a nickname taken from Denise. When she first came to the hotel from Philadelphia, I didn't know her yet, and I thought she was just one of these punks from out of town. She was wearing torn fishnets and stiletto heels and a leather skirt and bustier, elbow-length black gloves, and her hair was all teased up. And black lipstick. She was very sexy and beautiful. But I was very cynical at the time. Some of the punks who visited Sid's room were *real* punks and others were just having a little fashion show.

So I was lounging over to the side and I asked her. "Oh, what are you, a poseur or the real thing?"

And she said, "Fuck you." Which was kind of punk. They were into "fuck you" and spitting and being ornery. Because of that "Fuck you" I immediately fell in love with her and let her stay with me in my room.

Punks came to the Chelsea from all over. These were the alienated kids from all over the country, and Sid Vicious' room was sort of a shrine to them. They'd come to the front desk and ask "Where's Sid's room?" The desk clerks would brush them off and say, "It's not there anymore. We've changed things around." And in fact they had made the room into part of a suite, but of course the room was still there!

So Neicy wanted to see Sid's room. She knocked on the door with her friend. She was eighteen, and had all of this kind of sexy punk style, but she actually had this cute little bubbly personality.

When she came to the door, she said, "Oh! Oh! This is Sid's room! I see it!" Of course the guy who had rented the suite was not aware that he had rented Sid's room, but because she was so cute and young and charming, he let her in. She ran into the bathroom, because that's where Nancy died. And she was looking at the walls.

"Oh! Oh! There's bloodstains under the *sink*! There's bloodstains under the *sink*!" They may have been rust stains, or they could have been bloodstains, who knows? Maybe they hadn't quite done a good painting job. But the guy who was now living in the room probably never knew he had bloodstains and murder and horror under his sink until then!

Neicy was a very amusing girl, very bold. She liked to do what she called "bothering people" but it was all in a very fun spirit. She would walk down the street and engage complete strangers and talk to them, from the dowdiest looking person to the richest, most elegant person. She was full of life. One time there was a cop in the deli, and the cop wasn't very tall. She took off his hat with one hand and mussed up his hair with the other, and then put his hat back on. Pretty bold thing to do to a New York cop!

The cop was completely taken aback! He was flustered— he didn't know what to do, just standing there with a befuddled look on his face.

She came into New York and the Chelsea with one of her girlfriends from Philly. There was a girl in the lobby named Sasha, who was staying at the hotel and apparently had been taking some amphetamines. She was very nervous and talking a mile a minute. She was a manic and kind of nutty girl anyway. So Neicy and her girlfriend were in my room, and they invited Sasha up. They were very much into makeup and dressing up—plus it was really hot outside, in the middle of summer, so they were sitting around in their underwear and decided to paint Sasha sort of like Goldie Hawn on *Laugh-In*, with all sorts of funny little sayings and pictures and flowers painted on her skin.

All she was wearing were panties. And Neicy and her friend were only wearing their bras and panties, amusing themselves in the heat.

I was working as bellman at the time, and when I came through the lobby, the phone operator said to me, "Your crazy girlfriends have gone out with that nutty girl. They're almost completely naked, and they just went out the front door!" So I went out after them. And there they were, Neicy and her friend walking on either side of Sasha. Neicy and her friend had wrapped sheets around themselves, so it looked like they had gowns on. But the nutty girl only had on her panties and a little jean jacket.

Meanwhile, outside the Chelsea—this was in the evening—there was a black nightclub called *Savage*. Standing outside was a line of maybe one hundred black couples—high class black couples—waiting for the club to open. So as I was coming out of the Chelsea, Neicy and her friend and Sasha were strolling past this line of all these black people.

Neicy and her friend suddenly squealed "Take it off, Sasha! Show them your artwork! Show them your art!" So Sasha took off her jean jacket and just strutted topless by this whole line of people! I was running after them and I expected the people in line to have some sort of reaction to it. But they were completely in shock. I ran up to the girls and said, "You're not really dressed for that, are you? You're going to get a cold!" and coaxed them back into the hotel room. They probably would have gone clubbing half naked.

Pimp My Room

We've already established that some of the Chelsea's more colorful characters lived on the other side of the law. Stanley Bard would let them move in as part of his management strategy—remaining sensitive to the economy. When times were good, he rented rooms to a more respectable bunch of artists. When the economy stank, as it did during much of the 80s, he adapted by renting rooms to pimps, prostitutes, and drug dealers. They always paid on time.

In her book *At the Chelsea*, Florence Turner adds that she and her artist friends were always thankful when they saw a pimp had moved in. Then Stanley would ease the pressure on the artists who owed him money. "The pimps, unknowingly," she wrote, "were patrons of the arts."

PAUL VOLMER

Pimps lived there, even pimps with hookers who lived in their rooms. As long as they didn't turn tricks in the hotel, they could live there. Stanley would turn a blind eye to just about whatever went on.

MARLOWE WEST

Sometimes Paul and I and the guys in Skin Tight would get wind of a party in some room. We'd show up and be like "Whoa!" because it seemed like there was more than a party going on there; there was a feeling of some kind of business dealing about it, like a connection for drugs or prostitution. So we would just politely thank them and make our way out.

JERRY WEINSTEIN

We used to take in some pretty rough guys. We had several hookers, for example. One of the shticks I used on the hotel tours I used to give was that the Chelsea was "a very fertile place." Arthur Miller wrote many plays when he got here. Brendan Behan's only child was born when he lived here. A lot of writers do very well here. Jacob Dylan was conceived here. So it's a very creative place. We used to say that it was so fertile at the Chelsea that even the hookers got pregnant!

TIM SULLIVAN
Coffie was a big black guy, a pimp who had about five girls, and they were all gorgeous. He was your classic pimp, and a nice guy. Nobody bothered the pimps. If you want the truth though, it was scary! You had to kind of look over your shoulder and watch who you invited in your room.

PAUL VOLMER
One time when I was working, Coffie had a disagreement with me. I had asked him not to talk to my girlfriend, and he came in once late at night. He was high on crack, and he threw me against the wall and threatened me. I told Stanley that this guy should go, and the people at the desk backed me up. But because this guy was paid up on his rent, Stanley continued to let him stay there. A few weeks later, Coffie pulled a gun on Stanley. I guess Stanley saw this as reason enough to finally get rid of him.

TIM SULLIVAN
Andre the Russian was another pimp who had a couple of prostitutes working for him. They were all freebase cocaine addicts, always chasing the freebase. His girlfriend, who was a street prostitute, ended up getting her head cut off by a serial murderer who murdered all these prostitutes. His name was Bernie something.

She was a street prostitute, and life is rough for them.

ROBERT CAMPBELL
There was this guy Doc—he was a schoolteacher in New York City, but he also had these prostitutes. During the day he was a schoolteacher, and at night, he was a pimp! Doc and Viva, the former Warhol supserstar, used to get into these big fights forever. Doc would take his dog down in front of Viva's room every single morning and have the dog take a shit in front of her door on the doormat. Then Viva would go down to Stanley and raise hell about it. "Get Doc out of here!" She tried all kinds of ways to get Doc out of the Chelsea.

Frankie Nickel-and-Dime: The Candy Man

If Stanley couldn't find a dependable pimp to rent a room, he was sure to find a dependable drug dealer, and Frank Meyer was one reliable drug dealer.

PAUL VOLMER

Frank's room was like a pharmaceutical shop. You could go there and he would sell you whatever you wanted—heroin, cocaine, three kinds of pot. When some hallucinogens came through, he had those—he had a little bit of everything. And as long as they paid their rent, Stanley would let such people operate with impunity.

Former residents Paul and Anna Lee Romero were customers of Mr. Meyer, whom they nicknamed "Frankie Nickel-and-Dime." Once, though, Stanley Bard intervened. He had noticed Anna going up to Frank's apartment, so he took her aside and warned her to stay away from him because Frank was bad news. Bard told her he had seen how Meyers had gotten other women addicted to heroin and the results were not pretty. Anna Lee was touched by Stanley Bard's concern, but ignored his advice. The results were predictable.

What's especially interesting here is how Mr. Bard remained fully aware of Frank Meyer's dirty dealings, even warning people about the menace surrounding him, but did nothing to stop it. After all, Frank always paid his rent on time.

PAUL VOLMER

Frank sat in this chair in his room that was raised up on a platform in his room with a desk in front of him. People would come in to cop and they would have to sit down in a chair that was lower than his—he was like a corporate executive that way. He was also a carpenter, a really good carpenter. That's how he was able to make this platform. I helped him build that platform.

JAMES RASIN

His desk on its platform was completely surrounded by stereo equipment. Like racks of stereo receivers and speakers lining the walls. And two models—as in girls—tall blondes, screwed up on whatever drug, hanging around him, one on either side of him. Frank would sit there like Bartleby the Scrivener at this raised desk for days and days. He had lots of locks on his doors. He was sharing a room with Rene Ricard, and one day I went down to visit with Rene, and I saw this room. I thought, "What is it with this room? It has six dead bolts on the door!"

PAUL VOLMER

What was funny about Frank was that he had his own drug habit. He would snort these really, really skinny lines of heroin all the time. So he would sit there conducting drug deals all day, and never leave his chair. Eventually he got edema on his legs, just from sitting still all day doing small lines of heroin! All these different kinds of people parading through to buy this or that kind of drug, and between customers, he'd be doing his own drugs.

Eventually, a New York City SWAT team came through the lobby looking for Frank. They pulled a gun on the phone operator at the lobby desk. Apparently a lot of the phone operators in the lobby were being paid off by the drug dealers. If the cops came into the hotel, the operators downstairs would phone the drug dealers upstairs and tell them to dump everything down the toilet.

But this time when the cops came, they pulled a gun on the operator herself. The rest of the cops rushed past her upstairs and arrested Frank. He got thrown out of the hotel. Apparently, at that point he didn't have a criminal record at all, so he didn't go to prison. He had been dealing drugs for years and had never been busted.

But apparently he finally did get busted again just a couple of years ago. I suppose it was probably the best thing that ever happened to him, getting busted. He needed to get out of that chair!

I guess Frank really wasn't that bad a guy. After all, he was filling a need. Frank's a survivor. Some people are survivors.

The Chelsea Movie Palace

Numerous filmmakers have taken advantage of the Chelsea's shabby gothic *mise en scene*. The most famous, of course, is Alex Cox's *Sid and Nancy*.[114]

TIM SULLIVAN

When they made *Sid and Nancy* at the Chelsea, I remember watching the director, Alex Cox, telling Gary Oldman and Chloe Webb what they should do, how they should act. He was a real hands-on director—he also directed *Repo Man*. *Sid and Nancy* was the first feature film shot on a digital camera, and it came out in eighty-six. This was only seven years after the actual events.

JULIE EAKIN

For *Sid and Nancy,* the film crew had a huge electrical cord coming out of our room, so our door wouldn't close entirely because they were using part of our power. It knocked the lights out a couple of times, that sort of thing. We were used to people being there all the time. I don't know that it felt particularly glamorous, but then to see it on film is always great.

PAUL VOLMER

I got hold of this movie lamp that had been left behind from the filming of *Sid and Nancy.* It was the old-fashioned kind of movie light with a big cast metal housing and flaps on the sides, and at least five feet tall. It needed a new plug and a new bulb, so I fixed that stuff up. I painted it and put Marlowe's glitter on it, and then I went to a theatrical lighting shop on 42nd Street and bought all these different gels that you would smear on the glass housing over the bulb. At different times, it would light up the room all red, or all green, or purple. Finally, when I ran out of money, I sold it to the bellman Timur for a hundred bucks.

When they were making *Sid and Nancy,* the film crew noticed Fuchsia the dominatrix there. They wanted her to be in the movie. But they made a crucial mistake. She had a room like mine, without a shower, so the shower was down the hall. One morning they went by her room first, and she wasn't there. So they heard that someone was in the shower down the hall. They knocked on the shower door and said, "Um, hello, we're with the *Sid and Nancy* movie? We'd like to know if you would like to be in the movie?"

"Fuck you!" she yelled out at these movie guys. "I'm taking a shower! Who are you fuckers to bother me when I'm in the shower?"

She scared them off. It's kind of sad because she could have been in that movie and achieved a small amount of fame.

ROBERT CAMPBELL

Once, when they were making *Sid and Nancy*, Gary Oldman visited Paul's room. Paul must've made friends with the director, or some of the people in the movie. Gary Oldman got into Paul's room—I think he was still in his Sid Vicious costume—and he was appalled! It wasn't like they were laying out big, heavy drugs because Paul wasn't a heavy drug user. It was just a roomful of freaks smoking weed, but Oldman was just disgusted. I'm sure it was Paul's disgusting room, too. By the same token, Oldman must have liked something about the Chelsea because he's made four or five movies there. He did *Romeo's Bleeding*, and he did *The Professional*. Then he was in that *Basquiat* movie, some of which was shot inside the Chelsea.

In a 2011 interview, Oldman doesn't mention Volmer's room at the Chelsea but does describe his own room, where he stayed to do research for the film. "When I turned on the light," Oldman said, "there were cockroaches crawling over the phone. I immediately checked out."[115]

PAUL VOLMER

The film *Sid and Nancy* is a wonderful account of them and the scene at the time. It has a poetic undercurrent, even amidst all of this trashy stuff going on, Sid taking drugs and all. It's also sort of a fun and goofy love affair between them, almost endearing. That movie did more than anything else to make icons out of Sid and Nancy. If it hadn't been made, their story would probably have never reached the mainstream. The movie implies that there wasn't so much a suicide pact between them, but more that Nancy had a death wish and was bringing Sid along with her, goading him into it. Maybe that was true.

Sid and Nancy, as effective as it is artistically, accepts the official view that Sid Vicious killed Nancy Spungen. And thanks to the New York police, who didn't bother to conduct a thorough investigation because they assumed, naturally, that Sid was the culprit, and because Sid was in such a heroin stupor that he didn't remember a thing, we will probably never know what happened that night. But Chelsea residents have their own theories. Naturally, they contradict the party line.

TIM SULLIVAN

The theory around here is that Sid didn't kill Nancy, but this other guy, Rockets Redglare,[116] did. Rockets Redglare was this guy in a punk band, and also in the movie *Tree's Lounge*, and a lot of other movies. He always played a seedy character. Anyway, he was the last guy seen leaving the room. And he was a notorious thief and a heroin dealer. He probably went there and sold the heroin and wanted his money and got pissed off. He was a violent guy, and he probably killed her. He was also a misogynist—a very scary guy. We were at The World in 1986, and somebody said, "That's Rockets Redglare over there." He was this big fat guy with glasses and greasy hair. This friend of mine, Claudia, was being stalked by him. He was saying really scary things to her. I didn't know about the Sid Vicious thing at the time, but it was doubly spooky when I found out. Everybody told me, "Whoa, stay away from *that* guy." He was living here a few years ago, just before he died.

The rumor here in the hotel was that Rockets killed Nancy. Somebody even asked him once, and he answered sarcastically, "Yeah, I killed her."

JULIE EAKIN

Besides *Sid and Nancy,* there were several movies filmed when we were there. A film with Kim Basinger and Micky Rourke called *9½ Weeks* was also filmed there. I remember going up in the elevator a couple of times with Kim Basinger. She looked pretty distraught—I don't know if that was what was going on with her character too.

PAUL VOLMER

Warhol's movie *Chelsea Girls,* about girls who lived in the hotel, was the first example of reality TV.

TIM SULLIVAN

Warhol's *Chelsea Girls* film, you have to look at as art, and as a time capsule, and now with reality TV, the 15 minutes of fame thing has come absolutely true. Television now is 90 percent reality shows. Everybody's trying to get on the next reality show so they'll be famous for fifteen minutes. Warhol started it all.

Chelsea as Madhouse—Really

For wealthy people with mentally ill sons or daughters, the last resort was to put them in a mental institution. For those who weren't dangerous to themselves or others, another sort of institution might be in order, a residence hotel where the membrane between madness and sanity had long since frayed.

TIM SULLIVAN

The Chelsea is kind of a warehouse for rich families to put their crazy kids. It happens at any hotel, but this one in particular. During the seventies and eighties, a lot of families put their schizophrenic kids here. That way, the parents could keep an eye on them. I knew a lot of them. You realize pretty quickly that you can't get too close to them. Often, they had some kind of family money. One such guy lived on the first floor right over the front of the awning. He was super rich, but a horrible heroin addict with a two-thousand-dollar-a-day heroin habit. He was a musician with a big amplifier, and he would play up there. I think I went into his room once—it was just a wall of amplifiers. He spent the rest of his money on heroin. I remember seeing him fall down the stairs once. There were a lot of guys like that.

Stanley just dealt with them.

PAUL VOLMER

Winnie Purcell came from a family that owned a department store in Palm Beach, a very good family. She was one of these people whose family helped them out, and she was a really good artist. She took classes at the Art Students' League. One of her paintings is in the Chelsea lobby, in the phone room. She was a really good artist. She always wore sunglasses, and she was a short woman, attractive, and a drinker. She really liked to drink and paint. Of all the different kinds of artists I met at the Chelsea, for some reason it was the painters who drank the most. Alcohol seemed to be their drug of choice.

One time she painted a profile of this friend of ours, Rick. He had curly brown hair, and she did the painting in many different flat colors, like a Gauguin painting. It was beautiful. But because she had been so drunk, when I came in the next day, I asked, "Where's that beautiful painting of Rick?"

"I just painted it over."

She was a good person who had a husky dog. You were allowed to have a dog at the hotel, so there were a lot of dog people there, walking their dogs in and out. She was one of the dog people. She eventually moved back to Florida.

One of the things I did when I lived at the hotel was invite people I met in the lobby up to my room and sort of interview them, ask them about their lives. One man I invited up was named John Cram—a member of a very eminent family, and he had an indentation in his forehead, as if his skull were made out of Play-Doh and someone had pushed their thumb into it. How he got it was, he went to Africa as a graduate student, an anthropologist. The natives there threw a spear that stuck in his head and had to be removed. The hole was a remnant of his having a spear embedded in his head. He was intelligent, but he talked kind of slowly.

JERRY WEINSTEIN

John Cram was a resident for many, many years, a very, very wealthy guy who had a hole in his head. He woke up one day and didn't even know how he got it. But he wasn't very artistic. He was much more of a financial person, involved in the market. He woke up one day, and there it was, a hole in his head!

MARLOWE WEST

I'm telling you, the Chelsea was full of Dick Tracy type characters. I think this guy John Cram was German. He was very strict-seeming. The dent in his forehead made me think, "Oh, *shit!*"

Don Who?

PAUL VOLMER

Speaking of freaks, there was a character when I first arrived at the hotel named Don Normal. Don Normal had a ZZ Top-style red beard with two points, and he would wear a caveman sarong over one shoulder and platform shoes. And then he had a three-inch long piece of pipe, maybe one inch in diameter, that he had shoved through his ear. That was his nickname, Don Normal. After he moved out of the hotel, he ran a bar in the East Village called the Normal Bar.

The thing Chelsea dwellers all said about Don Normal was once you got past his Viking cave man get-up, he was actually a very normal guy with whom you could sit and have a very normal conversation.

And aren't dentists artists too? Especially those who specialize in cosmetic dentistry, as did Dr. Peter Ferro, in Room 614.

JOHN ZINSSER

On the sixth floor, there was a dentist's office![117] That's another thing that struck me as really creepy, like the guru's chanting group on the same floor. I couldn't imagine a creepier place to go to the dentist than at the Chelsea, and think about all the gas and syringes. It's like Dr. Benway in William Burroughs' *Naked Lunch*!

Children of the Chelsea

A lesser known aspect of the Chelsea scene was that children lived there. And not just Bohemian ragamuffins, but well-scrubbed children who went to school, had good manners and frolicked in the halls. One of the more famous children was Gaby Hoffman, daughter of Viva, the Warhol superstar. As mentioned earlier, Gaby has herself grown up to become a minor star.

JOHN ZINSSER

The little children who lived at the Chelsea seemed great! Every year on Halloween, the kids would trick or treat, and you could hear them at the top of the stairs because the stairs go all the way down. You could hear this rush of activity. They'd come streaming down and go to any room whose door was open. I always envied the parents because in the Chelsea, we were never privy to other peoples' rooms. Because of all these mysterious doorways and mysterious characters, you were always intensely curious as to what other rooms looked like. You would hear about things—like there were these beautiful apartments on the top floors that had roof gardens, but you never saw them! But the parents bringing their kids trick or treating could peek into other peoples' rooms.

Old Chelsea Haunts

Finally, when talking about residents of the Chelsea, you can't ignore the ghosts. They say the most haunted locales are hospitals and cemeteries, where people die and stay dead, respectively. But a lot of people die in apartment buildings and residence hotels like the Chelsea. It deserves ranking among America's most haunted. Most everyone who lived at the Chelsea has a ghost story or two. Some of them are playful—others troubling.

PAUL VOLMER

Once, a neighbor of mine gave me a couple hits of acid. Now I wasn't really sure if I was interested in acid, especially after seeing my acquaintance Adrian freak out when his leg absorbed the forty hits and he ended up on Letterman. So, I didn't want to bother with it. I put the acid aside on the dresser. So, of course, while I was doing my rounds as night watchman of the building, Neicy found it and took it.

I came down to the first floor, which is where Sid was supposed to have killed Nancy, and there was Neicy standing right there in that apartment and talking to someone. But no one was there talking back to her! Neicy was gesturing and having an animated conversation with, I guess, a ghost. A friendly talk. I could definitely tell it was a lively conversation she was having with this ghost! I walked up to her and said, "Neicy, who are you talking to?"

"I'm talking to Nancy," she said.

"Well, it's very late," I said. "I think it's time for you and Nancy to go to bed." I coaxed Neicy out of the room and brought her back home to sleep. I didn't think Nancy Spungen would be a very good influence. But Neicy had taken one of those hits of acid, and it made her go and talk with the spirit world.

Afterwards, Neicy didn't want to talk about it. I think it scared her and she didn't want to relive it.

Some people have said there are ghosts at the Chelsea, and it does seem like a possibility. There is a feeling of ghosts, such a feeling of serendipity there. I met people who had been on the fringes of the Kerouac scene, or of the Warhol scene. Ghosts of times past. I met one of Nico's ex-husbands. Lots of writers lived there. There were all of these lingering connections to bigger movements who felt like they were still there, kind of like ghosts.

MARLOWE WEST

You could feel stuff like ghosts at the hotel. It was creepy because of all the people who had died in there. It kind of had a glamor for death. But I was more into the happier things. Remember, I'm the one who used to stand out on the balcony and throw glitter!

JULIE EAKIN

There were two elevators—one of them would always stop on the first floor, no matter what you pushed. The first floor was where Edie Sedgwick had lived and I think it was also the Sid and Nancy floor. It was the doomed floor, and the elevator would always open there on its own. It was creepy, but in a good way. They were always trying to fix it, and it never got fixed.

TIM SULLIVAN

There are a lot of interesting ghost stories, but I've never experienced any ghosts here. One of the things that I've learned is that people who come here for the first time, and don't really know anything about the Chelsea, often have unusual experiences or unusual dreams. They'll see something—or something will visit them. There's a force here, a presence.

JOHN ZINSSER

The Chelsea Hotel definitely begins to occupy your dreams. You dream these imagined spaces. There's always a sense that there's a secret wall, or behind some door there's something else. I still have those dreams to this day, because it's so much about individual personalities occupying these kinds of spaces, and secrets, and layers of experience.

For what it's worth, one afternoon during my second research trip to the Chelsea, I had lain down on my creaky bed for a brief nap before my 1:30 interview with Tim Sullivan. Usually, with such little naps, I don't actually fall asleep, but rather settle into a reverie somewhere between waking and sleeping. After five or ten minutes, I'm completely refreshed.

This time, though, I was exhausted. I fell like a brick into solid sleep. Suddenly I felt a firm, distinct tap on my right shoulder, as if by someone's finger. Not aggressive, just determined. I woke up and turned to see what time it was: 1:25.

A Chelsea spirit, reminding me of my appointment?

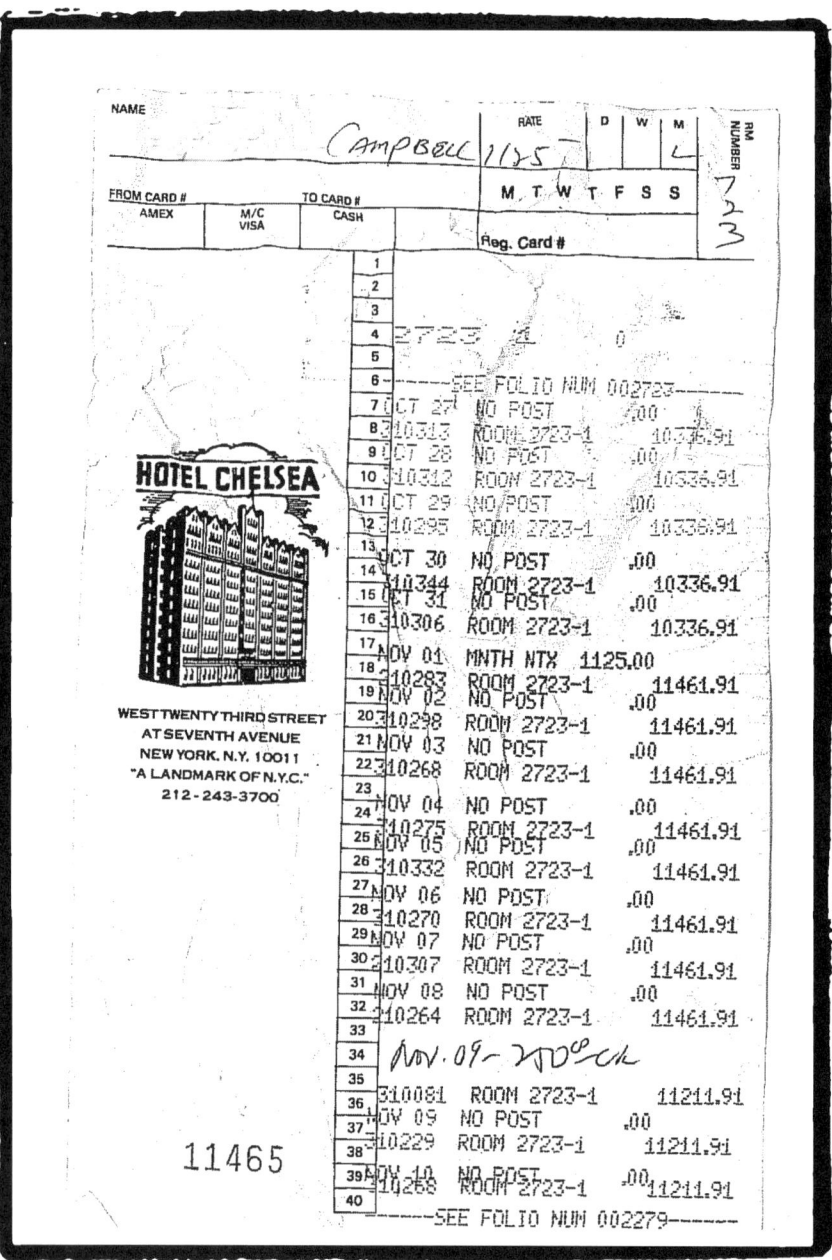

NAME			RATE	D	W	M	RM NUMBER

CAMPBELL 1125

FROM CARD #		TO CARD #	M	T	W	T	F	S	S
AMEX	M/C VISA	CASH							

Reg. Card #

```
 1
 2
 3
 4   2723    4         0
 5
 6  ------SEE FOLIO NUM 002723------
 7  OCT 27   NO POST        .00
 8  310313   ROOM 2723-1    10336.91
 9  OCT 28   NO POST        .00
10  310312   ROOM 2723-1    10336.91
11  OCT 29   NO POST        .00
12  310295   ROOM 2723-1    10336.91
13
14  OCT 30   NO POST        .00
15  310344   ROOM 2723-1    10336.91
16  OCT 31   NO POST        .00
    310306   ROOM 2723-1    10336.91
17
18  NOV 01   MNTH NTX   1125.00
19  310283   ROOM 2723-1    11461.91
20  NOV 02   NO POST        .00
21  310298   ROOM 2723-1    11461.91
22  NOV 03   NO POST        .00
23  310268   ROOM 2723-1    11461.91
24  NOV 04   NO POST        .00
25  310275   ROOM 2723-1    11461.91
26  NOV 05   NO POST        .00
27  310332   ROOM 2723-1    11461.91
28  NOV 06   NO POST        .00
29  310270   ROOM 2723-1    11461.91
30  NOV 07   NO POST        .00
31  310307   ROOM 2723-1    11461.91
32  NOV 08   NO POST        .00
33  310264   ROOM 2723-1    11461.91
34  Nov. 09 - 250 ck
35
36  310081   ROOM 2723-1    11211.91
37  NOV 09   NO POST        .00
38  310229   ROOM 2723-1    11211.91
39  NOV 10   NO POST        .00
40  310268   ROOM 2723-1    11211.91
    ------SEE FOLIO NUM 002279------
```

HOTEL CHELSEA

WEST TWENTY THIRD STREET
AT SEVENTH AVENUE
NEW YORK, N.Y. 10011
"A LANDMARK OF N.Y.C."
212-243-3700

11465

_Overdue rent bill sent to Robert Campbell detailing
the amount owed, accumulating month by month._

CHAPTER 8

Checking Out

I't's probably worth noting that none of our protagonists departed the Chelsea Hotel under the most genial circumstances. Some were pressured out—directly or indirectly by Stanley Bard. Others departed after plummeting so far into drug or alcohol abuse that staying at the Chelsea—which would supply their vices in spades—guaranteed breakdown or death. Still others departed because of people they had soured on: spouses, lovers, friends, roommates, people whose traits, once so attractive, now repulsed. Pretty much like our normal lives outside the Chelsea, but in more concentrated doses.

No matter how unpleasantly they left the Chelsea, every one of them had fond feelings for the old hotel. Most even managed to preserve some warm feelings toward Stanley Bard, even if they were still a little afraid of him.

Meet the New Boss

But something else was happening at the Chelsea, something bigger than personality conflicts. A new "take-no-prisoners" management philosophy marched into the hotel in the person of

Stanley's son, David Bard.

PAUL VOLMER

David basically took over most of the Chelsea's operation. He didn't want to give people so much slack, or have the same tolerant attitude with artists. This period began a grand-scale eviction of the old guard, these people who had gotten behind on their rent, including Robert and me.

It also included Viva. She was evicted with her daughter Gaby. That was a big event. They were cleansing the hotel of its Bohemian punk, trash-glam element. Viva represented, with the Warhol era, the Bohemian decadence that Warhol depicted in his underground films. So when Viva was evicted, it was symbolic. The new management under David Bard wanted all this Chelsea wildness gone. He wanted to make the place more of a world for yuppie artists, people who were less troubled, and dare I say less interesting.

In a 1999 article in *GQ* by Sarah Vowell, David Bard admits that when he got involved with the hotel, he wanted to renovate the building entirely, making it modern and clean. In other words he wanted to thoroughly change the Chelsea as it had been for nearly a century. But he changed his mind. According to the younger Bard, "A couple of the artists in the building, they said to me, 'David, you don't want to get rid of the cracks and the crevices in the building because that's where the ghosts hide. And if you get rid of the ghosts, the Chelsea will just be any other building.'" So the building underwent some renovation, but nothing extensive.

Nevertheless, it seems that while some cracks and corners were allowed to stay, a good number of living residents were summarily evicted. Even more troubling, the new management philosophy seemed to be rubbing off on Stanley.

JUDITH CHILDS

There is something about Stanley that's different now. He's not the old Stanley.

The new management style wasn't the only factor making the air less breathable at the hotel. Some residents' personal lives were beginning to stink.

MARLOWE WEST

When I was living in the Chelsea, and I'd go into my day job on Long Island during the day, Paul had a Bohemian friend who was from France. Now he had me down like clockwork. When I left the hotel to go to work, this guy came over and took my bed. And when I'd get home from work, he'd still be sleeping in my bed, and I'd have to wake him up! That was horrible! He wasn't paying any rent. There were things like this about living at the Chelsea which were becoming real bullshit. This guy didn't wash, so his smell was all over my bed. It was repulsive. I never made an acquaintance with him because I could never get past the fact that he was always crashing on my bed. I was thinking to myself, "Get the fuck outta here."

Typical of Marlowe, whose door-kicking, fire escape-tumbling episodes helped define his role at the Chelsea—his grand exit had to include a misstep.

MARLOWE WEST

On my final day at the Chelsea, when I just couldn't take that guy sleeping in my bed anymore, I called up my brother. He came out from Long Island with a pickup truck. Paul wasn't home, and I knew he wouldn't be home for a while. My brother had a friend with him, and we carried all of my stuff out of the room and just left.

On the way back to Long Island, as we were driving through the Midtown Tunnel, the steering on my brother's truck went bad. You couldn't steer it anymore. He had to crank the steering wheel all the way to the left to make the truck crawl a just little bit to the left. Then he'd crank the wheel all the way to the right, and the truck would inch a little to the right. Then all the way to the left again. We were zigging and zagging all the way through the tunnel, trying to keep straight by going all the way left and all the way right! Because we were basically out of control, my brother was driving as slowly as he could! Everybody behind us in the tunnel was beeping their horns at us.

When we finally got out of the tunnel, we got pulled over, because somebody had called the cops and told them there was some asshole blocking up the traffic in the tunnel. The cops were waiting for us at the other end. So we had to call another friend who came out with a van, and we loaded all of my stuff out of my brother's truck and into the van.

That was my exit from the Chelsea.

The things that led to my leaving were these strange people being in my belongings when I was wasn't there. I just got tired of it. Also, I was working and making money, but still living a desolate life because I was there at the Chelsea living like the rest of them. And the summers there were so hot! I had bought a fan at a yard sale in Long Island for five dollars. It was about an eight-inch diameter fan. I used to sleep with it facing my face. It was pretty rugged. But I guess the rough times at the Chelsea were less rough than out in the rest of the world.

If Marlowe's departure from the Chelsea came from being alienated from his own room, Paul Volmer's had to do with a woman, namely Neicy. With her as the root cause, Paul eventually landed in jail.

PAUL VOLMER

In a way, the worst thing I could have done was move in with Neicy. I had wanted to protect her, and I did. She was so lively that she was almost incapable of getting a job. She did do a little babysitting. But in taking care of her, I began my own decline. I really couldn't support both of us on what I was making. It was stressful. And Neicy had a very strong personality—she demanded a lot of attention. We were always on the edge financially.

Eventually, I wasn't able to keep up the rent. So I was a part of the "housecleaning" when Stanley's son, David, got rid of Robert and Viva and all the Bohemians in the hotel.

But Neicy was my weakness, my *femme fatale.* I would have

done anything for her, and that was my downfall. Other people had drugs as their downfall, but mine was a woman.

Stanley was always trying to break me up with Neicy because she wasn't paying any rent. One day he gave me an ultimatum: "If you don't get Neicy to leave, then I'm going to evict you."

So I started working as a bike messenger to earn extra money and pay Neicy's rent. Before, when I had been working for Stanley as bellman and night watchman, he had control over me then because I was working for him and paying off my rent that way. But now my loyalties were to Neicy, and she was making me fall further short on my rent. Stanley no longer had a reason to keep me.

I remembered how free I used to feel riding a bike as I kid, so I started the job with a small bike messenger company. It was headquartered in a rinky-dink office in an old warehouse. One time I bike-messengered pot to one of the members of the Allman Brothers. That's how I used to make a little extra money!

When this company hired bike messengers, they would always end up employing, say, two Pauls and three Johns, so they had to pick nicknames for people. Because I lived in the Chelsea, they nicknamed me "Sid."

Being a bike messenger was a wild job. It was grueling. But during the day, I would smoke pot in the various parks around Manhattan. I'd go uptown with my deliveries and stop by Central Park, where I would duck into the trees and have a smoke. I had my different spots that I *thought* were secure. But when Giuliani was mayor, he started this big, city-wide crackdown on crime, and I became caught up in that. He sent out all these crews of undercover cops. You couldn't tell they were cops—they dressed just like homeboys. I guess if I were hipper, I would've been able to tell.

These police were *hunting* us. They had the incident with Diallo,[118] the Haitian immigrant. Undercover cops stuck a broomstick up his ass. So one time I saw these guys a little way over from me, and they were sort of skipping happily back to their van. I didn't think anything of it because the way they danced back to their van, I thought they were probably gay and on their way back from the pier after a rendezvous or something.

 But then they walked over to me and said, "Don't throw that roach away." And they arrested me and put me in the back of their van. There were already some other people locked up in back.

These cops were doing a full-blown roundup. After they picked me up, they drove over to Washington Square Park and arrested a young kid. He was walking down the street with his girlfriend and smoking a joint. They pulled him right away from his girlfriend and threw him in the van.

"I'm not even selling real pot!" the kid said. "I've got *oregano* here!"

"Tell that to the judge!" the cops said.

This kid was only about sixteen, a black teenager. So when we got to the jail, they put me into the same cell with this kid. Probably because I'm a hippie-looking white dude, really no threat. I'm not a mean person.

In the cell, the kid started talking to the policeman.

"Have you ever heard of priapism?"[119] He explained it to the cop. "I have priapism and sickle cell anemia. At night, my dick gets hard and it won't go down. It's very, very painful. The only thing that'll get it down is some ice. Will you guys be able to give me ice?"

The policeman just brushed him off. "Shut up. I'm not dealing with you." The kid was dejected. He said to me, "I have sickle cell anemia, and every night when I fall asleep, I get a hard-on that hurts."

It was sort of like *Nightmare on Elm Street,* where if they fell asleep, suddenly the nightmare would happen. If this kid fell asleep, he would get this hard-on that was so incredibly painful that he'd have to get ice. It would be a horror show. But for some reason if he waited through the night and fell asleep in the morning, the painful condition would rarely happen. Every night, he had gone out to his deserted rooftop and stood out there, hoping he wouldn't go to sleep, hoping the pain wouldn't begin again.

So I told him what to do. I had learned that according to the law, the cops always have to ask you this formal question: "Do you need to see a doctor?" I told the kid that he had to make sure he got to see a doctor. It was his legal right. Then they wouldn't put him in jail with the rest of the general population—they'd put him in the hospital.

Then the police took me out of the cell and told me I could leave.

So because this was the first time I went to jail, I was so depressed. But when I got out, I thought to myself, "Compared to this kid, who's probably going to go to jail with this hard-on he can't get down, I have no problems at all!"

During his period of discouragement over Neicy, Paul would drop by Dimitri's for consolation.

DIMITRI MUGIANIS

Paul would come into my room looking to me for help. But I *myself* was a junkie mess! I'd try get myself together and compose myself: "I'll be right there with you, Paul!"

JULIE EAKIN

Right after Dimitri and I broke up, it was a very bad time for him. So my memories of the place are all just incredibly mixed—positive and negative. One the one hand, these people were delightful, but on the other hand, they were remarkably self-destructive.

DAVID LAWTON

Dimitri wasn't getting along with people as well. I used to say to myself, "Dimitri's different. Dimitri's not going to get sucked down into it."

But he did start to, so a little bit of tension developed between him and other people. There were even times when Huncke was mad at him.

DIMITRI MUGIANIS

These were years of complete garbage for me. Everything just stopped. The thing about being an addict was that I lived in New York. If you live in New York for a while, you've kind of seen the world, because the world comes to you. But I hadn't seen anything. I hadn't been beyond the corner of the block.

Robert Campbell left for reasons similar to Dimitri's—heroin and alcohol. He also owed the hotel a lot of money—roughly $14,000. Stanley had backed off Robert because he knew Robert had started a band with Dee Dee Ramone and assumed that they would make some money.

ROBERT CAMPBELL

Instead of making me move out of the Chelsea, I'm almost positive Stanley would have let me move to another room, a room that didn't cost as much. But I was so full of myself, and so pissed off at everybody at the time, that I left the hotel angry. That's how I left the Chelsea. Still, at the time, some part of me must have known that in the long run, it would be a good thing to get out.

NANCY ROGERS

When Robert left, it seemed that he had gotten much worse very quickly. A lot of it was when his girlfriend, Carol, an artist, a painter, moved out on him. I think she just couldn't take it anymore.

Robert did, on the way out, receive a little token of help from an unexpected source.

ROBERT CAMPBELL

There was this one drag queen whose name was Lena. I think she was from Cuba. She looked like a former welter-weight champion with her teeth busted out, that woman! She was tough as nails. I mean she was hard*core* tough. She had the fake boob implants, pure silicone, and the whole works. But she was a really cool person.

When I finally ran out of money at the end, before I got kicked out of the Chelsea, Lena gave me a five-pound tub of peanut butter. She also gave me a big old hunk of government cheese—it weighed like ten pounds. That was when the government started giving out tons of cheese to poor people. Lena was cool. I'll tell you what, though, you wouldn't want to screw with her because one hit from her and your neck would be broken.

It's not all hard luck. Painter John Zinsser moved out for benign, even normal reasons.

JOHN ZINSSER

We moved out just to have children. My wife was a little bit creeped out at the thought of having kids at the Chelsea, and we would have had to expand, which would've been expensive.

Airline steward Peter Johansson never actually left the Chelsea since he never actually lived there. But he did keep in touch.

PETER JOHANSSON

Later on, when I came as a flight attendant to the States—to the Chelsea—I would always give everybody a phone call. Of course I would still give Nicko a call. We were never able to actually connect again when I was in New York, but I would draw these little doodles on a slip of paper, or write these little messages on it, and ask the people at the Chelsea's front desk to put them in his mailbox.

Neicy's "Just say no thank you" to drugs friend Therese Zucal was less sanguine about her years in the Chelsea.

PAUL VOLMER

When I talked to Therese just recently, she said she wished she would have gone out and seen New York more. All she did was go to work and then come home and hang out in her Chelsea room. Because we had this cozy little world, this room in the back of the hotel, and we had created this womblike social atmosphere. In a way, I felt gratified when she said that because I had always been trying to protect Neicy and Therese at the time—they were younger than I, in their early twenties. Neicy, in fact, was eighteen. I was in my early thirties. So I guess I protected them well enough.

But unlike Therese, the rest of our Bohemian comrades, in spite of their dismaying ends at the Chelsea, had few regrets.

ROBERT CAMPBELL

I've seen people that were famous, I've seen celebrities, and I have realized that my dream was an empty dream—bullshit. So my dreams of being a rock star ended. Plus, I'm not as talented as I thought I was.

I feel like I went to the edge, and found out that it was meaningless. I want to be a square now.

DIMITRI MUGIANIS

A lot of lost opportunity, but it was incredible. I lived so much. I lived so much.

PAUL VOLMER

My eleven-year stay at the Chelsea was a little like Alice's stay in Wonderland, full of freaks and drugs. I learned more about freaks and drugs than anyone would know or could care to know. When I first came to the Chelsea, I had been traumatized. When I left, I was also traumatized, but in a new and better way.

The Chelsea's famous spiral staircase, site of numerous photo shoots, movie scenes, and suicides.

CHAPTER 9

Century 21 Aftermath

New York is the loneliest city. It doesn't smoke anymore, it doesn't drink much anymore, it doesn't do drugs, it's too rich and too expensive. The people who made the fun for the people who made the money have moved out. It's safe. But the city that doesn't sleep can now barely stay awake for dessert—if it ever ate dessert... In a generation, New York swapped Studio 54 for an African-dance class. We don't just connive in our own humiliation, but in our own loneliness, too.

A. A. GILL, "The Sorrow and the Pilates," *Vanity Fair*, January 2007.

As the Buddha made clear, everything changes. Transience rules. Manhattan is not exempt from this melancholy law of nature, and neither is the Chelsea Hotel.

The Place

PETER JOHANSSON

Afterward, I would drop by the Chelsea every once in a while and bring friends over to show them the better known spots, where people had lived and where people had died. I came in there one time and they had completely redone the lobby. And then I went up on the floors and I saw that they had redone all of the walls and everything. It was a totally different place. Except the staircase remained the same, with the same pretty iron handrails.

It was so sad. It wasn't the place that it used to be when, as a flight attendant, I would visit the Chelsea. It was now horrible. It was lighter, for one. Some of the floor was hardwood, not black and white linoleum like it had always been. Everything was cleaner and more antiseptic. It had no soul anymore. After that, I never went back.

JOHN ZINSSER

When we left the Chelsea, it had not been gentrified. It still had all its funkiness. However, they had fixed up the lobby and fixed up the hallways to some extent. That was when David Bard came in as a presence there. I went back maybe once or twice, once to introduce my baby daughter to Jerry at the front desk. But beyond that, I haven't gone back. I have bittersweet feelings about going back. At the time we left, it wasn't something that I really wanted to leave behind.

Maybe when my kids get older I can take them over and say "We lived here." But what am I gonna do now—just wander around the halls?

MARY ANNE ROSE

Originally, they didn't take much care of this place. But now they're doing all this work out in front—thank God. They're filling in the bricks with tuck pointing to prevent leaks. I used to have terrible leaks in the room. But, it's sort of better not to stir up dust and call much to Stanley's attention.

DIMITRI MUGIANIS

People still get the Bohemian experience, but I think it's getting harder and harder for young people because everything is so scattered. You know what people say about L.A., that "there's no there there." Well, "there's no there there" in this country anymore, and New York City has really taken that hit.

JOHN ZINSSER

Now, the artists are all out here in Brooklyn, but it's much, much more dispersed than it was in Manhattan. Brooklyn is so vast and spread out.

PAUL VOLMER

I'm sure people create there now as artists, but I seriously doubt with the rent so high, that a young person—a young artist could afford to live there.

I went back a year later, and this fragile ecosystem had disappeared. I know it isn't there now.

JERRY WEINSTEIN

I don't know where the Bohemians have gone. They can't afford these areas. They went to Brooklyn, to Williamsburg, but now *these* places are changing too. And the East Village, which we used to call the Lower East Side until they gave it a fancy name, is now gentrified, very expensive and very exclusive. Avenues A, B, and C, it used to be that you couldn't even go there for fear of getting mugged.

That's what's happening to the city. I don't know where they're going. Some are moving to Brooklyn. Hell's Kitchen has also been "redeemed." Even Harlem, where you had to be careful, forget it! Harlem is doing very well and the real estate is very expensive. Bohemians and people who aren't wealthy are being driven out of Harlem. They're probably going up to the Bronx. Brooklyn and the Bronx are improving also. Wherever they go, they keep being driven out because of the gentrification of the area.

MARY ANNE ROSE

One of the art dealers I work with has a gallery in the Chelsea District—he has got a ton of overhead—but he's living in a beautiful apartment up in Harlem. Sure, it would have been a lot better for him to live down here in Chelsea near his gallery, but he wouldn't have been able to afford a nice place. He'd get a tiny place with dorky furniture for three-thousand-dollars a month.

So Chelsea is too rich for art dealers! It's only for money people, people who *deal* in money.

JOHN ZINSSER

When I was living in Manhattan, I felt like I was living in a charged ionic atmosphere. You would run into people through serendipity and circumstance—things would happen in your life because you were literally in the right place at the right time. In Manhattan, so many of these things happened for me so quickly. One thing led to another, and one person led to another. And this was aside from the fact that I lived at the Chelsea.

Now in Brooklyn, I feel like, "Yes, *this* is where everybody is." In particular, in Greenpoint, I feel like, "This is where art is being made." Now I feel like I'm also "in the zone." But because the Brooklyn zone is so widespread, I don't see any other artists. I know everybody's out here somewhere, but the art geography and the art world have changed so much.

MARY ANNE ROSE

The whole Chelsea neighborhood used to be more alternative. But now people have moved in and changed the neighborhood, and that has taken a huge amount of money. Much of it has come from gays with money moving into Chelsea from the adjacent West Village. I mean, two men together earn a better income than a man and a woman.

JERRY WEINSTEIN

The hotel has changed along with the neighborhood. Some of our transients who stay here for short visits are business people, with Whole Foods executives, and Google is in the neighborhood. So the people we get now are a different bunch. And the rooms are much different. We've upgraded all the rooms.

JOHN ZINSSER

Gentrification is the easy answer. Now, when I go to the East Village, I still see all the people I saw in the 80s. They still live there! Everybody lives in these rent-controlled apartments, and what, at one time, was a group of young artists and musicians and writers—now they're all fifty years old and wandering around the same streets.

With all this talk of how New York has changed, it's all so much the same. If I go to Twenty-third Street, it's more the same than it is different. It's shockingly the same. But like everybody else, I go around pointing places out and saying, "This used to be here. That used to be there." This Rip Van Winkle-ism.

The People

MARY ANNE ROSE

These days, Stanley Bard is on the warpath against long-term tenants.[120] He feels we pay too little rent—and we do now, but hey, he overcharged at the beginning—and he tries to pick off people, threatening them, one by one. He tried to get me to agree to move from my studio apartment into "a nice room" with a bathroom down the hall. It costs one-thousand-five-hundred-dollars per month, and he told me he wanted three-thousand-two-hundred per month for my current four hundred square foot studio. Unfortunately for Stanley, the law is actually in the tenant's favor! I think we all appreciate the person Stanley once was, and feel badly for his current angst. So there are minor skirmishes being fought here, and not just by me. There are folks who, if Stanley gets on the elevator, they get off immediately.

PAUL VOLMER

Timur actually saw Fuchsia Gold, the dominatrix, a couple of years ago in the Chelsea lobby, handing out flyers to promote some party or event.

DIMITRI MUGIANIS

As an artist, I'm just getting back into it. After I got clean, I sat down wrote a poem, my first in five years. I've been writing for five years since. What happened when I got off of drugs—or maybe it was just a part of getting older and not being in my twenties and early thirties—was that I start realizing maybe I wasn't James Joyce.

I've been really blessed in my life to have older male figures, along with my father, who have been influential mentors. The ones who have chosen to reject their privilege, I've learned from them. I'm so lucky, having known Herbert Huncke and those guys. I'm forty-four, about to turn forty-five, and my parents are a little worried, but I know what's up for me. And it's not good.

It's not a nice thing to be poor and old in America. I've seen it with the hippie generation now, with people I admire. I know what I'm getting into. I've seen it, but I continue to live that type of life. I have no children, so I have the luxury to do that. But that's one of the many things that my male mentors who rejected their privileged backgrounds taught me—personal responsibility. The older I get, the more of an anarchist I am. I'm forty-five and living on a couch in an old yippie apartment.

MARY ANNE ROSE

All these older Chelsea people keep passing away. There's one woman who did all these slides of her husband's art—she just passed away this year. She was Russian, and such a lady, sort of a whole presence. A lot of people have left, folks that I knew.

Helen Johnson ended up having to go back to where she was from—Alabama or Louisiana—and be taken care of.

That's the thing about the Chelsea. A lot of the people who are new here, they weren't here when I first came here, there was an entire set of other people.

Nowadays young people are very different. They're very obedient, and all they worry about is getting a good job, and they do everything their parents say.

America is still as puritanical as could be.

ROBERT CAMPBELL

When Paul Volmer moved out of the Chelsea, he went to North Kingstown, Rhode Island, where he lives now. And get this -- they had some seaside downtown area that developers were going to close down and replace it all with a huge port, which would have ruined the ambiance of North Kingstown. And Paul managed to get the people in the city together and they fought against the federal government business conglomerate. This is regular old Paul, the bellman!

And they won! Paul and his people beat the government and these big businessmen! Because of this success, some local people even came to Paul and asked him to run for City Council of North Kingstown. Paul—the Chelsea bellman! That's the icing on the cake!

JAMES RASIN

Everyone has the tendency to idealize their own youth. So they'll say, "Oh, back then we really were outcasts. We were criminals. We couldn't get a job in regular society. We had to find each other at Max's Kansas City." I'm not saying that the Chelsea was a hotbed of creativity, or that *everyone* there was extremely talented, but there were certainly a lot of interesting people there!

MARY ANNE ROSE

I remember telling Stanley last fall—I was distracting him from his ever-present work. I don't remember what we were talking about, but he said, disgruntled, "But I *made* this place!"

"That's true, Stanley," I said, "And what you have in your memories is really, really important. And somebody should be doing your story about the whole thing."

The Chelsea Hotel was his life project. It's unique.

The infamous second floor hallway, prior to renovation.

Fauxhemia: Does the Death of Bohemia Matter?

The demise of the Chelsea Hotel as we knew it is a symptom of a much larger trend well underway in big cities nationwide: gentrification and homogenization of our urban culture. When neighborhoods—or entire cities—become gentrified, Bohemians move out. They don't leave out of principle. They leave because they can no longer afford to live in the very neighborhoods they helped make interesting and attractive.

Does it matter? So we're losing our urban, antiestablishment enclaves and the misfits who made them. Is it a real crisis? Have these creative radicals so enriched our culture that when they're gone, we will all feel the sting?

Bohemian culture has been living alongside bourgeois culture since the mid-1800s in Paris. As a phenomenon, it's about 170 years old. One might say it's a "tradition." But just being a tradition doesn't automatically make it worthy.

So let's put it this way: do we need our Picassos, Hemingways, Baudelaires, Toulouse-Lautrecs, Josephine Bakers, Richard Wrights, or Andy Warhols? Do we need the Impressionists, the Surrealists, the Imagists, the Abstract Expressionists?

Do we *need* art? Since the birth of the artistic counterculture, so much of our great art has come directly out of these urban petri dishes–Paris, New York, London, Berlin. Urban underworlds have served as the testing grounds, the informal universities, the sites of social networking where artists shared ideas, inspiration, arguments, and work.

Sure, a big segment of these cultural dissenters—probably around half ?—weren't great artists or even good ones. They were poseurs clinging barnacle-like to the scene for the fun times to be had. But the same is true about most *any* endeavor, from architecture to zoology. A select few people are extremely talented—the rest are middling or subpar. Just because poseurs proliferate doesn't mean we throw the talented ones out with the bathwater.

But as we settle into the Twenty-first Century, urban heretics, along with polar bears and ice caps, are becoming endangered. Their enemy isn't global warming but economic gentrification. Wealthy real estate speculators are forcing them out of their natural habitats, sketchy neighborhoods in lively metropolitan ecosystems.

There may be hope, however. A story that recently ran on public television profiled artists who had left Detroit but were now returning because of cheap rent. Apparently they're starting a small but lively scene. Rumor also has it that Austin, Texas is now a hopping place for artists, but one wonders if a small city can provide the vast stimulus that artists thrive on in big metropolitan cities. Portland, Oregon is said to house a viable counterculture. Also, we can't overlook the alternative communities that pop up briefly and then disappear, like the annual Burning Man Festival in Black Rock, Nevada. These "Temporary Autonomous Zones," according to theorist Hakim Bey, are not only the way of the future, but in some ways more resilient than monolithic, city-bound scenes of dissent. Their transience keeps them on their toes. It's harder for bourgeois day-trippers and their real estate agents to invade a TAZ. There are no cafés to turn into theme restaurants, no cold-water flats to jackhammer into luxury apartments.

The cultural commentator David Brooks, in his book *Bobos in Paradise,* has shown us one way in which something resembling a counterculture has managed to morph and survive the invasion of real estate. Bobos, as he calls them, are Bohemian Bourgeoisie, a new generation of middle-to-upper-middle-class Baby Boomers (and Gen-Xers and Millennial hipsters) who genuinely identify with the values of the fringe dwellers despite their bourgeois backgrounds. Instead of dropping out of their bourgeois culture of origin, they manage to cobble together the best of both worlds. Inside their BMWs, they blast the New York Dolls. They sit on their leather couches reading *Naked Lunch*. They eat whole-grain, honey-sweetened granola for breakfast atop their ten thousand dollar granite countertops. If someone bothers to point out the whiff of hypocrisy, they shrug and smirk. Irony is the Bobos best defense. These days, we call them hipsters.

But let us make no mistake: Bobo hipsters may admire the unorthodox and the outlanders—their ethic, their lifestyles, their art—but Bobos are not Bohemians. Most of them never spent a month, a day, or any fraction of their time in the counterculture. They may watch the right movies, know the right authors, talk about art, revolution and the underground, but they're too attached to bourgeois creature comforts to partake in them other than vicariously. To paraphrase Bob Dylan, their clothes are dirty, but their cars are chic.

And what *about* wealthy dropouts? What about the young artists who came from rich families but chose to live in underground enclaves and hang out with dropouts who weren't from money? Historically, as long as there have been Bohemias, there have been rich people slumming alongside them because the two shared some values. And the parties were better. For the most part, the less well-heeled heretics grudgingly welcomed the wealthy slummers, who were good for buying drinks, paying for a party, or in a pinch, a couple of weeks' rent. In return, the rich kids got to hang with colorful company. Wealth has its place in antiestablishment circles—Edie Sedgwick was hardly working class.

But let's bring the question to the present. Now, with few exceptions, *only* the wealthy can live in a city like New York. Can some sort of counterculture survive in an atmosphere almost entirely comprised of wealth? *The New York Times* printed a photo-essay featuring ten or twelve photographs of real live freaks from Manhattan. "Not all New York hipster culture," it read, "has moved to Brooklyn." But the Manhattan hipsters featured all looked suspiciously well-scrubbed. They had hip (read expensive) haircuts, and their black clothes looked fresh off the rack. It all smacked not of Bohemia, but Fauxhemia. *The Times* article ignored *why* hipster culture had moved to Brooklyn in the first place. And Brooklyn itself has fast become too expensive for dropouts who are not sons and daughters of wealth. Stanley Bard himself recently remarked, "We are very fortunate because a lot of the people who stay [at the Chelsea] became well known people and are comfortable financially, so they can afford to stay here."[122]

A "Bohemia" comprised only of wealthy members may be something, but it's not a Bohemia as we know it. When the neighborhood has become gentrified and made-over, and so have its artists, where are the seedier subterranean fixtures? Where are the bottom-dwellers who give the underground its local color, its edge, its real and present danger? Where are the prostitutes, or the men and women who only turn a trick occasionally for some quick cash? Where are the hippie gansters like Linda Twigg and the trenchcoat pharmacists like Frank Meyer to add a little delightful peril? And what about the poor suckers lying awake at night, alone on their mattresses in their tiny rooms, fingering their protruding ribs and worrying about how to pay next month's rent? Whether you enjoyed the company of misfits or merely tolerated it, these people who lived close to the streets, close to the bone, certainly added color and dimension to life.

Take, for example, the hustler's personality. A hustler's chief trait, the service he provides to his "customer" is his personality itself. It is his ability to charm and cajole and earn a person's trust. Herbert Huncke had it in spades.

This is not to romanticize those wacky, fun-loving, good-hearted hustlers and whores as portrayed in the film *Moulin Rouge,* but simply to say that real Bohemian life, by definition, is life on the edge, life without a safety net, a life of big dreams pressing against hard realities, of flights of hopeful fantasy, colorful baubles of the imagination (the first book sold, the first gallery exhibit, or the dream of "making it" in the art world) that often end up shattered against concrete sidewalks. High ideals fueled by cold soup.

Real artistic misfits, the ones who struggle, layer these hopes, dreams, and aspirations like blankets to cushion themselves from the concrete below. And if we peel those blankets away, one-by-one, only rejection, dejection and abjection remain. A real Bohemia, the real thing, is not only lively and fun. It is also sodden with the danger of failure, whose fetid stench permeates cheap rooms and wafts up from manholes.

For the bourgeoisie, such failure is simply not an option. When a middle-class rebel feels the moist breath of failure on the back of his neck, he stuffs his clothes into a gunny sack and applies to grad school, returning to his middle class roots. But if failure breathes on the neck of a working class rebel or lower, one without a bank account to back him up, then failure is all too real. It means being middle-aged and working as a waiter. Not as a stop-gap until things turn around – but until you can work no more.

In a real community at the fringes, you've got to scramble to keep body and soul together. And if scrambling means doing the song and dance to convince Stanley Bard to hold off a month on collecting rent, you will gladly do it. If that doesn't work, you'll scramble away from Stanley, around through El Quijote, so he won't have a chance to ask. Or you will take a lousy restaurant job, as Therese Zucal did. Or like Robert Campbell, you will proofread record covers at Atlantic Records. Like Marlowe, you will drive to Long Island every day to your full-time factory job. Or, like Paul Volmer, you might scramble to sell some weed. Maybe even, like Herbert Huncke, you will turn a trick or two, seizing whatever opportunity at your fingertips to make things tolerable for a few days. What you won't do is ask your parents for money – they don't have it to give.

The world is different now. Life's economic realities are harsher. Maybe it's just too risky to undertake a genuine "alternative lifestyle." The Chelsea itself has undergone the change—some say it has "sold out." But from one perspective, it can't help the gentrification it has undergone—it's just flowing with the tide of the times. Maybe we shouldn't even want to hold onto the past. Prosperity beats poverty. The great blues singer Bessie Smith once said, "I've been poor and I've been rich, and rich is better." I would warn any artist who rails righteously against "The Sellout" that he has the right to rail only *after* he has turned down the offer himself. The most principled critics of sellouts never had the option. When they do get the opportunity, and they turn it down, let them cast the first stone.

But let us not be mistaken—the Chelsea is not what it used to be. It has grown respectable. Its "Chelsea wildness" is gone. The old hotel will ossify into a museum of its former self, but not its entire former self, only the more presentable half. The charming side will remain. Real live artists may still walk the halls. No doubt they will add some of their new works to the Chelsea walls. But, under New Management, you can bet they won't do it in exchange for a month's rent. They're better business-men than that. It ain't no Holiday Inn, but it ain't no Bohemian rhapsody, either.

So to the creative dissidents still among us: however you manage it, live on! I celebrate your desire to live outside the norms and hope you can find an affordable, inspiring place to do it. I also celebrate your non-conformity and your "lifestyle experimentation." You are pioneers in the evolution of culture. Some of you will fly high—others will falter and drop. Still others will chicken out and return to the safe, conformist fold. And for those of you who choose to build your outpost outside the norms, don't automatically assume you're above them. No need to turn yourself into, as one of Paul Volmer's favorite books calls it, *Just Another Asshole*. Just produce your art. Great art is more important than Bohemianism. Art probably changes more people at deeper levels than countercultures ever can. Art is the beacon and banner that creates countercultures be-fore countercultures can turn around and create art. Rembrandt and Shakespeare, two of the greatest, were both solidly middle-class.

And to the members of the Bourgeoisie nodding smugly in your overstuffed chairs, I ask you to remember the following. In the big cities of this nation, commerce is devouring art. These cities used to provide the inspiration and the proving ground for fledgling artists. Beginning artists grow into mature artists, and it is the work of these mature art-ists that wealthy people like to purchase and hang on their walls for beauty and social status. That's all fine and good. The artists appreciate it, as do the gallery owners, theater producers, and book publishers who promote the artists' work and take their pieces of the pie. No artist can afford to take his audience for granted anymore.

So, in return, let's not take our artists for granted.

Where are they Now?

ROBERT CAMPBELL Since the inception of this book, Robert Campbell has played in three bands and learned a new trade—caning antique chairs. He lives in Charlotte, North Carolina with his fourteen-year-old son.

JUDITH CHILDS was married to the artist Bernard Childs for twenty years. She says she inherited the most fascinating job she ever had, promoting Childs' art after his death and securing its place in the future.

ELLIS DUNCAN During his thirteen years as a commodity trader and fifteen as a commercial real estate broker, Duncan had many occasions to visit the always interesting Chelsea Hotel and has many fond memories from those years.

JULIE EAKIN has pursued a career writing about architecture since graduating from the Chelsea. She credits her path (in part) to the building's magic appeal.

STEVE HOUSE teaches English in a secondary school in New York.

PETER JOHANSSON is living in Las Vegas and working in an art gallery.

DAVID LAWTON is a performer and writer who synthesizes his experiences in theatre, downtown rock and roll, and suburban ennui through the art of poetry. He has been featured at *Saturn Series, Brownstone Poets, The Back Fence, Stark* and the *Times Square Shout Out*, and at public libraries in East Orange NJ and his hometown of Woburn MA. He has been published in *Stained Sheets, Erato, Cripple*, and *CLWN WR*.

DIMITRI MUGIANIS is the subject of the 2010 documentary by Michel Negroponte, *I'm Dangerous With Love*. He works to help drug addicts rid themselves of their addictions.

JERRY POYNTON is a writer in New York City. He wrote the opening biographical sketch in *The Herbert Huncke Reader.*

WENDY PURCELL had a long career in the music industry and is now working as a voiceover artist.

NANCY ROGERS continues to work for Atlantic Records, now as Director of Production. She lives in Brooklyn.

JAMES RASIN'S 2010 film *Beautiful Darling* is about the influential Warhol scenester and actress/performer Candy Darling.

MARY ANNE ROSE still lives at the Chelsea Hotel. She has a Ph.D. in Art Education.

TIM SULLIVAN moved into the Chelsea Hotel in 1982 with a rockabilly-band the Stringbusters, and has lived there ever since. He was the co-founder and owner of Chelsea Music, the guitar store in the Chelsea Hotel from 1982-1992, and has put out ten albums with his surf band, The Supertones. He worked on the music for Abel Ferrara's film about the Chelsea Hotel, *Chelsea on the Rocks.*

PAUL VOLMER is living in Rhode Island, where he organized a grassroots movement to resist building an enormous port, and won.

JERRY WEINSTEIN has worked at the hotel for twenty-eight years. He used to be the Front Desk Manager, but now he just works the desk.

MARLOWE WEST is the author of *Go West: the Rock and Roll Memoir.* His previous book, entitled *Hollywood Revival*, is a musical fantasy. He is also affiliated with the Delray Beach Film Festival and has written two short screenplays, *Mary's Cross,* about Alzheimer's disease, and *Franklin and LaBrea,* named for the cross streets in West Hollywood where he was living when Jimi Hendrix's purple leather jacket came into his possession.

JOHN ZINSSER is an abstract painter, currently represented by James Graham & Sons Gallery in New York. He lectures on contemporary art at The New School and writes widely on the subject. He lives with his wife, Candace, and two children, in Brooklyn.

Acknowledgments

Thanks go to my late father, John Lough, for his enthusiastic support of this project, and to those who were there at the beginning: Robert Campbell, Ellis Duncan, Dimitri Mugianis, Paul Volmer, and Marlowe West. Thanks to those whose interviews comprise this book: Stanley Bard, Judith Childs, Steve Housepian, Peter Johansson, David Lawton, David Leonard, Edgar Oliver, Helen Oliver, Jerome Poynton, Wendy Purcell, James Rasin, Nancy Rogers, Anna Romero, Paul Romero, Mary Ann Rose Gentry, David Sands, Tim Sullivan, Jerry Weinstein, and others whose conversations are the building blocks of this particular Chelsea story.

Thanks to Tim Schaffner for recognizing the book's potential in utero and providing expert editing; to Alex Stein and Ken Morris for their astute editorial comments; and to Susan Olmetti for helping me score an interview with the Bard himself.

This project was funded through a Presidential Fellowship for Faculty Development from the Savannah College of Art and Design.

Endnotes

CHAPTER 1

1 Rene Shapshak, a Fellow of the Royal Society of Arts, created busts of Charles DeGaulle, Queen Elizabeth, and Harry Truman, the last of which is posted on the mantel over the fireplace in the Chelsea Hotel's lobby. Oddly, considering his subjects, he was also a renowned anarchist. "I still remain enthusiastic about anarchism, though I never took part in the movement," he wrote, in *Anarchist Voices: An Oral History of Anarchism in America.*

2 Larry Rivers is arguably the most famous painter who ever lived at the Chelsea Hotel. Born in the Bronx as Yitzroch Loiza (Irving) Grossberg, he was educated at Julliard, the Hans Hoffman School, and NYU. Rivers is largely associated with Pop Art. He was painting dollar bills and Camel packs well before Warhol's forays into popular culture, but his ever-expanding techniques and excellent draftsmanship seemed to qualify him for other movements as well. Some of his more well-known paintings are "Washington Crossing the Delaware" and the series of "Dutch Masters" paintings, one of which used to hang in the Chelsea's lobby. Rivers was also a respected jazz saxophone player, and he did text-image collaborations with poets from the New York School such as John Ashbery and Kenneth Koch. http://www.spaightwoodgalleries.com/Pages/Rivers.html

3 The abstract/Pop Artist Phillip Taaffe is associated with his collage work, repetition of patterns, and juxtaposing images in fresh new contexts. For an apt written description/celebration of some of Taaffe's work, see the poem by Quincy Troupe, "Fragmented Solos, Patterns, and Textures; Other Worlds; The Paintings of Phillip Taaffe," in his book *Transcircularities*. For a less positive review of his recent work, see Cassandra Neyenesch's review from The Brooklyn Rail. http://www.brooklynrail.org/2007/4/artseen/taafee

4 In her book *At the Chelsea*, Florence Turner, who lived at the hotel in the 60s and 70s, remarks on Stanley Bard's sincere interest in the works of art that he hung on the lobby's walls. But Turner adds, "His enthusiasm occasionally led him to extremes where he failed to distinguish the real thing from the fake." One might presume this also occasionally applied to the artists themselves.

5 One such fire happened in Edie Sedgwick's room. She didn't like sleeping in complete darkness, so she lit a few candles on her mantelpiece. A friend who happened to know something about the occult arts came to visit. He noticed

how the candles were arranged, and told her she had inadvertently placed them in a configuration that reeked of evil. She'd better move them, he said, or put them out. She ignored his advice, the candle flames spread to some drapes, and her room caught fire. Edie suffered burns to her arm and she spent a short time in the hospital.

6 Long-time Chelsea denizen, Herbert Gentry was an abstract expressionist painter who was born in Pittsburgh but grew up in Harlem during the Harlem Renaissance. After serving in World War II, Gentry stayed in Montparnasse, where he ran a nightclub frequented by Richard Wright, Jean-Paul Sartre, Simone de Beauvoir, Chester Himes, George Braque, Larry Rivers, Romare Bearden, Beauford Delaney, and Giacometti. In 1986, a Smithsonian magazine article featured Gentry alongside another notable African-American painter, Romare Bearden. http://www.herbertgentry.com/

7 Lawton comments, "If you saw *An American Family* on PBS, there's a scene when Lance Loud's mother comes to visit him at the Chelsea, and she says, "'I can't believe this is the famous Hotel Chelsea!'"

8 For more on Don Cherry, see http://www.furious.com/PERFECT/doncherry.html

9 Jazz sax player Ornette Coleman's atonal, improvisational playing marked him as a musical pioneer, and who had the confidence to entitle one of his pioneering albums "The Shape of Jazz to Come." He began by playing bebop, but his style began to follow a creative curve that originated what is now called Free Jazz. His career led him to Africa, where he incorporated Moroccan and Nigerian sounds into his music, and in the 80s he diversified again, playing with such dissimilar artists as Pat Metheny and The Grateful Dead. In 1994, he received a MacArthur "Genius" award, worth half a million dollars. In 2007, he received both a Grammy for Lifetime Achievement and a Pulitzer Prize. His influence upon music has been huge, descending even into Punk and No-Wave music, where his sax playing inspired the saxophonist James White of The Contortions. http://www.ornettecoleman.com/then.html

10 With all due respect to Grandmaster Flash, Gil Scott Heron was rapping twelve years before Flash's1982 hit, "The Message" was said to launch rap music. (Granted, Grandmaster Flash and Afrika Bambata were DJs, and Heron was not, and some critics argue that Heron's work resembles spoken word poetry more than rap.) Heron was a political artist , his much-sampled 1970 song "The Revolution will not be Televised" prophetic in outlook. He was largely critical of gansta rap, which glorifies young black men killing other young black men, as being antithetical to the Civil Rights movement. In addition to his many albums, Heron has also published two well-respected novels, *The Vulture* and *The Nigger Factory*. He died in 2011. http://www.gilscottheron.com/GILINTRO.htm

11 Depending on your generation, you would either know Julian Beck as the founder of the Living Theater or as the actor who played the Reverend Henry Kane in *Poltergeist II*. The Living Theater was an avant garde theater company in New York that featured actors leaving the stage to confront audience members, stretching them out of their comfort zones. This was revolutionary for its time: 1947. Beck's biggest artistic influence was Antonin Artaud and his Theater of Cruelty. He died of cancer in 1985. Even before he grew old, Julian Beck's face would best be described as severe—skull-like with piercing eyes.

12 Science fiction author Arthur C. Clarke was most famous for his novel *2001: A Space Odyssey,* which he adapted into film with Stanley Kubrick, who also spent time at the Chelsea. The collaboration was stressful, but mostly amicable. Later in his life, Clarke lived in Columbo, Sri Lanka, in an old hotel he called The Chelsea East. He died in 2008. http://www.visual-memory.co.uk/amk/doc/0073.html

13 Julian Schnabel's paintings composed on broken plates are celebrated by critics. His "neo-expressionism" came as a reaction against abstract, minimalist and conceptual painting popular in the 1970s and 80s. Schnabel also directed three movies, one of which was *Basquiat.* http://www.broadartfoundation.org/collection/schnabel.html

14 Turn-of-the-20th-Century writer O. Henry was most famous for his short Christmas story, "The Gift of the Magi" about a pocket watch, a shaved head, and a surprise ending featuring both. O. Henry's stories became known for their classic "O'Henry Endings," predictably featuring a surprise twist. For a time, he worked at the First National Bank of Austin (Texas) and was charged with embezzlement there. He skipped bail, and once caught, served in prison for three years. Once released, he enjoyed his most prolific period, living at the Chelsea. He often sat in the lobby taking notes on the characters walking in and out, which is still a favorite past-time there. http://www.online-literature.com/o_henry/

15 Unfortunately for Brendan Behan, he was born in the very long shadows of Irish literary geniuses James Joyce and Samuel Beckett. Politically active, Behan began working for the Irish Republican Army (IRA) at age 14 in its violent attempts to kick the British Empire out of Ireland. Growing up a Catholic in the slums of Dublin, he, always supported underdogs in his life and his writings. Several of his books, including *Borstal Boy,* were banned, and he spent a fair share of his post-adolescence in prison for IRA involvement and drunken mayhem. http://www.kirjasto.sci.fi/behan.htm

16 Beautiful, charismatic, doomed star of Andy Warhol's factory scene, Edie Sedgwick is the subject of the oral history, *Edie,* by Jean Stein and George Plimpton. Born into the Boston blueblood Sedgwick family, Edie rebelled tooth and nail, flagrantly spending old money and taking new drugs. In the

meantime, she worked as a model, dated Bob Dylan, whom she met at the Chelsea, and starred in Warhol's films, most notably *Chelsea Girls,* shot at the Chelsea Hotel. Like her siblings, she was the victim of her sadistic father and passive mother. Eventually, in 1971, in Los Angeles, she burned out and died as a result of booze and drug abuse. In 2007, the movie *Factory Girl* covered her years with Warhol and Dylan. Her cousin, Kyra Sedgwick, has had a long and illustrious acting career, most recently in the TV series *The Closer.* http://www.rams.demon.co.uk/esmain.htm

17 The GTOs (Girls Together Outrageously) were a gang of groupies who hung out with Frank Zappa and the Mothers of Invention. Beautiful and infectiously charming, they also had talent. In 1969, they cut their own album, "Permanent Damage," produced by Frank Zappa and Lowell George (later the lead singer of the band Little Feat). The album also featured Jeff Beck and Ry Cooder on guitar and Rod Stewart on vocals. The GTOs figure prominently in the semi-fictional 2000 movie *Almost Famous*, which chronicles the early career of rock writer Cameron Crowe.

18 Jobriath was the biggest pop star never to become a star. Though his career started in L.A.'s debut production of *Hair*, his rise to near fame came in rock and roll. A glam rocker a la David Bowie, Jobriath was, in 1973, given a half million dollar advance for his eponymous first album by Elektra records, a huge amount back then, and a first, especially for an artist without a track record. Elektra poured money into the album and its advertising, including an enormous billboard in Times Square and another in Paris. Despite the album's good reviews, it flopped.

Jobriath was also the first openly gay musical performer and one of the first wave of gay men to die of AIDS, which happened at the Chelsea Hotel, Room 1032.

19 Peter Brook is a film and stage director. Two of his more well-known films were *Meetings with Remarkable Men*, about Russian mystic Georges Gurdjieff, and a film based on the Indian epic *The Mahabharata*.

20 With all due respect to Mr. Lawton, a gracious and intelligent man, a malapropism is a humorously incorrect use of a word, so the "Debbie Gibson" example is not a malapropism at all. Mr. Lawton's use of the word malapropism is a malapropism.

21 Debbie Gibson was the Miley Cyrus of the late '80s. Her number one pop hit, "Foolish Beat," was one of her many successful songs. In 1990, in a desperate attempt to abandon her good girl image, she performed with the punk band The Circle Jerks at CBGB's and later posed naked for *Playboy*.

22 Ragged-voiced Tom Waits' most famous song is "Looking for the Heart of Saturday Night." He also acted in Jim Jarmusch's films *Down By Law* and

Coffee and Cigarettes, not to mention collaborating with William Burroughs and Robert Wilson on an opera, *The Black Rider.*

23 Philip Glass is a contemporary composer famous for repetitive soundscapes. He wrote the soundtrack for Godfrey Reggio's movie *Koyaanisqatsi.* Glass was one of the first orchestral composers to fess to being influenced by rock musicians like David Bowie and the Talking Heads.

CHAPTER 2

24 To read John Cale's amusing and literate article, "Chelsea Mourning," from which this quote was originally taken, see London's *Observer* online at http://www.xs4all.nl/~werksman/cale/text/chelsea_mourning.html

25 When the Texas writer Molly Ivins died in 2007, Kinky Friedman wrote her obituary for the editorial page of *The Los Angeles Times*, noting how the obituaries always sold her short because they were "the words we use when we don't know what to say." Molly Ivins' personality was too big to fit into a two-column obit.

The same could be said of Kinky Friedman, the colorful gadfly who began his eclectic career as the lead singer of Kinky Friedman and the Texas Jewboys, and whose most well-known song was "Asshole from El Paso." Another gem was called "They Don't Make Jews like Jesus Anymore," songs that only a Jewish Texan could get away with. Friedman's identity – like that of Molly Ivins – is inseparable from the state.

In the 1980s, Friedman picked up the pen, authoring twenty mystery novels with titles like *Roadkill, Elvis, Jesus and Coca-Cola* and *Kill Two Birds and Get Stoned.* He also wrote a regular column for *Texas Monthly.*

In 2006, Friedman received national attention by running for Governor of Texas, using the campaign slogan "Why the Hell Not?" While he did not win, he did receive thirteen percent of the vote.
http://www.newyorker.com/archive/2005/08/22/050822fa_fact
http://www.ellroy.com/ http://www.kinkyfriedman.com/

26 Marlowe West's miracle came not from Jesus, but from Jehovah. The church was actually an orthodox synagogue, the Congregation Emunath Israel since 1920. Earlier, since the mid-1800s, it had been the Third Reformed Presbyterian Church. According to a member, the synagogue's "President and Vice-President are both men, but with ponytails. The 60-year-old Berkowitz drives a motorcycle, wears a diamond stud in his ear and, as a plumber, does much of the repair work in the synagogue himself." The synagogue's vice president Joseph Max remarked, "there's lots of characters, varied stories, and a great opportunity to help here." Not unlike its secular neighbor next-door. http://home.nyc.rr.com/jkn/nysonglines/23st.htm

27 Former lead singer in The Animals, then in War, Eric Burdon's rock ca-

reer has undergone numerous permutations, but he's most famous for the Animals' song "House of the Rising Sun." With War, he sings the strangely compelling song "Spill the Wine," among others.

28 Chicago-born Quincy Jones is of course an immensely successful music producer, conductor and composer. http://www.quincyjones.com/

29 Mark From *Hendrix: Setting the Record Straight* by John McDermott and Edward Kramer; New York: Grand Central Publishing, 1992.

30 From *The Mammoth Book of Sex, Drugs, and Rock and Roll.* London: Robinson Publishing, 2001.

31 *Jimi Hendrix: The Intimate Story of a Betrayed Musical Legend* by Sharon Lawrence; New York; Harper Collins, 2006.

32 Devon Wilson's claim that she OD'd Hendrix is supported by her earlier antics. Lawrence recounts, "There were a number of incidents that year when Devon dosed Jimi unbeknownst to him." Once, in 1970, Hendrix had been playing at Madison Square Garden with Texas blues guitarist Johnny Winter. Halfway through a song, Hendrix started snapping back at the audience for begging him to play the old standards. He sat down on stage in passive resistance until stagehands finally led him offstage. Afterwards, Winter claimed Wilson had slipped drugs into Hendrix's drink before the concert.

The strongest evidence against Devon Wilson's confession is that the coroner's report showed no heroin in Hendrix's blood. Maybe Wilson slipped him some other drug that the coroner didn't test for? According to Ed Vulliamy in the *Guardian UK*, rock writer Keith Altham told him that Devon Wilson had not given Hendrix heroin but "black bomber" amphetamines. Danneman later gave him Vesarax to help him sleep. So maybe it was a cocktail of alcohol, speed, and downers that made Hendrix drown in his own vomit? We may never know. Nevertheless, this new piece of the puzzle begs to be looked into. Especially given the hostile response Marlowe West received when he looked too closely into the whole affair.

33 Since 1964, the Whiskey A Go Go has been a major rock and roll club on L.A.'s Sunset Strip. Some feel that without the Whiskey, L.A. would have no rock scene at all. Numerous bands played and even recorded there, but its heyday was during the Punk and New Wave era of the 1970s and early 1980s. The club—like the Chelsea Hotel—is a shadow of its former self, mainly serving now as a performance space where bands pay to play. http://www.whiskyagogo.com/whiskysite/home_fs.html

34 Arthur Lee died of leukemia on Thursday, August 2, 2006 in Memphis. His psychedelic rock band Love was hugely influential on bands like the Rolling Stones, The Byrds, and The Doors. It was Lee who persuaded Elektra Records

to sign The Doors.

Lee referred to himself as "the first black hippie," and his sound was acoustic folk mixed with trippy electric orchestration. Love's one song to hit the Billboard Top 40 was called "7&7 Is". In 1970 he recorded an album, never released, with Jimi Hendrix. In the 1990s, he served six months in prison for illegally possessing a gun. http://www.lovewitharthurlee.com/ http://www.nytimes.com/2006/08/05/arts/05lee.html?_r=1&oref=slogin Also *Time* magazine, in the August 2006 issue, features his brief obituary.

35 Charles Bermant wrote a pertinent article for *Rolling Stone,* "Hendrix Family Feud Continues." It appears, in an abridged form, at http://www.rollingstone. com/artists/jimihendrix/articles/story/5933717/hendrix_family_feud_ David Kramer's documentary on Hendrix seems to be still in the planning stage.

36 See Brian Hay's article, "Behind the Curtain: Guest Suicides at Hotels and Tourist Attractions," http://eresearch.qmu.ac.uk/2199/

37 Judith Gould is the pseudonym of Nick Bienes and Rhea (pronounced "Ray") Gallaher. Their successful trashy novel *Sins* inspired an equally successful TV movie starring Joan Collins,. http://www.judithgould.com/story.php

38 Ice is apparently, once again, all the rage. http://www.msnbc.msn.com/ id/17859998/

CHAPTER 3

39 *Goodie* magazine devoted an issue to Roger Richards, which is still available for purchase at their website http://www.goodie.org/goodiemag/18richards. html. For a poignant eulogy of both Richards and Claude Pelieu, check out the *Literary Kicks* website at http://www.litkicks.com/BeatPages/msg. jsp?what=RichardsPelieu

40 In the 1980s and '90s, Raymond Foye, with the backing of Expressionist painter Francesco Clemente, founded and ran Hanuman Books. They published mostly beat writers, but also rockers (Patti Smith, Richard Hell) painters (Willem de Kooning) and photographers (Robert Frank). The most striking thing about the books themselves was their size, about 4" by 3". Their tiny size and vibrant covers were modeled after traditional Hindu prayer books. Hanuman is the Hindu monkey god.

41 From *Literary Outlaw: The Life and Times of William Burroughs.*

42 The annual Lowell Celebrates Kerouac Festival is featured at http://lckorg. tripod.com/

43 Riker's Island, New York City's main jail, houses around 14,000 prisoners

and has been the subject of numerous abuse scandals in the last five years.

44 Pop artist and graphic designer Richard Bernstein was most famous for working with Andy Warhol and eventually providing the distinctive cover art for Warhol's *Interview* magazine, in which he enhanced photographs of celebrities with pastel crayons and airbrush, creating a soft glow similar to that of antique colorized photographs.

45 Linda Twigg's sometime friend Margaret Morton, in her memoir *Glass Houses*, about the Lower East Side squatter's scene, said this about Twigg in high school: "She was a superstitious kind of Catholic girl who said novenas to St. Dismas, the patron saint of thieves."

46 For Mark Kramer's entertaining story about Linda Twigg's "salon," see http://www.bmezine.com/dib/19/index.html

47 According to Al Aronowitz's obituary, "it was Al who introduced beat poet Allen Ginsberg to Bob Dylan, Dylan to the Beatles, and the Beatles to marijuana." Al Aronowitz was a music journalist before there was such a thing. He wrote for the *New York Post* and authored many books, including *Bob Dylan And The Beatles, Volume One of the Best Of the Blacklisted Journalist*. He hung out with the Beats for many decades. For a sample of his writings, see http://www.bigmagic.com/pages/blackj/

48 The "Pope of Pot" is the late Mickey Cezar. According to *Screw* magazine reporter Mark Kramer, the Pope used to brag about "fellating one tenth of the U.S.S. Intrepid's crew while on a Navy tour of duty in 1959." For an interesting article on the Pope of Pot's influence in the Ibogaine movement, see http://www.cures-not-wars.org/ibogaine/chap08.html
For more about Cezar, see http://www.bmezine.com/dib/19/index.html

49 For more on the Bernard Goetz case, see http://www.berniegoetz.net/

50 Jack Kerouac wrote the introduction to Robert Frank's photo book *The Americans,* summing it up with, "Robert Frank, Swiss, unobtrusive, nice, with that little camera that he raises and snaps with one hand he sucked a sad poem right out of America onto film, taking rank among the tragic poets of the world."

51 From http://www.blacklistedjournalist.com/

52 Johnny Thunders died under mysterious circumstances in New Orleans, where he had fled New York to get away from drugs. Mysterious because he apparently "overdosed" on LSD, despite the fact that people don't overdose on LSD. According to sources close to him, Thunders had never liked acid and didn't take it. Nina Antonia, author of *Johnny Thunders ... In Cold Blood: The Of-*

ficial Biography of the ex New York Dolls and Heartbreakers Guitarist, claims the New Orleans police did not investigate his death because they thought he was just another no-name junky whose death didn't warrant an autopsy.

53 Methadone is the synthetic opioid used by medical professionals to get people to kick heroin. It is relatively harmless, and doesn't provide the heroin "high" but does prevent the serious withdrawal symptoms of heroin: extreme, convulsive nausea, trembling, pain in the muscles and bones, diarrhea and vomiting.

54 *The Herbert Huncke Reader*, edited by Ben Shafer, published by William Morrow and Co., and with a foreword by Jerome Poynton.

55 Colonel Parker — Elvis Presley's manager, promoter, and some said conman — once was engaged in a high stakes poker game in Las Vegas. Eddie Murphy was watching. For good luck, Colonel Parker went up to Murphy and rubbed his head, a racist tradition that supposedly attracts good luck.

56 According to *Filmmaker* magazine, "Jeremiah Newton has written a one-character play on Candy Darling that was part of [2007's] Howl Festival. He is credited in the 1996 film *I Shot Andy Warhol* with 'Additional scenes and dialogue' and his character is portrayed by actor Danny Morganstern. He is the Film and Television Industry Liaison for New York University." http://www.filmmakermagazine.com/archives/online_features/glitter.php

57 In *Huncke and Louie,* a moving documentary made by Laki Vazakis about Herbert Huncke and Louis Cartwright, the two destitute old men still manage to exude a sparkly-eyed spiritual freedom. http://www.metaclick.com/huncke/

58 Whatever else you say about actress Tatum O'Neal or her actor father Ryan O'Neil and their family problems, they were both excellent in *Paper Moon.*

59 Poet Edgar Oliver writes like Baudelaire and speaks like Bela Lugosi's Dracula. Originally from Savannah, Georgia, he and his sister Ellen, a talented painter, moved to New York to escape their mentally ill mother. Oliver tells the tragicomic story in his spoken word performance with The Moth. http://themoth.org/

60 Poet John Wieners was central to the 1950s San Francisco Renaissance in poetry, when the mainstream was finally discovering work by the Beats. He studied under Charles Olson at Black Mountain College. For his ability to combine Beat street jargon with high surrealistic imagery, Wieners' work is reminiscent of Marty Matz's. http://www.lib.udel.edu/ud/spec/findaids/wieners.htm

61 In a 1957 issue of the journal *Dissent*, Norman Mailer published a controversial essay called "The White Negro: Superficial Reflections on the Hipster." Mailer claimed the countercultural Beats and hipsters of the time were mainly white men imitating the archetypal streetwise black man. According to Mailer, African-American males, unable to gain acceptance in mainstream white culture, chose instead to reject it, turning to the lawless, violent life of the streets. While Mailer's analysis of crime in the African American community is simplistic, he was spot on about white men wanting to be as cool as black men.

62 Copyright David Lawton, by permission.

63 For more on Gregory Corso's poem "Gasoline," see http://www.english. uiuc.edu/maps/poets/a_f/corso/bio.htm and http://www.litkicks.com/ Texts/Bomb.html

64 From Levi Asher's literary website, *LitKicks*. http://www.litkicks.com/ MartyMatz

65 The Cedar Tavern was a Village bar that attracted artists—nay, whole artistic movements—like the Abstract Expressionist painters and the Beat Poets. Jack Kerouac was famously kicked out of the Tavern for peeing in an ash tray.

66 From LitKicks. http://www.litkicks.com/MartyMatz

CHAPTER 4

67 From *Love Goes to Buildings on Fire: Five Years in New York that Changed Music Forever,"* by Will Hermes (New York: Faber and Faber, 2011).

68 G. G. Allin's achievement was to serve as an example of Punk at its most extreme: extremely nihilistic and extremely destructive. Allin specialized in provoking audiences by pulling stunts like performing naked or taking Ex-Lax before performances and crapping and pissing on stage. Later, he served time in prison for torturing a woman.

69 Stax Records (Volt was one of their subsidiaries) out of Memphis, was the premier record label of Soul music. In contrast to Motown's slick, smooth, pop sound, Stax's songs were rawer and more powerfully emotional. According to Robert Campbell, the main musical difference between Stax and Motown is that Stax used a 2/4 beat, while Motown used a 4/4. Some of the luminaries launched by Stax were Booker T. and the MGs, Isaac Hayes, Sam and Dave, Otis Redding, The Staples Singers, and Albert King. PBS aired an excellent documentary on Stax: *Respect Yourself —The Stax Records Story.*

70 According to Richard Hell in Leggs McNeill and Gillian McCain's excellent book *Please Kill Me: The Uncensored Oral History of Punk*, "Dee Dee was one of these guys who was really wide-eyed dumb. But his dumbness was so smart that you never really knew how much of it was his style of dealing with the world. He played it. Everything he said was really on the money and funny." Dee Dee himself commented on this faux innocent coping strategy. In his book *Surviving the Ramones*, he describes how the band's manager Monte Melnick could get really impatient and difficult. Dee Dee's response to such difficult behavior—"I tried to play innocent to keep him level."

71 According to the Spectator News Agency, "On September 27, 1989 Dee Dee was arrested in Washington Square Park, New York on marijuana possession charges." www.spectator.co.nz/culture/ramones.html

72 Stiv Bators made his name in the punk band The Dead Boys. He later performed with The Lords of the New Church and The Whores of Babylon, a short-lived band including both Dee Dee Ramone and Johnny Thunders. Bators also played Bubo Ballinger in John Waters' 1981 film *Polyester*.

73 Richard Hell (aka Richard Meyers) founded the seminal band Television with Tom Verlaine (Tom Miller). Hell modeled himself after the poet Baudelaire and took his name after Rimbaud's book *A Season in Hell*. (Malcom McLaren credits Hell's image as inspiration for the look of the Sex Pistols.) Television was one of the first of the "punk" bands to play CBGBs. Hell, its bassist, would later play with Johnny Thunders in the Heartbreakers. From *Love Goes to Buildings on Fire: Five Years in New York that Changed Music Forever*, by Mark Hermes.

74 Junior Walker and the All Stars was a rowdy Rhythm & Blues band who did songs like "Shotgun," their biggest hit, and a version of "How Sweet it is (To be loved by you)" later made into a hit by James Taylor.

75 Not to be confused with Tramps Nightclub in Worcester or Tramps of Tenerife, New York's Tramps has featured about every famous and not famous musician in the world.

76 The manuscript was eventually published, in a different form, under the title *My Right to Survive*.

77 Laura Allen was a fashion model, not to be confused with the Laura Allen who starred in "All My Children" and "Mona Lisa Smile."

78 D Generation released two albums, *D Generation* in 1994, and *No Lunch* in 1996. John Carco seems to have left the band before they recorded the albums.

CHAPTER 5

79 From *Poets & Writers*, March/April 2007.

80 For more on the painter and interior designer Willem Van Es, who died in 2009, see his memorial website at http://memorialwebsites.legacy.com/willemvanes/Homepage.aspx

81 The Chelsea's basement is also the setting for the climactic scene in Dee Dee Ramone's 2001 novel *Chelsea Horror Hotel,* a mix of factually-based memoiric anecdotes, paranoid hallucinations and revenge fantasies. The basement, according to Ramone, "is one of the rawest and largest spaces available in the building, but no one ever uses it. It's too horrible to be an apartment and too creepy to be a workspace for an artist. About the only use I could think for it would be a rehearsal studio for punk and death-metal bands."

82 If you're dying to see Long Dong's long dong, log onto http://web.archive.org/web/20051221041656/http://www.sasserlone.de/bild.0067-long-dong-silver-2.html

83 Florence Turner refers to the staff with affection, mostly, and with sympathy for their taxing roles as keepers of the madhouse. "The staff, black and white, were unusually united. There were two reasons for this: low pay, and the unbelievable behavior of the tenants, cause for gossip and mirth, enlivening a day that began in Harlem at five o'clock and ended in Manhattan at six in the evening with a long subway trip ahead."

84 Called "Ginger" because of his red hair, Baker is almost as wild a drummer as Keith Moon was. He was the drummer for Cream but also went on to play for Blind Faith and other bands. He always considered himself a jazz drummer, and bristled when called a rock and roll drummer. (http://www.drummerworld.com/drummers/Ginger_Baker.html)
http://allmusic.com/cg/amg.dll?p=amg&sql=11:aifqxqw5ldse~T1

85 Next to Jackson Pollock, Willem DeKooning was the other bright star of New York's abstract expressionist movement in painting, which, for the first time, moved the center of the art world from Paris to New York. DeKooning is famous for his depiction of threatening, toothy women, the classic "teeth mothers" of mythology. For this, some feminists have objected to these unflattering depictions.

CHAPTER 6

86 John Sloan was one of the celebrated Realist "Ashcan School" of painters—a term Sloan disliked intensely—in late 19th Century New York. He painted gritty urban scenes including prostitutes, laborers, and life in restaurants and

saloons.

87 One of the U.S.'s greatest playwrights, Arthur Miller authored such classics as *The Crucible* and *Death of a Salesman*, which won the Pulitzer Prize for Drama in 1949. He was also famous for marrying Marilyn Monroe, who served as the inspiration for his screenplay of the movie *The Misfits*.

88 According to Florence Turner, one hotel maid commented, "If Stanley's heart was made of gold, he'd sell it."

89 Joe Andoe's large canvases featuring modern rural scenes—old Fords running down highways in flat, barren landscapes, fields dotted with an occasional farm animal, irrigation ditches—are like something out of Sam Shephard. An article in the *New Yorker* called his work "cowboy noir with a fashionista twist." Andoe's memoir *Jubliee City* received good reviews.

90 Playwright Edward Albee's most famous play *Who's Afraid of Virginia Woolf* was made into a classic film starring Elizabeth Taylor and Richard Burton at their most vicious and funny. He also wrote *A Delicate Balance* (1967), *Seascape* (1975), and *Three Tall Women* (1994), and has received a Tony Award for lifetime achievement.

91 Carl Andre, on top of being an important minimalist sculptor influenced by Constantin Brancusi and painter Frank Stella, was also the subject of a 1985 inquiry into his wife's death, all of which was covered in detail in the book *Naked by the Window,* by Robert Katz.

    Carl Andre's wife was the Cuban-American sculptor Anna Mendieta. In 1985 she either jumped to kill herself, fell by accident, or was pushed from the window of their apartment in Soho. Katz's book creates a pretty strong case for her being pushed by Andre, and ever since, Andre's name has been associated with the event. But instead of going to a jury trial, Andre chose to stand in front of a judge and was acquitted of all charges. The trial created a schism within the New York art world—those who supported Andre versus those whose sympathy lay with Mendieta. In the biography of Andre that appears on the Guggenheim Museum's website, there is no mention of the trial. More on Carl Andre at http://www.guggenheimcollection.org/site/artist_bio_3.html

92 Sadly, Capitol Fish and Tackle no longer rents the space on the Chelsea's ground floor. Amazingly, the fisherman's supply shop in the middle of New York City had occupied that space since 1897. http://home.nyc.rr.com/jkn/nysonglines/23st.htm

93 From Ed Hamilton's *Living with Legends* blog: http://legends.typepad.com/living_with_legends_the_h/rock_roll/index.html

CHAPTER 7

94 Joni Mitchell's quote was taken from http://jmdl.com/library/view.cfm?id=1756

95 For an account of Jaco Pastorius's contributions to music, written by jazz great Pat Metheny, go to Pastorius' official website. http://www.jacopastorius.com/

96 For a quick description of the Lone Star written at the time of Jaco Pastorius's gigs there, see the following website: http://squattheatre.com/article04m.html Also, former Chelsea dweller Kinky Friedman wrote a mystery novel set at the Lone Star Café entitled *A Case of Lone Star.*

97 The bouncer, Luc Havan, was sentenced to two years in prison for involuntary manslaughter. He served eight months. http://www.browardpalmbeach.com/2006-11-30/news/jaco-incorporated/6/

98 From "Memphis Beau," by Richard B. Woodward, *Vanity Fair,* October 1991.

99 en.wikipedia.org/wiki/William_Eggleston

100 For a valiant attempt at summing up everything the filmmaker-painter-ethnologist-occultist-music historian-anthropologist Harry Smith really did accomplish, see http://www.harrysmitharchives.com/1_bio/index.html

101 Mary Beach is a multi-award-winning painter. When she worked at City Lights bookstore in San Francisco, she discovered Beat writer Bob Kaufman, published work of William Burroughs, and was close with Allen Ginsberg, of whom she made a famous portrait. Claude Pelieu, her partner later in life and also a companion of the Beats, made stunning surrealistic cut-up photo collages.

102 Paola Igliori published the book *American Magus Harry Smith: A Modern Alchemist* (1996) as part of her INANDOUTPRESS series. She made the film version in 2001. In an interesting interview about Harry Smith that Igliori conducted with Allen Ginsberg, Ginsberg recollects, "Every time I went there [Smith would] get me very high, sort of hypnotize me with the grass and film! And then he'd hit me up for money! Twenty dollars, thirty dollars, fifty dollars." http://www.milkmag.org/interview3.htm
For a photographic portrait of Ms. Igliori by Jeannette Montgomery Baron, see http://www.jeannette-montgomery-barron.com/portraits/zooms/zoom13.html

103 Gaby Hoffman, a baby-faced actress with her mother's big, fetching eyes,

appeared in such movies as *Field of Dreams, Sleepless in Seattle,* and Woody Allen's *Everyone Says I Love You.* She's also made numerous TV appearances. http://www.imdb.com/name/nm0000451/

104 For more on Vali Myers, see http://www.valimyers.com/HTML/ColFrmst.htm

105 The first international fashion superstar, Roy Halston Frowick, born in 1932 in Des Moines, Iowa, started out by designing hats, including the pillbox hat that Jackie Kennedy wore to her husband's 1960 inauguration. Contrary to the "peasant" style popular in the 1970s, Halston's designs were miminalist, sleek, and elegant. His most famous design feat—other than the cosmopolitan design for Banff Airlines' employee uniforms—was the ultrasuede, shirtwaist dress. Halston was equally well-known for his social life, hanging out in the late '70s with the likes of Bianca Jagger at the disco-on-steroids Studio 54. Liz Taylor and Liza Minelli were also friends. In 1990, he died of AIDS in San Francisco. http://www.glbtq.com/arts/halston.html

106 "Fashion Victim: The Rise and Demise of Halston, America's Superstar Designer" by Carina Chocano. http://www.salon.com/1999/09/17/halston/

107 Cynthia Plaster Caster was a Chicago artist famous in the 1960s for making plaster casts of rock stars' erections and marketing them as sculptures. More recently, she's expanded into casting women's breasts. Jessica Villenes made a documentary film, *Plaster Caster*, about Plaster Caster's work. http://www.cynthiaplastercaster.com/ www.blockbuster.com/browse/catalog/personDetails/310258

108 When Holly Solomon died in 2002, Charlie Finch wrote her adoring if catty obituary in which he calls her "the original sultry bitch," and "the fag hag's fag hag." http://www.artnet.com/Magazine/features/cfinch/finch6-19-02.asp

109 Robert Palmer—not to be confused with the "Addicted to Love" Robert Palmer—wrote *Deep Blues,* which covers the Blues' development in the Mississippi Delta, emphasizing the life and myths surrounding Robert Johnson. http://www.amazon.com/exec/obidos/tg/detail/-/0140062238/qid=/sr=/ref=cm_lm_asin/103-6980159-3023044?v=glance

110 The Stonewall was a Greenwich Village gay bar at a time when gays were still undercover. The 1969 Stonewall Riots launched the gay rights movement.

111 In 1996, Michael Alig confessed to murdering Angel Menendez, a drug dealer central to the club scene at the time. The extraordinarily gruesome murder—and the Club Kids' scene—are chronicled in detail by Alig's friend and mentor James St. James, himself a club-scene impresario, in the book *Disco Bloodbath: A Fabulous But True Tale of Murder in Clubland.*

112 From "The Hotel in Chelsea That Art Calls Home," *New York Times*, October 14, 2010.

113 Nina Hagen makes Lady Gaga seem like Taylor Swift. Hagen is an opera singer who converted to 80s alternative rock, but to call Nina Hagen a punk or New Wave musician is too limiting. She is also into Asian mysticism and New Age spirituality. Her vocal performances are extraordinary and funny— roaring and screeching as well as singing. Her hair and clothes were as outrageous as her music: brightly-dyed hair, elaborately stylized makeup, color-collided clothing. Her album *Nun/Sex/Monk/Rock (Nonsense Punk Rock?)* is a good place to get a feel for her range.

114 Alex Cox's movie *Sid and Nancy* is a better anti-drug show than anything done by D.A.R.E. Its scenes in the Chelsea Hotel are ideal for portraying the heroin milieu, the shadowy, squalid lower floors and the clammy faces and glazed stares of Gary Oldman and Chloe Webb, whose performances are astonishing. Courtney Love plays a supporting role.
http://www.geocities.com/Hollywood/Set/7601/sidnancy.htm

115 From *Starpulse*: www.starpulse.com/.../gary_oldman_sad_to_see_sid_vicious_hot.

116 Rockets Redglare lived a fascinating, sordid life and had a surprisingly full acting career. He was born to a fifteen-year-old heroin addict, and doctors had to feed him minute doses of opiates to keep him from spiraling into withdrawal. By most accounts, he grew up to be a complete creep. In 2001, he died of everything he had ever done. There's a decent interview with him, in which he comes across as a jovial, decent fellow, at http://www.nyhangover.com/issues/0601/rockets.htm

117 During the great purge detailed in Chapter 8, Dr. Ferro vacated the Chelsea Hotel for new digs on Madison Avenue. He's still open for business at http://www.peterpferrodmd.com/

CHAPTER 8

118 On February 4, 1999, a Haitian immigrant, Amadou Bailo Diallo, who had commited no crimes, was killed in front of his apartment's front door by New York police. When he reached for his wallet to show police his identification, the police thought he was reaching for a gun. Diallo had nineteen bullet holes in him (out of 41 fired). http://www.nyc.gov/html/records/rwg/html/bio.html http://www.nchr.org/crp/archive/crp_archive.htm http://www.amadoudiallofoundation.org/lifehistory.html

Less than two years earlier, on August 9, 1997, Abner Louima, another Haitian immigrant, had been beaten and sodomized with a broomstick by New York's finest. The story was covered internationally. Policeman Justin

Volpe was sentenced to 30 years without possibility of parole. Another cop, Charles Schwarz, received 15 years. Louima received $5.8 million in a civil suit against the city of New York. He has contributed some of the money to charities in Haiti, New York, and Florida, where he now lives. He has remained active with anti-police-brutality organizations.

119 As Paul Volmer indicates, Priapism is a documented medical condition. Its name comes from Priapus, the ancient Greek fertility god, son of Aphrodite and Dionysius, who was enormously well-endowed. According to The Mayo Clinic, the syndrome is "most common in boys between ages 5 and 10 years old and in men from ages 20 to 50 years." http://www.goaskalice.columbia.edu/1133.html http://www.mayoclinic.com/health/priapism/DS00873

CHAPTER 9

120 At the time Mary Anne Rose made this comment, the hotel's Board of Directors majority, comprised of Marlene Krauss and David Elder, had not yet forced the third board member, Stanley Bard, to step down from his position as manager. But it's likely that the they were already lighting a fire under him to evict delinquent tenants and boost the hotel's profits. After all, this was why they finally used their majority status to leverage Bard out of the hotel.

EPILOGUE

121 From *New York Times*, September 10, 2006. http://query.nytimes.com/gst/fullpage.html?res=9E02EEDD1631F933A2575AC0A9609C8B63

122 From *Chelsea Now* by Chris Shott, October 26, 2007.

Photo/Image Credits

Cover photo courtesy of Chio Flores,
www.chioflores.com; chiostudio.tumblr.com

Introduction/Facing page: Chelsea Hotel postcard and brochure, courtesy of Robert Campbell

Introduction, xii: Chelsea Hotel lobby, courtesy of David Leonard

P. 24: Nicko Gentry and Paul Volmer, photo courtesy of Tim Sullivan

P. 54/Top: Marty Matz and Herbert Huncke, photo courtesy of David A. Sands

P.54/Bottom: Gregory Corso, photo courtesy of Tim Sullivan

P.104: Dee Dee Ramone and Robert Campbell, photo courtesy of Robert Campbell

P.132: Dee Dee Ramone and Robert Campbell at Continental Divide, photo courtesy of Robert Campbell

P.144: Stanley Bard photo, courtesy of Erik

P.164: Stormé DeLarverié, photo courtesy of Tim Sullivan

P.220: Rent Bill, courtesy of Robert Campbell

P.232: Chelsea staircase, photo courtesy of Tim Sullivan

P. 240: Chelsea hallway, photo courtesy of Tim Sullivan

Cover and Interior Design by James Kiehle

About the Author

James Lough teaches in the Writing Dept.
of the Savannah College of Art and Design,
and is the winner of the Frank Waters
Southwestern Writing Award. He lives
with his family in Savannah, Georgia.

To find out more about the author and this
book, visit: www.jameslough.com